W9-APQ-803

The Capitalist's Bible

The Capitalist's Bible

*The Essential Guide to Free Markets—
and Why They Matter to You*

Edited by
Gretchen Morgenson

HARPER
BUSINESS

NEW YORK · LONDON · TORONTO · SYDNEY

HARPER
BUSINESS

THE CAPITALIST'S BIBLE. Copyright © 2009 by HarperCollins Publishers. All rights reserved. Printed in the United States of America. No part of this book may be used or reproduced in any manner whatsoever without written permission except in the case of brief quotations embodied in critical articles and reviews. For information address HarperCollins Publishers, 10 East 53rd Street, New York, NY 10022.

HarperCollins books may be purchased for educational, business, or sales promotional use. For information please write: Special Markets Department, HarperCollins Publishers, 10 East 53rd Street, New York, NY 10022.

FIRST EDITION

Produced by GOLSON MEDIA
President and Editor   J. Geoffrey Golson
Staff Writer   Bill Kte'pi
Layout Editors   Mary Jo Scibetta, Cinnamon Kennedy
Copyeditor   Kenneth Heller
Proofreader   Mary Le Rouge
Indexer   J S Editorial

Library of Congress Cataloging-in-Publication Data

The capitalist's bible : the essential guide to free markets—and why they matter to you / edited by Gretchen Morgenson.
     p. cm.
  Includes index.
  ISBN 978-0-06-156098-9
  1. Capitalism. 2. Free enterprise. I. Morgenson, Gretchen. II. Title.

HB501.C24278 2009
330.12'2—dc22   2009005720

09 10 11 12 13   OV/RRD   10 9 8 7 6 5 4 3 2 1

CONTENTS

Preface **vii**
Hard Times by Gretchen Morgenson

Introduction **xiii**
The Rebirth of Capitalism by Robert J. Samuelson

Chapter 1: Capitalism 101 **1**

Chapter 2: Capitalist Chronology **43**

Chapter 3: People Every Capitalist Should Know **71**

Chapter 4: Capitalist Successes **107**

Chapter 5: Disasters in Capitalism **153**

Chapter 6: Capitalism Around the World **189**

Chapter 7: Must-Reading for Capitalists **217**

Appendix A: Capitalist Glossary **235**

Appendix B: Capitalist Resources **261**

Index **279**

Hard Times

Gretchen Morgenson

A few years ago, a friend of mine lost his job. He was facing some tough times and when the phone rang at his home, he thought it might be a response to a resume he had sent out. Instead it was the bank. "Good news," the bank salesperson said. "We are prepared to offer you an equity credit line on your house for $150,000."

"That's nice," my friend replied, "but I'm unemployed and I don't know how I would qualify for such a loan."

"Not a problem at all," said the salesperson. "No income verification required. The money is yours."

My friend didn't understand. "But wait a minute. I already have a mortgage on my house, a big one at that and I'm worried about making that monthly payment."

"Not a problem," the salesperson repeated. "The way house values are rising, you're guaranteed the credit line. Shall I send you the paperwork today?"

My friend knew then something was not right. Bank deregulation had led to some downright risky business practices from institutions that should be conservative. This was the "bank"—those guys who should be the most risk-averse of all. What were they doing? In the end, my friend did not take the credit line despite being sorely tempted, did not get a new job, but he did start his own home-based business.

Getting wise to the ways of world financial markets—real estate, credit, investments, stocks, IRAs, 401(k)s, and such—has never been more crucial than it is right now. When times are good, the penalties are few for drifting along without a clear understanding of how markets, businesses, and investments operate. But during periods of economic turmoil, like the one that began in mid-2007 when world credit markets seized up, financial education becomes a necessity. For those hoping to avoid a devastated 401(k) or investment portfolio, or for anyone trying to decode what can seem like bewildering events, financial fundamentals are the key.

Moments of peril in markets or economies are never easy to endure, of course. But they do come and go. So for those who recognize the powers at work and know how similar periods in history turned out, surviving the chaos is more likely.

In fact, knowing how to thrive in tumultuous economic times has been a hallmark of capitalistic icons everywhere. Capitalism's winners, after all, have risen to the top by embracing change. They understand that capitalism is, by its nature, protean, and that the status quo never lasts for long. Companies that are leaders in their industries rarely remain so forever. Corporate upstarts with game-changing inventions come along to upset the apple cart, providing profits to investors who saw their promise and losses to those who thought their place in the hierarchy was assured. Today's blue chip can quickly become tomorrow's has-been.

The same goes for talented investors. Rare is the money manager who beats the market year in, year out, over decades. Nevertheless, it is in this world of constant change that dreams are realized and goals achieved. To be sure, change is intimidating. But it is also integral to markets and companies where thousands of participants make choices everyday.

The American style of capitalism is unique in its populist twist. It allows everyday people to enrich not only themselves, but their investors and their employees as well. That may be hard to believe in an era of high unemployment, store closures, and stock losses. The solutions are sometimes hard to fathom. Talk of a nearly $1 trillion economic stimulus plan can spin one's head: consider that $1 trillion is nearly half the gross domestic product of the entire country of France—nearly half of what that country produces in one year. That's a lot of money.

To help understand what capitalism is all about is the reason for this book: *The Capitalist's Bible* is not a another how-to invest guide, but rather a primer on the basics of the economic system to help you understand what it is all about, how it came to be, and perhaps where it is going. And how it affects your daily life.

We begin with an introduction by Robert J. Samuelson, the noted *Newsweek* and *Washington Post* columnist. He offers his perspective on the "Rebirth of Capitalism," noting its recent heyday and the fact that regulated capitalism, despite its current downward cycle, is a recent worldwide phenomenon, a dominant economic system in our era of globalization.

Our first chapter, "Capitalism 101," explores the basics of capiatlism: economic theories from the great thinkers and explanations of core capitalist concepts, such as supply and demand, business cycles, globalization, economic indicators, banking, stocks, bonds, venture capital, and even the black market.

Chapter 2, "Capitalist Chronology," goes into the history of the economic system from the first days of mercantilism and the first investment craze (Tulip Mania, of all things) to the panics of the 19th century to the first decade of the 21st century and our current situation. It's the "story" behind the "history."

Chapter 3 explores the personal stories of famous capitalists and thinkers, "People Every Capitalist Should Know," and offers the experiences of why some capitalists succeeded. Unfortunately these biographies are dominated with white-haired white men, as is much of the history of western civilization—a situation we can all expect to change dramatically as time and equality progress. But from David Hume to Bill Gates, there is something to learn from these men who have either provided great insight into economics or have succeeded at capitalism beyond their own dreams.

Chapter 4, "Capitalist Successes," went through some major changes as we edited this book. We had included companies like AIG and Citigroup originally. They had been, up until recently, great companies in the history of capitalism. But they are no more. Even companies like Boeing, Starbucks, Google, and Toyota have experienced huge losses in 2008. But they are still exemplars of capitalist success, perhaps most notably by their survival despite unprecedented worldwide economic challenges.

Chapter 5 is about "Disasters in Capitalism." When this book was conceived, the Great Depression of the 1930s was considered the greatest disaster in capitalism; perhaps its status has been challenged. There are other economic downturns worth noting, from the Long Depression of the 1890s to the Savings and Loan crisis of the 1980s, to the Asian financial meltdown of 1997.

"Capitalism Around the World" is the subject of Chapter 6, and here we provide a bird's-eye view of how capitalism is practiced around the globe. The spread of capitalism is indeed impressive, where it has supplanted socialist or command economies in major countries like Russia and China. Today, you can count on one hand the truly noncapitalist countries, such as North Korea and Cuba.

In Chapter 7, "Must-Reading for Capitalists," we have excerpted short samples of texts from seminal works on capitalism, from the *Wealth of Nations* by Adam Smith to the *The World is Flat* by Thomas L. Friedman. These are just a few leads to what is out there that can illuminate the story and workings of capitalism. Further reading is encouraged.

Finally, we provide two appendices for easy reference: a Capitalist Glossary that defines many often-used terms (that are rarely defined in the media) and a Capitalist Resources section that provides a sample of Websites, magazines, and books that are available to understand better and understand more.

There you have it. As a reporter and columnist for *The New York Times*, I often receive questions and requests for advice from readers about investments and capitalism. *The Capitalist's Bible* is a start at providing some answers for those readers, as well as for my friend who was offered that ill-conceived equity line. How's he doing? Well, his home-based business just broke through the $1 million gross sales mark—and he did it without borrowing. He reports a 23 percent profit margin. I'll take that any day. My friend's example is a small example of why America is still the place where even the most impoverished strivers can become millionaires. It is to America that hardworking hopefuls still come to make their fortunes.

American capitalism has survived recessions, depressions, panics, and crises, and has triumphed in times of booms and growth. Wherever we are in the capitalist cycle, the information in this book stands the test of time.

Introduction

The Rebirth of Capitalism

Robert J. Samuelson

One of the remarkable stories of contemporary history is the fall and rise, and some would say in recent times, the fall again, of capitalism. But it will rise once more; it always does. In the 1960s or the 1970s, hardly anyone talked about "capitalism." The word existed in dictionaries and history books, but it had virtually disappeared from everyday conversation and political debate. It connoted a bygone era (it was thought) of cruel and crude business titans who abused their workers and presided over an inherently unstable economic system. People thought the economic system had fundamentally changed for the better. Government supervised markets; modern managers, not the old moguls, were more sensitive to workers and communities. They had more "social responsibility." A new vocabulary was needed to signify the progress.

People talked of a "mixed economy" of shared power between government and business. Sometimes there was mention of "free enterprise" and "private enterprise." Hardly anyone advocated unadulterated "capitalism." There were a few conspicuous exceptions. In 1962 a little-known economist named Milton Friedman published a book titled *Capitalism and Freedom*. The title was catchy precisely because it praised a system that was so unfashionable that it was hardly mentionable. More than five decades later, we have come a long way. Friedman became famous and won a Nobel Prize. His title no longer seems controversial, and the relationship it suggests—that capitalism promotes political freedom—is widely, if not universally, accepted. Friedman cited many connections. By allowing consumers more choices, capitalism nurtures a taste for choice in many areas, including politics. Capitalism dilutes political power with widely dispersed economic power. And it enables people to criticize government because most workers do not depend on government for employment.

What explains the reversal? Well, the answer isn't shrinking government. When Friedman wrote his book, government did less than it does now. It spent less as a percentage of national income (Gross Domestic Product—GDP) and taxed less. It had fewer regulations. In 1965 Congress created Medicare and Medicaid, federal health insurance programs for the elderly and poor. Programs to provide college aid, food assistance, and housing expanded. In 1960 governments at all levels—federal, state, and local—spent 26 percent of the GDP. By the early 2000s they spent 32 percent of a much larger GDP. Government regulation of the environment, workplace safety, and consumer products increased dramatically.

Generally speaking, the story is similar in Europe. In the 1980s and 1990s some nationalized industries (airlines, telecommunications, and steel) were converted to private companies. But government spending had progressively grown, as had regulation. Almost everywhere the "welfare state" has grown. With a new Democratic administration in the United States after the 2008 election, that trend will increase. Still, capitalism has regained permanent respectability for two reasons: the alternative (socialism) has been proven not to work, and the Cold War ended.

Nothing discredited capitalism more than the Great Depression, a climactic crisis. In the 1930s the unemployment rate in the United

States averaged 18 percent. High joblessness in Europe helped cause World War II by bringing Adolf Hitler to power. Raw capitalism, in the popular view, could no longer be trusted. At a minimum, it needed to be reformed and regulated. Other critics thought it should be abolished. The Great Depression is mentioned frequently in analysis of the 2007–09 economic crisis; generally it serves as a benchmark for catastrophe. But the difference is that in the Great Depression, many people were ready to toss the baby out with the bathwater; today economists realize deregulation may not be a good idea, but are willing to keep the baby.

Among some intellectuals in the 1930s, Communism was fashionable. So much suffering and political instability made capitalism a scourge. But as the Depression-era generation has died, so have the personal memories of the decade's horrors. The anticapitalist stigma faded, albeit it was having a rough time at the end of the 2000s.

For roughly four decades, Communism (and its many variants) vied with free enterprise to see which could do better. Under Communism, government ruled the economy. There was collective ownership of industry and agriculture in Communist states; in socialist countries, the government controlled critical industries (power, communications, railroads, airlines, oil). Central planners coordinated production, made investment decisions, and dictated which industries would expand. On the other side was free enterprise. Private companies competed for customers and profits. Private markets—responding to consumers' preferences and corporate profitability—made the basic decisions of what would be produced, what prices would be charged, and what sectors would flourish or falter.

By the early 1980s, even before Communism's political collapse, the economic competition was essentially over. People could see that the Communist world (the old Soviet Union, most of Eastern Europe, China, and Cuba) was vastly poorer than Western Europe, the United States, and Japan. They could see that it wasn't just elites who benefited; average families enjoyed riches that, 50 years earlier, had been virtually unimaginable. The contrast was so obvious that even some Communist states began abandoning the orthodoxy. In the late 1970s China started to introduce personal ownership and private markets into its farming system. Once the Soviet Union and Eastern Europe discarded Communism, it became commonplace to dramatize the outcome: capitalism and freedom had conquered Communism and tyranny. The collapse of Communism in the 1980s and the early 1990s seemed to confirm capitalism's superiority as a wealth-generating machine, a system that could raise mass living standards. Governments everywhere were obsessed with improving the well being of their citizens.

But if "capitalism" was no longer a dirty word, its triumph was also misleading. Lost in all the celebration and rhetoric was a simple reality: capitalism is a vague concept. Its meaning is unclear. Capitalism requires more than the legality of private property, or the ability to accumulate wealth. Even feudal societies had private property and permitted some members (such as monarchs, lords, barons) to become rich. But feudal societies restricted property ownership and, through law and custom, decided what people could do. Serfs were tied to lords, who promised them protection. In turn, the serfs had to farm their lords' lands. Capitalism is larger than property and profits. It's an economic system that depends on some common social and political arrangements that guide the behavior of people and enterprises.

A capitalist society has at least three defining characteristics. First, it settles most economic questions through decentralized markets and free prices. If people want more widgets, then widget prices rise and production increases. If there are too many widgets, prices will drop, profits will fall and, ultimately, production will decline. Decisions about which industries will grow (or shrink) and what occupations will increase (or decline) are mostly resolved by markets.

Second, it creates a motivational system because it allows people and companies to keep much of the reward from their own work. Capitalism presumes that people want to better themselves. The theory is that they will work harder, invest more, and take more risks if they benefit from their own ambition, inventiveness, or imagination. Incomes are generally not determined by law, custom, or politically set "needs." Finally, capitalism establishes a permanent system of trial and error. Without centralized control of what's produced—and because people and firms can profit from satisfying the market—everyone is free to experiment.

The experimentation is a basic source of higher living standards because it leads to new technologies, products, and services or better ways (including cheaper ways) of making and selling existing products and services. What this means is that, as a social system, capitalism inevitably involves inequality. Some win more than others. The whole theory is that the possibility of exceptional reward inspires people to make exceptional effort.

Similarly, capitalism virtually ensures constant change. The market is not wedded to the present. Its demands and desires can shift. The economist Joseph Schumpeter (1883–1950) called this process "creative destruction." At its best, it improves people's well-being. But sometimes the constant change leads to economic and social instability—financial panics, depressions, and industrial and agricultural displacement. Economic stability requires that supply and demand roughly match; that workers who want jobs can find them; that what's produced will be consumed; that what's saved will be invested.

Though the market does well at making these matches, it doesn't succeed at all times and in all places. Because all societies cope with these twin problems—inequality and instability—there is no ideal form of capitalism. Every country, including the United States, modifies capitalism's dictates to satisfy its own political preferences and cultural tastes.

Few markets are totally free. Most involve some government regulation. Labor markets in the United States have, among other things, a minimum wage, limits on working hours, and rules for pensions. Some prices are regulated or controlled; in many countries, governments set power, water, and phone rates. People and companies typically can't keep everything they earn; there are taxes. Government regulation and social custom limit trial and error.

In Japan, government regulations protected small family-owned stores against larger chains. Almost all societies regulate scientific experimentation. Capitalism is thus an art. All advanced economies remain mixed economies, with power shared between private markets and government. It is a matter of degree. Similarly, capitalism is conditioned by culture. It is not the same in the United States as in, say, Japan, Brazil, Germany, or South Korea. If government suppresses the power of markets too much—through taxes, restrictions, regulations, subsidies, and politically inspired privileges—then capitalism is a label without meaning. Similarly, if culture checks markets too much—by, for example, awarding wealth and status on the basis of birth, custom, political connections, or corruption—then capitalism is also a misnomer.

Capitalism is always a work in progress, and at the start of the 21st century, this is especially true. In the past half century, it has grown more global in two senses. First, more countries are trying the capitalist model—China, India, and Russia the largest of recent converts—and hoping to fit it to their own values and social systems. Because Friedman was at least partially correct, the global spread of capitalism involves social and political transformations, as well as economic change. Relying more on markets means giving people more freedom and allowing status and income to be settled more by economic competition, rather than by birth, ethnic background, or political standing. Conflicts between the past and present are not only possible; they are inevitable. Capitalism has also grown more global in a second sense: reduced barriers to international trade and investment have resulted in more of these exchanges. Countries that decide to try capitalism need not decide simultaneously to join the world economy; they can keep their capitalism at home and restrict dealings with the outside world.

But in practice, countries are doing both. Almost all countries have become more dependent on worldwide flows of trade and investment funds for their own prosperity. This creates new opportunities for gains—cross-border flows of products, technologies, and management techniques. Countries can specialize in what they do best; investors can seek out the highest returns. But the same interdependence also creates new opportunities for instability if there's a breakdown in global trade or investment flows. There has been a rebirth of capitalism, but it is not the capitalism of 30, 50, or 100 years ago. It is a new version—or rather many new versions—of an old idea. How it evolves and fares is a fascinating story.

Robert J. Samuelson writes a column for *Newsweek* and the *Washington Post*. He is the author of *The Good Life and Its Discontents: The American Dream in the Age of Entitlement* (1995) and *The Great Inflation and Its Aftermath* (2008).

Chapter 1

Capitalism 101

Don't let the "ism" throw you. When you think of "isms," you may think of beliefs—abstract things, nothing hands-on, philosophers arguing in the campus coffee shop about the chicken and the egg. There is more to capitalism than just a belief system and a way of looking at economics. There are good and bad ways to be a capitalist, and we're not just talking about morals, we're talking about effective business practices. Capitalists are unified by core beliefs, values, and goals.

Capitalism is an ever-evolving concept. Always pressured by market growth and hardship, it is constantly manipulated by governments and business leaders in an attempt to make the free market—or some derivative thereof—as fair and profitable as possible. *The Capitalist's Bible* contains no commandments. As you will see as you read further, even capitalism's chief engineers—its prophets and leaders—generally engaged in their study of capitalism with respectful curiosity, not dogmatic assurance. This book is the ultimate guide to where capitalism has been, and it provides tools for the building of what capitalism will become. We're going to go over those tools in a few different ways. We'll talk about the great success stories and the most devastating disasters, and how we've learned from both.

We will start by covering some of the basic concepts important to capitalism, economics, and modern finance. If you run across an unfamiliar term, check the glossary in the back of the book.

Theoretical Foundations

Classical Economic Theory

Classical economic theory evolved from the philosophy of British classical liberals like Thomas Hobbes and John Locke, who popularized the idea that everyone metaphorically signs a contract with the government to receive only those services that they can't provide themselves. In modern context the word *liberal* is generally applied to those favoring social freedoms, but in the days of Hobbes and Locke it signified those favoring maximum economic freedoms for the individual. Hobbes thought the contract couldn't be broken, while Locke argued that the government had a responsibility to the individuals who had created it, individuals who were born with inalienable rights (life, liberty, and property) that no government could take away. Rational individuals were capable of governing themselves, Locke said—and classical liberals embraced the idea of laissez-faire, or hands-off government.

The economic side of this is that the government has a responsibility to leave the market alone and let it regulate itself. Classical economists following in Locke's footsteps said that the three basic functions of government were domestic protection, national security, and public works (such as roads, canals, hospitals). Since human nature would lead self-interested people to grab as much of the limited resources as possible, the public good would be best served by allowing unrestricted competition to act as a counter to that natural greed. Classical economics emphasized individual liberty and the ability of each person to determine his own best interests, and there-

Drafting the Declaration of Independence: American colonists wanted not only political, but also economic freedom.

fore the goods and services that prove most prosperous will be the ones that benefit the most people affordably.

The American founding fathers were classical liberals. The Declaration of Independence refers to the inalienable rights of life, liberty, and the pursuit of happiness (rather than property). The Constitution established a laissez-faire federal government, and most state governments were similarly hands-off. The easy availability of land and seemingly unlimited human and natural resources proved a fertile ground for classical economic theories. In the next century, though, industrialization brought to light the weaknesses of classical economic theory.

Unchecked greed can actually restrict economic liberty for the common man, leading to monopolies and collusion, which are harmful to consumers. Competition can also lead to wages that fall below the subsistence level, especially if workers don't have many other options, or are kept in debt to their employers (as with sharecropping).

In the wake of the Great Depression, the American government began to regulate such areas of economic life as the stock market, banking, antitrust, interstate commerce, labor, and trade. Classical economics still formed the backbone of American thought—this change didn't abandon that; the goals were the same. But gaps in the safety net were sewn up, and wrinkles smoothed out. Classical economics, meanwhile, had begun its segue into neoclassical economics thanks to the marginal revolution, when the concepts of marginal utility and marginal productivity were introduced at the end of the 19th century.

Neoclassical Economic Theory

The changes of the Industrial Revolution were too much for classical economics. Like a doctor treating a patient who had developed some new symptoms, economists had to change their prescription. The biggest event in the transition from classical to neoclassical economics was the marginal revolution, named for the theories of marginal utility proposed by four economists in four countries.

Marginal utility is a subjective theory of value—one that focuses on the value of a thing to consumers, not the cost that producers put into it. When we talk about something having sentimental value, we're on the same page as marginal utility. When people buy designer sneakers at many times the cost of production, marginal utility is also involved. Philosopher Jeremy Bentham had defined utility as the total pleasure—and pain—inducing character of a particular thing, the sum total of all the pluses and minuses. In economic terms, this was a function of the quantity of a particular good. Marginal productivity provided a way to assess the value or labor, as well as a unified theory of production and distribution, which classical economics had insisted were separate spheres. The marginal revolution marked a shift in thinking, away from economics as theory or philosophy, and toward the idea that economics can be knowable and quantifiable—even predictable. Neoclassical economists began to look at the cost and value of any good or service in terms of supply and demand: when demand goes up or supply goes down, the value rises, even though the item has not changed.

Apart from substantive theoretical shifts like the marginal revolution, the biggest development in the second half of the 20th century was a shift to mathematics as the preferred mode of expression. Modern economic texts tend to be heavy on graphs and equations, a far cry from the philosophical origins of classical economics.

Neoclassical economics, as practiced and taught for most of the 20th century, became a theory of static resource allocation. Capital and population are treated as given parameters. It is not that neoclassical economists are uninterested in growth and development; it's just that the mathematical methods developed because of the marginal revolution are so good at what they do that people limited their subject matter. A question for the future is whether economics will be driven by its methods, or by its subject matter.

Insiders and outsiders have long questioned the adequacy of comparative statics to represent a dynamic world. In *Capitalism, Socialism, and Democracy*, Joseph Schumpeter contrasted the standard neoclassical conclusion that monopoly is harmful to consumers with the empirical observation that the great increase in the average standard of living occurred precisely with the concentration of ownership in industry. His point was that it is highly misleading to judge the performance of an economic system with static models—sooner or later you have to hang your head out the window and see what's actually going on out there.

Marxian Economic Theory

As the economies built by classical economists threatened to jeopardize their own workers and consumers in the 19th century as theory collided with the Industrial Revolution, neoclassical economists revised their views to take these developments into account. Karl Marx saw the imminent death of capitalism, and its replacement by Communism.

Like classical economics, Marxian economics is based on the labor theory of value. In the first volume of *Capital*, Marx built his economics on the assumption that the price of a thing is proportional to its value, and proceeded to demonstrate that under capitalism, the control and ownership of the means of production had been taken away from the workers who were integral to the production process, and that more work was extracted from workers than was necessary. Industrial innovations like scientific management and the assembly line had only increased the control of the owners over the workers.

In *Capital*, Marx examined the capital accumulation process to discover the "laws of motion" of capitalism. Marx contended that competition between capitalist firms forces them to invest in new technology to save on labor costs and increase profits. The new technology makes more money for the company, at the expense of other capitalists, since their composition of capital—or the ratio of dead elements (tools) to living elements (workers)—rises. At the same time, using the new technique lowers the value of the commodity by reducing the amount of necessary labor.

Other companies have to adopt the technique—or something with similar advantages, in the case of patented technologies—in order to stay competitive. Eventually the surplus value is no longer transferred between companies, and the profit advantage disappears. Capitalist companies as a whole find themselves with a higher composition of capital, lowering profit at a constant rate of exploitation. In other words, the spread of innovation and increased ease of production will increase competition, and ultimately lower profit margins.

Marx's theory of the falling rate of profit is at the core of his theory of the crisis and breakdown of capitalism. Other theories of crisis are either underconsumptionist or disproportionality theories. The underconsumptionist theories suggest that since workers only receive a fraction of the value they create as wages, their consumption demand always falls short of the value produced, leaving an excess supply on the market. The disproportionality theories focus on Marx's dynamic analysis of accumulation, and argue that disproportional growth between various interdependent sectors of economy would result in a capitalist breakdown.

Laissez-Faire

"Let it be," we might call it if the French had not coined a term first: laissez-faire literally means "let do," and the phrase was popularized in the 17th and 18th centuries by French and English economists of the classical school. The principle of laissez-faire says simply that government controls on economic behavior—trade, companies, prices, wages—limit the freedom of the individuals involved. Because the economic world touches all others, it isn't strictly economic freedoms that are limited. Laissez-faire isn't an exclusively liberal or conservative principle, and its proponents have held all sorts of political allegiances.

Even before Adam Smith famously promoted laissez-faire principles in his 1776 seminal work, *The Wealth of Nations*, the term was in use to condemn mercantilism, the doctrine according to which the government controls trade (especially international trade). Locke had argued that humans were essentially good despite their self-interest, and that governments were formed for mutual benefits, not the sacrifice of natural liberties.

Competition among humans for their share of the public domain is natural and not harmful, as long as there is more than enough to satisfy every person's needs. Private property, one of Locke's fundamental natural rights shared by all humans, derives from a person putting forth labor to acquire goods from the public domain. Private property is therefore not evil, and neither is the competition to acquire it.

In mid-18th century France, the intellectual group known as the Physiocrats called for laissez-faire reforms as well. The French economy was still under the thumb of the old regime of land-owning aristocrats, an almost feudal structure that limited the trade and capital of the French countryside. According to the Physiocrats, the problem was the trade limit imposed by the government, and the heavy taxes farmers had to pay. A freer exchange, a less restricted market, would lead to greater personal and political freedom, to the betterment of all concerned.

Smith is usually categorized as a classical liberal, because he combined his optimistic view of economic competition and restrained self-interest with the liberal assumptions of man's inherent goodness and collective goal to work for the interests of the common good. Unlike modern liberals, Smith believed that economic behavior did not require government intervention to achieve the maximum good for society. In his view, goodness couldn't be imposed—it would be a natural consequence of human behavior, human nature.

Thanks in large part to the influence of Smith and Thomas Jefferson—a strong economic liberal who believed in limited government, free trade, and the admirability of the agricultural way of life—the United States' economic policies and practices were built on laissez-faire principles.

One of the strangest distortions of laissez-faire philosophy involved the Populists of the 1890s. The Populists were a political party made up of farmers of the American South and Midwest. Suffering from the exploitation of railroad monopolies that set high prices for transporting farm produce, the Populists advocated government intervention to establish a society and economy consistent with Jeffersonian principles and economic liberalism. In other words, the Populists believed that economic self-interest among farmers resulted in activities for the common good, but corrupt industrialists, monopolists, and politicians were thwarting traditional American economic liberalism. The situation could be remedied only by involvement of the federal government into the economy by means of government ownership of railroads and other utilities, a rejection of the monetary gold standard, and the adoption of a national income tax.

The Populist political program only succeeded with the rise to political power and socioeconomic influence of the Progressives. The Progressives possessed the heritage of American economic liberalism, but at the same time recognized the varied problems brought about by the Industrial Revolution and wanted to solve them.

It was under the influence of the Progressives that the first two decades of the 20th century in America witnessed the onset of the income tax; legislation putting restrictions on business practices and monopolies; a constitutional amendment to make U.S. senators more directly answerable to the people; the creation of the Federal Reserve, the nation's central bank; and the achievement of women's suffrage.

The Great Depression of the 1930s was the watershed in the history of laissez-faire economics. The Depression weakened and destroyed the economies of great nations, and caused such panic and anxiety that no Western industrial government would advocate a return to the principles of laissez-faire. Even the conservative Republicans were forced to concede the failure of economic liberalism. Pure laissez-faire economics had come to an end.

Concepts of Capitalism

Supply and Demand

Supply is one of the most fundamental concepts of economics. In microeconomic theory (the study of how individuals, firms, and certain market sectors make economic decisions), supply refers to the production of markets and is a function of prices and costs of production. In macroeconomics (the study of the performance, behavior, and structure of national or regional economies), aggregate supply refers to the production of whole economies and is, depending on the macroeconomic theory, thought to depend on factors such as household savings, capital stock, labor force, and technology. Since goods and services are—with the exception of household production—supplied by businesses, the supply side is often synonymous with the business sector.

One of the pillars of microeconomic price theory is the law of supply: all things being equal, the quantity of a good rises as the market price rises, and falls as the price falls. The amount supplied is a function of several independent variables: the selling price, the cost of the things used to make it, the technology of production, taxes and subsidies, and expectations of future prices and costs. If price changes, the quantity supplied will change along the supply curve; if one of the other factors changes, the supply curve shifts.

Demand is the desire of consumers for a particular good, regardless of price—quantity demanded, a related and sometimes confused concept, is the total amount of a product that consumers are willing and able to buy at a particular price. The existence of demand doesn't mean that consumers will buy as much of a thing as is made available. It's a critical distinction, as any amount of window-shopping or flipping through a *SkyMall* catalog will tell you that there are plenty of things consumers are interested in, but rarely purchase. Our desire for a product, the demand we create for it, is based on how much we think we need it—as in the case of "useful" purchases—and how much satisfaction or pleasure we think we'll get out of it. This is an example of marginal utility.

Demand plays an important role in the capitalist economy, because it serves as a sign of how people want to divide their scarce resources. It's like a voting mechanism: barbecue-flavored potato chips continue to be made by virtually every potato chip maker, because that's a flavor consumers have consistently "voted" for by buying it time and again. That desire is communicated not only to a particular potato chip company, but, to its competitors, to industry analysts, to competing industries like pretzel manufacturers who may use that information to try to lure consumers.

Supply and demand each affect price: the quantity demanded may rise as the price falls, which can lead to a more profitable situation for the producer if they lower the price in order to let more consumers afford the item, especially if doing so affects the cost of the supply. By being able to afford a larger and more efficient factory because of the larger-scale production called for by the quantity demanded, the cost of supply decreases.

Business Cycles

Business cycles are the recurrent, alternating, but unpredictable phases of expansions and contractions in business and economic activity. One business cycle is the length of time from one peak (high) or trough (low) to the next peak or trough. The fluctuations in the business cycle are commonly referred to as periods of economic recovery, expansion or prosperity, and recession or depression. Given the complex structure of modern economies, it is not surprising that fluctuations in business and economic activity persist. However accurately predicting or even confirming the precise shifting points, the peaks and the troughs, in the business cycle can be problematic. For instance, since 1820, the American economy has experienced tremendous growth in its real Gross Domestic Product (the measure of total output produced by the economy), which has increased by an average of 3.6 percent per year. Just describing the upward trend, though, glosses over the many short-term fluctuations when the economy contracted—the depressions, recessions, slumps, and so on. This cycle of expansion-peak-contraction-trough-expansion repeats itself over and over again throughout the history of any capitalist economy.

Business cycles are very irregular. The phases do not last for any set duration, and since the Civil War the U.S. economy has passed through 29 complete business cycles, varying in length from 17 months to 10½ years. Expansions tend to be longer than contractions, and both phases have been subject to different labels and analyses over time. Contractions were once commonly called panics, and then crises, and depressions—all terms eventually rejected because they implied a dire situation that might not have been present. The neutral term "recession" is common now, and you will sometimes hear "growth correction." Depending on the context, expansions are often called booms, or recoveries.

The most well-known business cycle in American history began in August 1929 and ended in May 1937, roughly corresponding to the Great Depression. Though contractions covered only 56 of the 120 months of the cycle, the general trend of the economy was faltering during the entire period. Many saw this as the death knell of capitalism, particularly given the rise of socialism in the previous decades, and the corresponding Bolshevik Revolution in Russia. However there is an upside to business cycles. Once the economy reaches a trough at the end of a recession, real GDP begins to rise, employment begins to recover, and most economic things look brighter. For example during the expansion of the Clinton years—the longest in U.S. history, running from March 1991 to March 2001—the economy seemed to be booming. Real GDP rose 3.5 percent per year, the unemployment rate averaged 4 percent, and the stock market experienced its largest increase in history. In many ways, the U.S. economy was healthy and prosperous. Expansions, as the counterpart to contractions, are the positive side of the business cycle.

Fortunately, in the United States, business cycles have diminished in severity. Since World War II there have been 10 cycles, with expansions averaging 57 months, and contractions averaging only 10 months. In the most severe recession during this time (July 1981 to November 1982), output fell 2.9 percent, and unemployment reached a maximum of 11 percent. In contrast, in the years between the Civil War and World War II there were 19 cycles, with expansions averaging 28 months and contractions averaging 22 months.

In the most severe contraction during this time, the Great Depression, output fell 27 percent, and unemployment was at times over 25 percent. With output falling farther and longer, and unemployment reaching much higher levels, pre-World War II recessions were both more frequent and more severe than those of the past 70 years. Expansions are now twice as long as they previously were, and contractions average one-half of their former duration, so that the balance between the two has improved significantly. In December 2008 the National Bureau of Economic Research officially declared that the United States had entered into recession one year previously. The country lost 533,000 jobs in November 2008, the biggest monthly job loss since 1974. By early 2009, the unemployment rate reached 7.6 percent.

Globalization

According to international relations expert Joseph Nye, a truly globalized world "would mean free flows of goods, people, and capital, and similar interest rates." We're not there yet. From antiquity, with the Roman Empire and the early spread of Christianity and Islam, through the Silk Road connecting Europe and China, the age of revolutions across Europe and the Americas, up to the modern era and the rise of democracies and Communist states around the world, there has been an internationalization of some aspects of culture. Certain things have spread across regions much larger than countries, and in fact surviving the rise and fall of those countries. But only in recent decades has globalization replaced internationalization as a buzzword.

Since the late 1970s, deregulated and privatized globalization has been the basic goal of the United Nations (UN) institutions that deal with global economics: the World Bank, the International Monetary Fund (IMF), and the World Trade Organization (WTO), the successor to the General Agreements on Trade Tariffs (GATT). The United States has taken the lead in developing lending policies and economic development models in the tool kits of UN financial lenders and managers. This model of economic development for the poor and transitional countries of the world is called "the Washington Consensus."

For most developing countries without oil to export, one of the only opportunities for economic development is international financing for projects beyond the capabilities of the local economy. To qualify for international loans from most major banks, the IMF or World Bank must certify the borrower's willingness to service the debt. IMF counselors have established a standard, that requires the loan recipient to agree to structural adjustment plans. These often include trade liberalization to encourage international investors, reducing and ending tariffs that may have protected infant industries, privatization of public sector enterprises and rationalizing public sector work by downsizing and reducing the number of public employees, ending subsidies for food products and services, devaluation of local currency, and expanding export production.

From the perspective of the bankers, investors, and multinational corporations, these structural adjustments provide a stable environment in which to invest, they hasten movement from barter to a monetized economies, remove inefficiencies of publicly owned enterprises and surplus labor, and assure that, at least the interest, if not the principal, on previous loans will be repaid.

From the perspective of the workers, farmers, and the poor, however, the effects of these policies have been to increase the cost of food and services; to increase the unemployment rate; often to discourage enforcement of labor law, thereby reducing union membership and power; to lower the number of school attendees and the availability of medical care; and to drive many economic refugees behind the fences of international sweatshop and *maquiladora* or "offshore" production facilities.

In its structural adjustment plans, the Washington Consensus does not provide a clear means to improving the economic situation of the labor pool, as imports are discouraged, and the increased money from exports can be used to service the debt. Companies threatening to move further erode the bargaining power of workers, in both industrial and poor countries. Some are willing to abandon their disposable fixed capital, even after bargaining to gain concessions, in large part because of the incentives provided by the new host nation in the form of rapid depreciation, lower taxes, low or no environmental regulation, and wages a fraction of the rates at home, in pursuit of much higher profits and lower costs in even lower-wage countries.

Globalization faces considerable opposition and criticism. As tariff barriers are removed, inefficient producers of commodities such as food grains in poor countries can no longer compete with the often highly subsidized and sophisticated agribusinesses, which now have new markets for their corn, rice, and wheat.

For instance, price caps and subsidies for tortillas in Mexico must be removed as one condition of the structural adjustment plans required of a debtor country, or for membership in the WTO (World Trade Organization, an international trade organization designed to liberalize and supervise trade) or NAFTA (the North American Free

Trade Agreement, a trilateral trade bloc for North America—Canada, the United States, and Mexico —designed to free up trade between the three nations). Thus, subsistence farmers who used to be able to sell their small surplus are now required to participate in a monetized economy and to pay for "cheap" imported grain from the industrial societies in order to eat.

Economics and Game Theory

Everyone has played games, but most people don't analyze the structure of the game in terms of its basic elements—players, rules, strategies, timing, outcomes, and payoffs. Game theory is the branch of mathematics that does exactly that, and while it studies real games— board games, computer games, card games—many of the "games" it studies are real-world scenarios examined from a game-theorist point of view in order to distill a complicated whole into those constituent parts.

Modern game theory came to prominence after the 1944 publication of *The Theory of Games and Economic Behavior* by mathematician Jon von Neumann and economist Oskar Morgenstern, and so right from the start was married to the notion of exploring economics in terms of game-like behavior.

There are two distinct, but related ways of describing a game mathematically. The extensive form is the most detailed way. It describes play by means of a game tree (picture it as a "Choose Your Own Adventure" type of flowchart) that explicitly indicates when players move, which moves are available, and what they know about the moves of other players and the "state of nature" when they move. Most importantly, it specifies the payoffs that players receive at the end of the game. Equilibria to such games are often gotten by examining the payoffs at the right of the tree, and working one's way left to the choices that would have been made by each player to get there.

A "pure" strategy is a set of instructions. Generally, strategies are contingent responses. An alternative to the extensive form is the normal or strategic form. This is less detailed than the extensive form, specifying the list of strategies available to each player, and the pay-offs that accrue to each when the strategies meet.

A zero-sum game is one in which the total payoff to all players in the game adds to zero. In other words, each player benefits only at the expense of others. Chess and poker are zero-sum games, because one wins exactly the amount one's opponents lose. Business and politics are non-zero-sum games, because some outcomes are good for all players or bad for all players. A cooperative game is one in which the players may freely communicate among themselves before making game decisions, and may make bargains to influence those decisions. Monopoly is a cooperative game, and so are most board games we remember from family game night. The Prisoners' Dilemma, a thought experiment in which two prisoners are segregated from each other, each of them given a choice with an outcome determined by the other's choice, is not a cooperative game. A complete information game is a game in which each player has the same game-relevant information as every other player. Chess is a complete information game, while poker is not.

The notions of self-interest, utility, and optimization created early links between game theory and economics. The key link is rationality, the attribute of people that guides them to do things in their own self-interest only if the perceived benefits exceed the perceived costs. As trivial as games may seem, especially when they have no consequences, people tend to play them to win—which, from the game's point of view, is rational behavior.

Economics is based on the assumption that human beings, and the institutions they create, are absolutely rational in their economic choices. Specifically, the assumption is that each person or institution maximizes their rewards—profits, incomes, or subjective benefits—in the circumstances that they face. The game theory framework is ideal for this, and theorists like Augustin Cournot have devised famous applications of it.

Market failures such as the overexploitation of fisheries, global warming, and inadequate resources committed to research are additional examples of games. In this realm, the individual pursuing self-interest is pitted against the broader goals of society. Modern game theory texts are filled with such examples, and game theory also permeates many other disciplines. Over time, this phenomenon's influence will likely grow.

Economic Indicators

Economic indicators are bits of information used by economists and investors to take stock of economic events in the past and present, and to anticipate similar events in the future. They are the equivalent of the rainfall, wind patterns, barometric shifts, and cold fronts scrutinized by meteorologists to prepare the weather report. These indicators can be related to general conditions like the country's Gross Domestic Product, or to more specific areas, like the state of affairs in manufacturing or labor. Production levels, spending habits, the amount of money people are investing or saving, the unemployment rate, inflation, and exchange rates are among the events that economists examine and correlate to various indicators.

There are three basic types of indicators that policy-makers and analysts pay attention to: leading, coincident, and lagging. Leading indicators are the indicators that tend to move in anticipation of turning points or changes in general conditions or the business cycle. A variable that consistently reaches its peak before the peak of the business cycle can be reliably used to forecast an upcoming business cycle high point. Interest rates, changes in the money supply, building permits, and automobile sales are all examples of leading economic indicators—things that go up or down right before the business cycle itself does likewise.

Coincident indicators move with the changes in the general business cycle, give or take a month. Unemployment, hours worked, weekly earnings, those are all coincident indicators, reaching their peaks and lows at the same time as the business cycle.

Finally, lagging indicators are the ones that tend not to move until after the business cycle has moved, following behind the general trend.

Job vacancies, productivity, and the average prime rate charged by commercial banks are all lagging indicators.

Generally, leading indicators are a sign of business expectations; coincident indicators give a sense of current conditions; and lagging indicators show how production costs and economic conditions have changed. Like the weather, nothing is exact. The amount of lag time between an indicator and the business cycle can vary from cycle to cycle.

Even though there are about 20 commonly-accepted indicators used in leading composite indexes of indicators, there are literally dozens of indicators that could be used by economists and financial and public-policy analysts to evaluate current and future economic trends. And since economic analysis and forecasting is less than an exact science, there are some disagreements about the classification and effectiveness of some indicators. Indicators are also reevaluated over time to consider whether or not they remain useful.

Despite these drawbacks, economic indicators can reveal relative changes in economic conditions. One method for increasing the probability of correctly estimating changes in economic conditions is to employ more than one indicator.

For practical reasons, indicators are used in clusters to approximate the end of a period of expansion or the end of a contraction phase. Since identifying the precise timing of the end of one phase and the beginning of the next in a business cycle can be difficult, making use of a number of economic or social indicators increases the likelihood of positioning the specific turning points in the business cycle, and for assessing relative strengths or weaknesses in an economy.

Central Banks

Charged with critical monetary and financial responsibilities, a central bank is the most powerful financial institution in a nation's economy. Central banks issue currency, serve the banking needs of the national government, maintain foreign exchange reserves, support the banking system (including serving as a clearinghouse for bank drafts and as a lender of last resort), and perhaps most importantly, protect the value of the currency through monetary policy. Examples of central banks include the Federal Reserve in the United States, the Bank of England, the Bank of Japan, and the recently created European Central Bank, which serves the European Union.

Modern banking operates on the principle of fractional reserve banking. Under this system, banks accept currency deposits and make loans. Because banks use some of the deposited money for lending activities, they do not hold all the currency they receive—they reserve only a fraction of it. Consequently the total amount of money in circulation is greater than the total amount of currency.

This system functions effectively as long as depositors do not wish to withdraw all the funds at the same time. If such a situation occurs, the system experiences a bank run (when the rush to take out cash happens at one institution) or a bank panic (when the mania infects many banks at the same time, though you sometimes also hear this called a run on the banks). In these situations banks desperately need access to additional currency to calm the fears of depositors.

Because bank runs have the potential to turn into bank panics, individual banks don't like dipping into their cash reserves to assist other banks in trouble. After repeated bank panics in the 1800s, central banks took on this role of lender of last resort. In this capacity, the central bank stands prepared to provide emergency currency reserves to any bank that faces a run. By the early 20th century this role was well established, and central banks had emerged as banking leaders rather than competitors.

In the heyday of the international gold standard (1870–1914), central banks were responsible for maintaining the convertibility of a nation's currency into gold. Under normal conditions this responsibility limited the issuance of currency.

In times of war, financing government debt took precedence (generally requiring central banks to issue additional currency) and convertibility was suspended. When the international gold standard was suspended at the outbreak of World War I, the convertibility constraint disappeared. Despite several attempts to restore the gold standard and modified versions of the gold standard (including the Bretton Woods System that lasted into the early 1970s), monetary policy changed forever in 1914.

During the early 20th century, central banks discovered the power of monetary policy, and have been exercising this power to influence macroeconomic events ever since. Monetary policy refers to the manipulation of the money supply and interest rates in order to meet particular goals on a macroeconomic (that is, affecting the whole economy) scale.

Central banks have a variety of tools at their disposal to conduct monetary policy, including altering the interest rate banks pay when they borrow from the central bank (known as the discount rate in the United States), changing reserve requirements (the portion of depositors' funds that banks must hold in cash), and engaging in "open market operations" (that is, buying or selling bonds to alter the amount of cash reserves in the banking system.)

Monetary policy objectives generally focus on price stability (that is, restricting inflation), unemployment, or economic growth. Experience has shown that these objectives often conflict with one another and therefore must be prioritized. Although the Great Depression of the 1930s raised awareness of prolonged unemployment as a concern, central banks have historically emphasized maintaining their currency's value, a role most compatible with the price stability objective.

No central bank today can ignore the needs and perceptions of financial markets. With stock market volatility the norm and global capital flows at historic highs, public statements made by central banks often invoke strong market reactions. With the power to calm public concerns or induce fear merely through a speech or press conference, central banks have inherited additional power. Consequently central banking in the 21st century extends beyond the realm of banking and monetary policy, and necessarily encompasses the entire financial sector.

Commercial Banking

Commercial banks provide services to individuals, small businesses, and government organizations; these are the banks most people have contact with on a daily basis. They act as intermediaries by accepting funds in a variety of forms, and lending a portion of them out, making their profit on interest and fees. Most of a consumer's contact with the bank will be through deposit accounts, bonds, and loans.

A print titled "The Panic—Run on the Fourth National Bank in 1873."

Deposit accounts include checking accounts, savings accounts, and money market funds (MMFs). Negotiable Order of Withdrawal (NOW) accounts, interest-accruing checking accounts, were introduced in 1981 to compete with MMFs. Until the 1980s, the interest paid on savings accounts was limited to 5.25 percent (5.5 percent for savings and loans), because the federal government was afraid competition would lead to bank failures. The regulation was repealed when inflation caused people to move their funds from savings accounts to nonregulated MMFs.

The common uses of bank funds include bank loans, investment in securities, federal funds sold, repurchase agreements, Eurodollar loans, and fixed assets. In addition banks hold cash in order to maintain liquidity, and accommodate withdrawals by depositors. The amount of cash a bank maintains is determined by the requirements imposed by the Federal Reserve (also known as "the Fed")—a power the Fed uses to control the money supply.

The main use of bank funds is for loans. A common business loan is the working capital loan, a short-term loan that may be renewed frequently; it's used by a business to purchase short-term assets such as inventory. Term loans, with a fixed interest rate and a maturity ranging from two to 10 years, are commonly used to purchased fixed assets like machinery; the terms of the loan limit what the funds can be used for, and the assets purchased by the loan serve as collateral, to be repossessed if its interest is not paid.

Commercial banks also provide individuals with installment loans to finance cars and other big-ticket items, and real estate loans, typically with a 15- to 30-year mortgage, sometimes shortened with a large balloon (one-time) payment. Banks typically also provide credit cards, through an agreement with VISA or MasterCard; their interest rates are regulated by the relevant state laws.

When seen as too big to fail, some troubled banks have received special treatment from bank regulators. One well-known example is Continental Illinois Bank, which was rescued by the federal government in 1984. Roughly 75 percent of the time deposits at Continental were in accounts in excess of $100,000, and therefore not guaranteed against default by the FDIC. The government bailed out all depositors, reasoning that if a bank this size failed, the loss of confidence in the American banking system would lead to a run on other banks. As a consequence, though, large banks are seen as safer ventures, more capable of taking risks because of the promise of a bailout. The 2008–09 $700 billion bailout of many leading American investment firms and banks (and corresponding bank bailouts in nations throughout Europe and Asia) was a new test for capitalism: a guarantee of bailout and the actuality of bailout may mean different things for a nation's economy.

Investment Banking

Investment banks assist with a variety of transactions, particularly those involving the restructuring of the ownership of firms: private placements, initial public offerings (IPOs), mergers and acquisitions, leverage buyouts, and securitization. Unlike commercial banks, an investment bank makes most of its profit in fees, since it acts as an intermediary.

Private placements are stock issues that don't have to be registered with the Securities and Exchange Commission (SEC), and the purchase of which is highly restricted. The purchasers can include an unlimited number of accredited investors—institutions, the officers and director of the company, wealthy individuals—and no more than 35 nonaccredited investors. None of the stock can be resold to the general public. For most startup companies, the first private placements are sold to a small number of wealthy investors called angel investors. They usually have some understanding of the relevant industry and are given a position on the new company's board of directors.

As a company grows, the next step is to seek the support of a venture capital fund—a private limited partnership that raises money from a group of investors (usually institutions). The managers of such funds are called venture capitalists, and are typically very well-versed in a particular industry, and limit their investments to that industry.

An IPO—often much-anticipated in the case of well-known private companies on the rise—is the first sale of stock to outside investors, at which point it can be bought and sold among the general public, in markets like the New York Stock Exchange. Taking companies public is the primary business of most investment banks. Investment bankers assist firms by helping to determine the stock's initial offering price and selling the stock to its clients—generally a mix of institutional investors and high net-worth individuals. After the stock is sold, the bank will have an analyst cover the stock to maintain investor interest in it.

In a merger, two or more firms become one firm with control of the combined firm going to both management teams. An acquisition occurs when one firm takes control of another firm. There are a variety of pros and cons to mergers and acquisitions, both to the stockholders and the general public.

The Justice Department's antitrust division regulates mergers for this reason. They are also a good example of a situation in which what's best for the company may not be best for its shareholders: when a company becomes more diversified by acquiring other companies, it takes in income from a wider variety of sources. But a stockholder is able to diversify his portfolio already, and it may not be to his benefit to have the companies in which he owns shares seek diversification on their own.

A leveraged buyout is a "going private" transaction, in which all the equity of a publicly held company is purchased by a small group of investors (often including the company's management)— specifically, one in which substantial borrowing is necessary in order to make the purchase.

Securitization is the process of combining debt instruments and selling various slices of the combinations to investors depending upon their risk profiles. Asset securitization began with the mortgage-backed market, in which individual home mortgages were combined into pools, and bonds were issued using the pools as collateral. Everything from auto loans, credit card balances, student loans, and the cash flow from David Bowie's album sales became subject to securitization.

The subprime mortgage crisis spelled the end of Wall Street as a group of lightly regulated investment banks. On September 15, 2008 Lehman Brothers filed for Chapter 11 bankruptcy protection, the largest such filing in U.S. history. When the U.S. government refused to bail out Lehman Brothers (but did rescue the government-sponsored lenders Fannie Mae and Freddie Mac, as well as insurance giant AIG), investment banks had no choice but to redefine themselves as traditional banks (Goldman Sachs and Morgan Stanley did) or to be sold (like Merrill Lynch and parts of Lehman Brothers). The age of free-wheeling investment banks had come to a close.

Stocks and the Stock Market

Stocks—shares of ownership in companies—are the main form of securities traded in stock markets. Stockholders usually receive dividends as a portion of the company's profits, and benefit from stock trades by buying at a lower price and selling it at a higher one. The risk is that the price may not rise—and dividends may be suspended when the company is encountering difficulties.

The concept of stocks and stock markets is not new. Originally known as stock exchanges, these markets were established to organize the trade of securities, which now include stocks, bonds, futures, and options. The ability to buy and sell shares in a company without taking an investment back from the company itself gives investors a flexibility that may make them more willing to put their money down, knowing they can get out any time they want—and makes investing a more reasonable proposition for everyday people.

Modern stock markets are an integral part of global capitalism. In the United States, the New York Stock Exchange (NYSE) and American Stock Exchange (AMEX) are the two largest markets, but there are nine regional exchanges, as well as NASDAQ for over-the-counter (unlisted) stock exchanges. Around the world, there are major exchanges in London, Paris, and Tokyo, among other cities. Dealers buy and sell from their own portfolios, or inventories of securities. Brokers execute trades representing clients and receive commissions and fees for their services. Sometimes the same firm can act in both roles.

Although corporations or companies may not be involved in the secondary markets, they monitor the stock value of the company on the secondary market. The better the stock performs or trades in value, the better the company's future borrowing position with investment banks will be; a well-performing stock is like a good review. A company's success is measured not only by how well it performs in terms of profit and loss in capitalistic trade markets, but also by how well or poorly the company stock performs in the market. A company can only list its stock on one exchange, and strict regulations apply to the buying and selling of shares.

Some exchanges like the NYSE set the bar high so that only the largest of companies can meet their requirements. A company must have at least 1.1 million shares outstanding, for instance, and must be valued at $100 million or more. Over-the-counter trades like those done at NASDAQ are one option for stocks that can't meet the requirements of major markets—as a result, many of the good performers are the small technology companies with highly perceived potential that hasn't been reached yet. The rapid generation of new technology means there will always be companies of interest to investors, even though they haven't had the opportunity to demonstrate their longevity and dependability the way giants like General Electric or IBM have.

Much of the securities trade is conducted by brokerage firms that act as intermediaries for individuals and institutions. Only members of the stock exchange can actually conduct a stock transaction, and seats on exchanges are limited and expensive. In 2005 an NYSE member seat sold for $3 million. Membership has its privileges, and brokerage firms also get to vote on exchange policy. The cost of a seat is offset by the fees firms charge for transactions, both sales and purchases. At traditional stock exchanges like the NYSE, which currently has five trading floors in New York City, a typical trade revolves around a post. A stockholder or client places an order to trade a security such as a stock with a stockbroker of a firm. Sometimes institutional brokers are used if the client is a bank or institution and the purchase is large. The order is moved to the exchange floor by a variety of traditional and electronic methods, so that a floor broker for the stockbroker firm or institutional broker actually carries the order to a post where all stocks associated with that company are traded. A specialist at the post will manage the auction process as different floor brokers exchange, buy, and sell orders or trade the company stock. The specialist informs the floor brokers of the final price agreed upon in the ongoing auction. After hours trade also takes place when markets are closed, but such trading is light and can be highly volatile because fewer investors are participating.

The markets move on anything that affects investor confidence, not only in an individual company, but also in the economy itself— which can include noneconomic events. The September 11 terrorist attacks, the end of the Cold War, and closely-watched election results are all among the major world events that are reflected in market activity. The economic turmoil of that late 2000s carried investor confidence to Great Depression–era lows, and that economic fear became the driving force.

Bonds

Bonds are publicly traded long-term debt instruments, issued by a variety of governmental agencies and corporations. The issuer promises to pay bondholders some fixed amount of interest according to a particular schedule, until a future date when the bond matures. At maturity, the bond issuer repays the amount borrowed, also called the face value of the bond. Bond maturities are always more than 10 years, and usually 20 to 30 years long. Technically, any maturity is legally permissible by the bond issuer, and in 1993, the Walt Disney Corporation offered 100-year bonds in order to lock in low interest rates.

Let's say a bondholder purchases a 20-year bond for $1,000 with an interest rate of 5 percent. The bondholder will receive a fixed return of $50 dollars every year for 20 years, plus the face value of the bond ($1,000) when it matures. The face value of a single bond is usually a multiple of $1,000. The 5 percent interest is commonly referred to as the coupon interest rate, dating from the time when bonds had coupons attached to them that owners would clip and cash in.

Since bonds bring in a constant interest payment, bonds can and will be sold at different prices later on. But bonds aren't considered very liquid assets. The enormous bond market primarily deals with newly issued bonds, and a seasoned bond—one that has already collected some of its return—is a tougher sell. Discount bonds are those sold at a price below their face value, and premium bonds are those that have sold for more than face value.

Bonds are generally considered a safe investment, but there are inherent risks. The behavior of interest rates has a big effect on the bond market—when rates rise, prices of existing bonds fall, and vice versa. Most bonds have a call provision, which gives the issuer the right to pay off the bonds under specific terms, before maturity. When prevailing interest rates fall, many issuers call their bonds—paying off the owners—and issue newer bonds at the lower interest rate. While the investor probably hasn't lost money in this case, he has made less income than he hoped.

There is also the risk of inflation. Since bonds have long maturities, the purchasing power of the interest generated by the bond and its inflation-adjusted value at redemption may decline. Index-linked bonds take care of this risk by paying interest linked to some index (such as the Consumer Price Index) that adjusts to inflation, rather than a fixed rate. Another risk is that the issuer may default. Unlike stocks in the stock market, bonds do not give the bondholder any ownership stake in the company. Many bonds are immune to this risk—U.S. Treasury bonds and municipal bonds (issued by towns, cities, states, and so on, often to pay for some major project), for instance. Municipal bonds, though, are usually revenue bonds, which don't pay out until a specific level of revenue has been generated. Local municipalities sometimes have the option of defaulting on their debt, as do corporations.

Venture Capital

The business practice of venture capital is a form of hands-on investing that had its heyday in the late 1990s dot-com boom, and still exists in business sectors throughout the country, particularly in Silicon Valley, California. Although it's no longer exclusively practiced in the United States, it is a distinctively American institution. Venture capital was once also called risk capital, highlighting its riskier nature relative to guaranteed investments like bonds. Venture capital invests in funding, or is available for investments. These investments are, by nature, funneled into enterprises that offer the probability of profit with accompanying high risks of no return. Many startup companies are funded by venture capital, notably technology and biotechnology firms.

Venture capital isn't just used to start a company, though. It can also provide seed money—small amounts loaned to inventors or entrepreneurs so that they can prove or demonstrate the profitability of their ideas. It can be used to finance a leveraged buyout, a major expansion of the company, or the preparation for an initial public offering of stock.

The venture capital investment decision-making process requires an extensive and arduous analysis to examine management capabilities, financial health, market trends, and investment strategy; sometimes a venture capital firm must be adaptable to choice and structuring of investment. Although venture capital investment is relatively smaller to Gross Domestic Product (GDP), it is a major source of funding for new technology-based firms. Firms using venture capital are given financial support at a crucial moment to create innovations for the market place.

Originally, venture capital resembled the old patronage system of the Renaissance: wealthy individuals supported new ventures in return for a piece of the pie. Now, venture capital is disbursed by funds gathered from individual and institutional sources and managed by a venture capitalist who has extensive knowledge of a particular industry or type of technology. Banks need to be conservative about who they lend money to, and to err on the side of caution; the promise of the possibility of a high return is less likely to entice them when there is a real risk of failure. Venture capital funds are not so hesitant, and the way to minimize the risk is to know as much as possible about the types of businesses they are going to fund, specializing in a way that is unnecessary to banks.

While investors playing the stock market might be able to succeed without knowing much about the products and activities of the companies in which they invest—depending on what other factors guide them—a venture capitalist needs to be able to evaluate whether a new idea has profit potential, and whether a new company's goals are realistic.

Arbitrage

Arbitrage is the simultaneous purchase and sale of similar or identical assets to try to earn a profit from the price difference. The concept of arbitrage is very closely related to the law of one price, which says that in competitive markets, identical assets should have the same price. If prices are different, the activity of arbitrageurs will act to equalize the prices. Arbitrage is essentially that which reinforces the law of one price. For instance, assume that the price of gold is $250 an ounce in New York, and $300 an ounce in Los Angeles. The $50 price difference, minus the cost of transporting gold across the country, is a chance for profit. As more arbitrageurs move in to take advantage of this, buying up New York gold, the prices in New York go up. As more gold arrives in Los Angeles, increasing supply, the prices in L.A. go down. Prices will continue to move until the price difference between L.A. and New York is the same as, or less than, the cost of transport. Such opportunities don't last long, and there are more expenses than just transport.

Arbitrage carries over into financial markets as well. The price of a share of stock on the NYSE and the London Stock Exchange is usually almost identical, because trading costs are low. If a significant price differential existed, arbitrageurs would quickly take the opportunity to make a profit, and the price would once again equalize.

Interest rates are also affected by arbitrage. If two bonds on the market are similar in characteristics, you can expect that they'll pay almost the same interest rate. Corporations use the concept of interest rate arbitrage to calculate how much interest they should pay on bonds when they need to borrow money. They just look at what the market is paying on a similar bond to the one they plan to issue.

Arbitrage is also connected to the foreign currency exchange rate. The exchange rate is the rate at which one country's currency can be traded for another's, and directly affects international trade. A given commodity should have the same price across countries, so purchasing power is at parity. If that is not the case, then traders can buy a commodity from a country where it is cheap, and sell in a country where it is expensive at a profit. This commodity arbitrage will result in equal commodity prices across countries.

This assumes no trade barriers and ignores the practical cost of trade. In real life, exchange rates tend to be proportional to relative changes in price levels in the two countries, over long periods of time—but on a day-to-day basis, there can be significant discrepancies.

Debt

People think of debt as something you "go into," "fall into," or are "buried under," but economists speak of debt as being issued. Like credit, it's a liability for the borrower, who promises to make future payments to the lender—though "lender" here can be a misleading term, when the debts are phone or electric bills, which represent goods or services provided in advance of payment. In both those cases, though, there is a formal binding contract that enforces the borrower's requirement to pay.

The economic basis of debt is the mismatch between the resources and needs of the parties involved. A debt contract matches a borrower, who is short of current resources but long in potential future resources, and a lender, who is currently long and therefore can afford to be patient. Debt can be seen as the exchange of funds over time—paying tomorrow for a hamburger today. The lender sacrifices current use of these funds in exchange for financial return. The return is usually referred to as the rate of interest, and the profit to the lender is obviously the same as the cost to the borrower. Student loans are a case where the benefits of the loan—the increase to future earnings—are forecast to outweigh the cost to the borrower.

Both lender and borrower take risks with debt. That student may never finish college, or a startup business that borrowed money to begin operations may never earn a profit—such are the lenders' obvious risks, and why they sometimes require collateral to back the loan, a physical asset belonging to the borrower that the lender can repossess and sell. In the case of businesses, some part of the collateral will often be the company's equipment used for its operations.

There are different types of instruments that can be used to issue debt. Short-term debt instruments generally maturing in less than a year are traded in the money market. These instruments include short-term bonds (bills), negotiable bank certificates of deposit (only large denominations), commercial paper, and repurchase agreements. Long-term debt instruments are traded in the capital market. These instruments include long-term government and corporate bonds (bonds); residential, commercial, and farm mortgages; and commercial and consumer loans.

Credit

Credit is an arrangement under which resources are acquired now, but paid for later. The eventual payment, whether it's made all at once or in installments, usually includes interest—the creditor has essentially made a loan. The extension of credit is almost as old as economic culture, and is a way of life for many: consider the case of farmers, for instance, who would buy seed and equipment on credit, and pay for them with the profits of the eventual harvest. The emergence of capitalism has meant a boom in the number, frequency, and complexity of credit transactions. Just like with those farmers, credit lets businesses and individuals spend against tomorrow's earnings—which is sometimes the only way to make the earnings in the first place.

Various instruments of credit are negotiable and traded in the markets. There are three types of credit. Consumer credit is a short-term loan extended to the public for the purchase of goods and services. The main economic function of consumer credit is to allow consumers to make purchases sooner, which in turn allows businesses to make sales sooner. Consumer credit can be either noninstallment—repaid in a lump sum—or more commonly, installment credit, paid in regular (usually monthly) payments.

The second type of credit is trade credit. This is a credit extended by a trader or producer to other business firms through terms that allow payment sometime in the future. It may be extended by material suppliers to manufacturers, or by manufacturers to wholesalers or retailers. Trade credit is a principal channel through which credit flows across the economy.

The third type of credit is bank credit, money lent by banking institutions through advances, overdrafts, discounting bills, or purchasing securities. Overdrafts are more often seen as a penalty in the United States—rather than bouncing, a check drawn against insufficient funds is honored, and the account-holder is billed a fee or interest—but in the United Kingdom it is treated simply as another credit limit, much like that on a credit card. The line between a penalty and the fee associated with credit can be slim—another case is that of the discount that is offered to people who pay back a debt early, which in a sense acts as a penalty for those who do not. It's all a matter of perspective.

All forms of credit, including home mortgages and automobile financing, took a bad fall in the late 2000s, as banks shored up their interests. For a period of time in 2008 and 2009, a consumer needed an excellent credit rating above 700 to even be considered for a basic loan that could have been approved a few years earlier with a credit rating of perhaps 600.

Audit

Like democracy, capitalism has evolved some facets that ensure fairness by means of checks and balances. In most capitalist systems, auditing guards against corruption and ensures compliance with government regulations and tax laws.

An audit is a process in which a company's or individual's financial statements are examined by a third party, to confirm their accuracy. The familiar example is the tax audit, during which the auditor examines the taxpayer's deductions and other claims, comparing them against receipts and other evidence, as well as judging whether the preparer of the tax return followed the letter of the law. This is only one example of the sorts of audits that are conducted, though one that happens to be well-known because all taxpayers may be subjected to an audit.

Audits are often thought of as a fault-finding mission, but that's not exactly the case. When the annual Academy Awards votes are audited, it's not conducted out of a desire to uncover wrongdoing or errors, but to prove that no wrongdoing occurred, and to ensure public confidence in the results. Audits evaluate all sorts of information and data, of three broad categories.

A compliance audit determines that a set of activities conforms to specific rules and regulations—like the audit of the Academy Awards. An operational audit assesses efficiency according to particular operating objectives—the domain of the famed efficiency expert. And that tax audit would fall under the financial statement audit. The auditor's report following a financial statement audit includes the audit opinion, which summarizes whether or not the examined financial statements and records accord with the Generally Accepted Accounting Principles (GAAP). If they do, the auditor issues what's called an unqualified opinion—meaning that the opinion is without further specification or disclaimers.

A qualified opinion, in contrast, is one expressing reservations about the audit—maybe there is insufficient evidence to draw conclusions in one area of the books. An adverse opinion is issued when there is a significant or material departure from GAAP—when a significant amount is wrong, deceitful, erroneous, or improperly presented. A disclaimer of opinion is equivalent to the auditor declining to comment; for whatever reason, maybe conflicting information or a lack of data, no opinion is given.

The Generally Accepted Auditing Standards (GAAS) are the most recognized set of auditing standards in the industry, and include 10 standards in three categories. GAAS aren't laws, but because they were adopted by the American Institute for Certified Public Accountants, they are the standard used in industry, by government agencies, and in courts of law.

The execution of an audit is a complicated and varied process. The auditor, with a healthy skepticism, adopts a preliminary audit strategy to assess materiality and risk. Materiality is the measure of magnitude of an omission or misstatement—such an error is material if its inclusion is enough to affect someone's opinion of the data; typing "teh" instead of "the" is an immaterial typo, but typing "can" instead of "can't" is not. Audit risk is the risk that the auditor may unknowingly fail to flag in the opinion that the statements were materially misstated.

The overall methodology of an audit comes down to identifying what needs to be proven. The auditor collects relevant evidence upon which the judgment is based, and assesses the fairness of the data through the use of various tests. In applying a range of tests, the auditor deals in probabilities through statistical sampling. Small sample units that represent larger populations are observed to evaluate relevant characteristics that the auditor needs to identify.

Auditing also involves less systematic means of evidence collection such as inquiring, observing, and the application of analytical procedures. The auditor may observe and inquire about procedures for recording transactions, or apply analytical procedures to compare current year assertions to the prior year, often helping to pinpoint items that may need to be investigated further.

It is important to remember that the auditing of financial statements is an attest function, meaning that after conducting an audit of the accounting system of a business, the independent auditor issues an opinion on the fairness of the presentation of the financial statements and their conformity to GAAP. Essentially, an attestation is an evaluation of the quality of the information presented under GAAP rules.

An attest function differs from the definitive substantiation of facts or truths because "attest" merely means to "bear witness" or, more specifically, to attest to the reliability of an entity's financial statements. The financial statement assertions of a company are the responsibility of its management. The auditor is merely expressing judgment—in a separate report—on the basis of being a trained observer performing a critical review of the data.

Bankruptcy

In antiquity, bankruptcy—when a business or individual is unable to pay their outstanding debts—was a type of fraud. Those who were bankrupt were severely punished, and the laws were all aimed at making sure the creditors were repaid. Rather than declaring bankruptcy, as in the modern world, a business would be accused of bankruptcy—and the punishment could include a public flogging. Even a few centuries ago, bankrupt individuals in England had their ears cut off and nailed to a wall. Debtors' prisons never suffered from a lack of inmates. The accusatory origins of the word are reflected when we refer to someone as being "morally bankrupt."

Today, though, bankruptcy is declared by the debtor, rather than starting as an accusation made by the creditor; in most cases there is no crime in being bankrupt. The declaration of bankruptcy seeks to eliminate debt, especially when personal bankruptcy is declared—it provides the possibility of a fresh start and relief from creditors. The modern version of bankruptcy developed over the course of the 19th century, as state and federal laws were repeatedly softened—offering some relief from debt, and reducing penalties—in response to economic crises that left many Americans without the ability to repay their debts.

In the aftermath of the Great Depression, Chapter 13 bankruptcy was introduced, which gave debtors the ability to repay over a three to five year plan, while retaining their property and residence. In the late 1970s, Chapter 11 bankruptcy was introduced, to help the reorganization of bankrupt businesses. In the aftermath of the farm crisis, Chapter 12 provided options for family farms. The end of the 20th century saw a boom in bankruptcy for both businesses and individuals—one in 76 Americans filed for personal bankruptcy in 1997. Bankruptcy filings in the United States neared the one million mark in 2008, exceeding 5,000 filings per day in November of that year.

Well-known businesses like Continental Airlines and Texaco filed for corporate bankruptcy, soon joined in the next decade by Worldcom and Enron. Chapter 11 reorganizations are the most common form of bankruptcy in the business world. Under this program, businesses are allowed to continue operations with their management teams in place, while assets are protected from creditors. Management has 120 days to propose a plan of reorganization to creditors, but the deadline can be extended for years.

Cash Flow

Cash flow is the transfer of money in and out of a given operation. Assessed in a company's statement of cash flows, the analysis starts from net income that has accrued from the previous year, adds non-cash (or paper only) charges such as depreciation or amortization, subtracts or adds changes in asset and liability accounts, then adds or subtracts payments and receipts related to investing and financing, and arrives at a cash basis net income. The end result of a cash flow statement is to emphasize the change in cash and cash equivalents for the year.

There are various components of an enterprise that affect cash flow, such as inventory, accounts receivable, accounts payable, and in addition, investment and financing activities undertaken by the enterprise. By performing a cash flow analysis on these components, business managers are able to more easily identify potential cash flow problems and find ways to fix them. Cash flow is meant to capture all real cash outlays of the present, and analyzing this in detail helps an entrepreneur to determine the ability of a business to generate cash from its current operations. While cash flow is not a fashionable point of focus among the majority of business media, to financial professionals it is generally a valuable indicator of a company's immediate financial health and its ability to stay solvent.

A business enterprise succeeds in generating earning power when it uses cash to generate more cash. Earning power, in turn, increases an enterprise's monetary wealth so that it may pass on this wealth to its owners, and this denotes a healthy cash flow. The passing of wealth may be to a single proprietor or a series of partners, or in the case of the corporation, it may be shareholders. Both investors and creditors rely on healthy cash flows of an enterprise to which they have committed funds, because the motive for committing funds is to earn a favorable rate of return from the investment, whether the funds were exchanged for a percentage of ownership and dividends, or for an interest-bearing loan. Whereas solvency problems can be hidden beneath revenue growth and satisfactory profits, the financial reporting of cash flows allows prospective investors, creditors, and business partners to assess the viability of the enterprise.

Barter

Barter—the exchange of one thing for another without using money—evolved in prehistory, when humans exchanged basic goods like animal and plant products. Living in groups exposed individuals to a wide array of skills, and built trust between individuals and families. It wasn't long before people were able to recognize the benefit of trading among themselves, in order to share the wealth. Even when skills were equal, there's only so much time in the day, and barter allowed for a division of labor.

Division of labor in turn allows for specialization, a driving force in improving productivity and living standards. Though barter made that possible, it has been supplanted by a monetary system in nearly every modern country. While the use of barter allowed for previously unknown prosperity, the substantial transaction costs limited social and economic advancements.

For one thing, barter required what has become known as the double coincidence of wants. A pig farmer who finds himself in need of a sweater would have to find an individual who had sweaters to trade, and who also wanted pork. If the pig farmer could not find a sweater-maker in need of pork, the search costs could be prohibitive, and hence the pig farmer may choose to retreat to a self-sufficient lifestyle.

Even if the pig farmer were able to overcome the double coincidence of wants, other problems exist. The durability and portability of the pigs may pose a problem should the farmer live a great distance from the sweater-producer. Assessing the true value of the pigs may prove difficult, as pigs are neither uniform in size nor quality. Because one pig is likely to be worth more than one sweater, barter may be further hindered due to the fact that pigs are not divisible. The pig farmer would have to agree to take ownership of a large number of sweaters, or find something other than a pig to offer for the sweater. Despite the near-uniform displacement of barter by money, barter did not disappear altogether. It continued to crop up throughout modern history, particularly during periods of high inflation (and hyperinflations). During the German hyperinflation of 1923, for example, due to rapid declines in the purchasing power of money, lifetime savings vanished overnight, while economic life was reduced to barter. Similar episodes occurred as recently as the early 1990s at which time hyperinflations in Yugo-slavia caused many individuals to return to barter as their primary means of exchange.

Black Market

The black market is the sector of economic activity involving illegal activities. This can refer to everything from goods that are intrinsi-cally illegal—like drugs and some firearms—to goods which are ren-dered illegal by context, such as stolen goods, smuggled contraband, or cases where the seller has avoided a tax. Black markets flourish under government restrictions, such as during Prohibition or under the regimes of Nazi Germany or the Soviet Union. Organized crime is often involved in the black market, though not all black market activity stems from organized groups.

Legal restrictions cause a decrease in supply, and the price will rise as long as demand stays the same, or at least doesn't fall as much. At the same time, some black market goods are typically cheaper than they would be if they were legal, because of a change in production costs—like cigarettes without tax stamps, stolen goods, or illegally bootlegged DVDs.

Black markets represent an important sector of any national economy, but in some cases the contribution is extraordinary. Underground markets represent the largest section of the domestic products of dictatorial regimes in developing countries: 65 percent of the Gross Domestic Product in Bolivia and 76 percent in Nigeria, to name the most extreme cases. Black markets continue to prosper in former Communist states as well: 39 percent in Estonia, 45 percent in Russia, and 51 percent in Ukraine. The currency used in these foreign black markets is the American dollar. This phenomenon started in the late 1960s and peaked in the 1990s, when about 75 percent of the $100 bills in circulation were overseas. Some market analysts suspect that the 1996 redesign of the $100 bill was due to the creation of an extremely convincing fake from Middle Eastern forgers that was undermining the real bill in unofficial operations.

In the United States, there is little market regulation relative to these other countries. Black market activity covers about a tenth of the American GDP, a parallel economy with its own secretive and well-hidden structure, labor demand, prices, and commodities. Much of the market is created by the clash of American practices. For instance, Americans consume more marijuana than the rest of the world, but also imprison more people for marijuana-related crimes. American laws guarantee maximum freedom to Californian agricultural employers, so migrant workers are mainly illegal immigrants from Mexico. The shadow economy is inextricably linked to the mainstream, and the parallels are striking. Both tycoons and gangsters rise and fall; new technology shapes both markets; government intervention can reinvigorate black markets as well as mainstream ones; and big business learns and profits from the underground, just as drug dealers adopt brand names for their products in emulation of legitimate vendors.

The black market provides an interesting model for the study of unregulated capitalism, because the 2008 financial crisis signaled an increase in capitalist regulation. Many major global corporations were collapsing or being rescued by government intervention. Many people believed that more government oversight of business practices would solve the financial crisis, while others argued that government policies were too restrictive and were making the markets behave artificially. Experts in capitalism were baffled (Alan Greenspan called the crisis a "once-in-a-century credit tsunami"), political leaders were in disagreement, and the general public was in outrage. As you will read in the next chapter, the quest for a perfect balance between regulation and free trade is far from new to the evolution of capitalism: in fact it is the story of the capitalist chronology itself.

Chapter 2

Capitalist Chronology

Capitalism is a living piece of history. That's the nature of doing business, the nature of economics—everything is in motion, everything started somewhere and is headed somewhere else. Capitalism is a living thing, an adapting thing—and adaptability is the capitalist's greatest tool. There are reasons modern capitalism has taken its current shape—reasons for both its strengths and weaknesses. It has been shaped that way, in response to past successes and failures. Like everything else in the world, we have to assume that it hasn't taken its final shape—or attained its ideal form. In order to participate fully as capitalists and be part of the next generation of capitalists, it is necessary to know what came before.

Ancient History

It is tricky talking about the history of capitalism, because it's been around longer than anyone has had a name for it. Capitalist transactions are at the heart of human society—the basic principle of "give me that, I'll give you this" has been around since prehistory, and may even predate *homo sapiens*. Trade and trade routes developed early, to take advantage of the different natural resources of various regions. That kind of barter never went away. Two everyday illustrations give a sense of how quickly this kind of economy develops: in armies where soldiers are given cigarette rations along with their meals, nonsmokers have always saved up their cigarettes to trade with the smokers—both parties profiting from the transaction. And after every Halloween, kids across America dump out their bags of candy and trade Almond Joys for Skittles, turning one kid's trash into another's treasure. Sometimes there's even some entrepreneurial kid who can turn Sally's dislike of Almond Joys and Jimmy's abundance of Skittles into a profit for himself, acting as intermediary.

Early societies in the 9th and 10th millennia B.C.E. were formed by hunter-gatherer tribes that settled down and became farmers—domesticating animals, building permanent shelters, and cultivating crops instead of relying on foraging. These stable communities produced surpluses of food and other goods, which could be stored or traded. Specialization developed on both the micro level—individuals acting as hunters, potters, hut builders, farmers—and the macro level, as settlements took advantage of their natural resources (such as the ocean with its fish and shells, fertile soil and its agricultural possibilities, and fields with wild game). Just as communities depended on the cooperation between those specialists—the potter needed some of the hunter's meat, and the hunter needed the builder to make him a hut—they came to depend on the cooperation between disparate communities, to share innovations, trade goods, and improve the gene pool through intermarriage.

Trade networks and well-formed trade routes developed so early that we have probably not yet uncovered the first of them, and they sometimes covered vast distances, as evidenced by the types of seashells found in the remains of inland communities.

Writing developed alongside, and partly in the service of, commerce. Some of the earliest writings are long lists of inventories of grain, cattle, and sheep etched into soft clay tablets with a sharpened reed. Number systems generally came before alphabets for that reason, and many alphabets began as symbols for those items to be tallied.

Code of Hammurabi

Civilizations spread and became more sophisticated, with economic systems adapting to suit new needs. In the Near East, the ideas of credit and debt were well-established by the 18th century B.C.E., when the Code of Hammurabi was enacted. A king of the first dynasty of the Babylonian Empire, Hammurabi called for the laws of the land (defining offenses and their punishments, including "an eye for an eye") to be written down and erected in public view, so that the law would outlive the will of any one king. It was a symbolic gesture—few people could read—but an important one, and this first code of immutable laws included a number of banking and trade regulations.

Coins had not yet been developed, but trade was often done with silver and grain. Creditors made loans and collected interest (as high as 300 percent per year, usually between 20 percent and 33.5 percent). Contracts and promissory notes governing these loans had to be drawn up in front of a public official and agreed to in the presence of witnesses—a lot like what judges and notaries public do now. In the case of natural disasters, the debt was forgiven unless a crop had been lost only through the debtor's negligence. The law also protected debtors from being unreasonably abused by creditors.

Hammurabi's code provided laws governing the leasing of land and profit sharing between landowners and tenant farmers, the sale of property, the hiring of labor, and fixed prices for beer and shipbuilding, while regulating other goods and services. Responsibility was central to the code, determining for instance that the captain of a ship was responsible for replacing freight lost in transit, and whether a traveling merchant carrying goods on consignment was responsible for replacing them if they were stolen. He wasn't, but he did have to make up the difference out of his own pocket if he sold them and was unable to get a good price. Even marriage involved financial arrangements—the division of debt, the result of divorce, the process of inheritance—all outlined in the code.

Coins

When silver and other precious metals were used as money in Hammurabi's time, they were usually put into small, portable forms—ingots, easily identified coils, or sometimes rings. Beginning around 600 B.C.E., precious metals were made into coins. The small kingdom of Lydia, part of modern-day Turkey, made coins from electrum—a naturally-occurring alloy of gold and silver. Each coin was stamped with the image of a lion's head, to show that it was made under royal authority. There is some question as to how much the coins were worth in trade, but a coin likely represented some specific trade equivalent—a certain number of bushels of wheat, or the annual income of a certain kind of worker.

The idea of the coin spread quickly, and it became integral to the swiftly sophisticating economies of Greece, Rome, Egypt, and the many kingdoms of the Near East and Asia. The coinage system of ancient Rome was particularly developed, with coins of different values made of copper, silver, gold, bronze, and brass—often with a legal value greater than the mere value of the metal.

That is a hugely important difference: when the coin and its metal have the same value, the act of making a coin is just a way for someone to say "we certify that this is 1/100th of an ounce of silver." It's like the sticker on a package of ground beef stating its weight. But when a coin's value exceeds that of the metal, the act of making a coin becomes an act of creating value—making money from nothing. Rome took on a remarkable power in this way, and the value creation has been used (sometimes wisely, sometimes not) by governments and banks ever since.

Trade between these far-flung regions was common, and one of the greatest trade routes was the Silk Road, a 5,000-mile series of routes over land and sea that brought travelers back and forth between China and Rome, and to all points in between. Some of these routes had been in use for thousands of years; others, especially those in India and Persia, had been established during the reign of Alexander the Great as he tried to unify and rule his known world.

In some periods, trade relations were aggressively pursued, and the Silk Road came to particular prominence around 114 B.C.E., during the Han Dynasty of China. Nomads, monks, and soldiers followed the road, as well as merchants. Along the Silk Road oranges were brought from Persia and India to Rome, which is why the word "orange" (both the color and the fruit) in most European romance languages is a corruption of the Sanskrit *narangah* and the Persian *narang*. The routes of the Silk Road accounted for most of the exchanges running east to west through the 15th century C.E.—not limited to trade, but including culture, art, religion, and technology.

Mercantilism

The spice trade was a critical and lucrative source of income during the period of exploration and expansion that began during the early Renaissance. Spices are natural products from a particular region that are in demand beyond their point of origin because of their flavor or odor. Peppercorns, vanilla, cinnamon, and nutmeg—all things that are commonplace for us—had to be carried vast distances, and were often worth more than their weight in gold. The creation of the Dutch East India Company gave the Dutch a near monopoly over the trade in fine spices, and a heavy portion of the market for black pepper. This was achieved not only by Dutch influence on European markets, but also by the company's success in controlling production of spices in its colonies, influencing commodity prices by stockpiling product in years of high production, ending the Silk Road trade, disrupting native trade arrangements, and replacing them with Dutch ships.

The spice trade was essential for the development of capitalism in its cultural and economic outcomes: profits from long-distance trade were huge and concentrated (not dissipated among middlemen, as was the case with the grain trade); the spice trade was the most efficiently-organized of all the European markets, and caused the expansion of distribution networks; it generated connections between two zones of the young global economy; and crucially, it created among Europeans the long-term interest in accumulation and consumption fundamental to the success of capitalism.

The desire for spices may have contributed to the contraction of European money supply at the end of the 15th century. It was an important factor in motivating the desire of the Spanish crown to import American silver, which expanded the European money supply (and fed a steady inflation) in the 16th century. International business contacts fed the development both of financial instruments like the bill of exchange (a means of international currency exchange and money transfer before the advent of banking), and formal and informal institutions that guaranteed the enforceability of contracts. Increased business aided the development of uniform accounting procedures.

In the 15th century, European monarchs began consolidating their territories. They brought more money to their coffers by overturning medieval trade restrictions that had created tolls at virtually every city or river crossing. Having consolidated at home, they tried to extend their power at the expense of their rivals. Spain's New World possessions were rich in gold and silver, which, through trade, aided other rising powers—such as Holland, France, and England—as they built empires of their own. But there was never enough bullion to make everyone happy.

All of this led to Europe dallying with what Adam Smith would later call mercantilism. To get into a mercantile mindset, think of the major difference between then and now: when talking about wealth and money now, we're usually talking about bits and bytes and the numbers on an account statement, as money slips out of accounts at the swipe of a debit card, and lands back in them via direct deposit. Most of the money a person makes or spends is intangible. But three centuries ago, mercantilists considered gold and silver the only "real" money—they could touch it, they could dig it out of the ground, but they couldn't make more of it. However much was in the world, that's as much as there would ever be, and all they could do was move it around.

Mercantilism was a closed system in which each participant attempted to acquire as much tangible wealth—gold and silver—as possible. To do so, mercantilists discouraged unfavorable balances of trade, emphasized home self-sufficiency supplemented by colonial possessions that provided material the homeland couldn't make for itself, and provided guaranteed markets for domestic items.

The system required high tariffs on competing goods, but low tariffs on colonial output needed at home. It also generated an activist government willing to impose navigation restrictions and tight central controls over the quality and types of goods produced. Colonial trade meant strong merchant fleets, usually armed, for both practical and symbolic reasons. The spread of the flag also made large populations desirable, both to produce at home, and to populate abroad. Thrift was a mercantile virtue, given the finite stock of wealth.

When the easy money disappeared, the mercantilist nations debased their coin in order to finance their debt. The result was an economic crisis. The Netherlands stepped in once again to turn crisis into opportunity. Dutch merchants—no longer as strongly state-controlled as in most other European countries—took over trade, introduced new banking and shipping methods, cut costs, and quickly regained their dominance. Some economists consider the Dutch the first modern capitalists, controlling European commerce 1648–72. Dutch cities were dominant trading centers because of their aggressiveness, innovation, and ability to economize. The Amsterdam Stock Exchange was the first full-fledged stock exchange, and home to the first asset-inflation bubble—the famous tulip mania.

Tulip Mania

Tulips had been introduced to the European market by Dutch traders in the 1500s, who had acquired them from the Ottoman Empire.

Tulip mania in the 1630s marked one of the first speculative crazes.

It gradually became a popular status symbol and a luxury good, especially once Dutch gardeners got their hands on it and began breeding different, more vividly-colored tulip flowers. (Dutch horticulture was as alive and well as its economy was—around the same time, the Dutch developed the first orange-colored carrots, among the dozens of other types growing in their gardens.) The most impressive of the new tulips were those that were deliberately infected with a plant disease that had the side effect of causing brilliant stripes and other patterns to appear on the brightly-colored petals when the plant matured.

In 1636 tulips were traded on the Amsterdam Stock Exchange, along with the stock exchanges of smaller Dutch towns, and according to some accounts, this encouraged the nonwealthy to engage in tulip speculation. Citizens bought tulips they couldn't really afford (by putting off other purchases or by selling necessities) and tried to resell them at a higher price to recoup their capital, and used the profits to buy still more tulips.

There are many modern examples of manias—the dot-com stock boom, the Beanie Baby craze—but what fed the tulip bubble was the sale of tulip futures, when the supply of tulips ran out and the demand persisted. Growers began to sell, in essence, promises of tulips from future crops.

Eventually a panic developed when the belief spread that, at this point, the demand could increase no further—and that if it couldn't increase, it would have to decrease. The market collapsed. Some accounts paint this as a major economic crisis in the Netherlands— others suggest it was just a curious little incident that probably ruined few people beyond some of the riskiest speculators. Since the most widely-read accounts were written 200 years later, it's hard to know, and certainly makes for more drama if we imagine panicked Dutch tulip speculators leaping out of their windows.

In any case, Dutch dominance did not last forever, though nobody blamed tulips for that. The Dutch lacked the military resources and strong leadership they needed, and the English proved too able a military enemy throughout the 17th century. Dutch holdings remained strongest in Asia, where they were least-contested.

Restless Colonies

English mercantilism took its most familiar form in the series of Navigation Acts, which were resented by colonists and (over time) contributed to the feeling that they were being exploited by the motherland. England's colonies were intended for the motherland's benefit—they were places meant to purchase finished products made in England in exchange for raw materials and cash. England regulated shipping to reflect this (through unequal tariffs, among other things) as early as the time of Richard II in the 14th century, but it was sporadic; as late as 1642 the Long Parliament was exempting American goods from import and export fees.

Under Oliver Cromwell, England restricted imports from America, Asia, and Africa to British ships only. Imports from Europe were restricted to ships of England or the producing country. This act was directed primarily at the Dutch, with little consideration given to its impact on the colonies.

Mercantilist practices varied, as did degrees of success, but all attempted to use the same rules to attain the same goals. As wealth consisted mostly of bullion (gold and silver in the form of bars or ingots), the goal was to maximize the amount under the state's control. To do that, countries either acquired colonies or worked toward favorable balances of trade with their rivals. The governments aggressively promoted economic development, restricted colonies to providers of raw materials and markets, and tried to keep the system closed through navigation acts and other laws to control competition. As long as economic theorists assumed that the supply of wealth was finite, limited to the world supply of gold and silver, mercantilism was logical.

Meanwhile the New World began to take on an economic life and identity of its own, despite England's disregard. The English colony at Jamestown, Virginia struggled in its first years just to survive; later it struggled to become financially viable. Chartered as a commercial venture, the earliest colonists had come to the New World expecting to find the ground littered with gold and precious gems, but when that proved not to be the case, they began searching for an alternate product or cash crop. Salvation came in 1610, when a man named John Rolfe arrived from England with a small cache of tiny seeds in his luggage. At that time, Spain was the world's preeminent supplier of tobacco, a crop that grew well in their southern hemisphere colonies. Virginia colonists found the local tribes cultivating tobacco, but their *nicotiana rustica* was not pleasing to the English palate, and could not find a market.

Rolfe got a hold of a small supply of Spanish *nicotiana tabacum* seeds—illegal for him to possess—and joined the Third Fleet bound for Virginia in May 1609. The fleet was caught in a hurricane and forced to ditch in Bermuda, so he was unable to plant his first crop until 1611. His Orinoco tobacco was an instant success, and quickly became the currency of the colony. In 1614 Rolfe married the Native-American princess Pocahontas, and took her and their son home to England as visiting royalty in 1616. She died there in 1617; Rolfe returned to Virginia, where he died in 1622. His crop lived on, though, and in the 1620s, Virginia was producing about 40,000 pounds a year for export. By 1765 output had climbed to 75 million pounds annually.

Tobacco proved the viability of American colonization. Although overtaken by cotton as the crop of the South, it remained a crucial revenue source for more than 200 years, and is still an important crop today.

An Industrial Revolution

Adam Smith's two-volume masterwork, *An Inquiry into the Nature and Causes of the Wealth of Nations*, was published in 1776. He identified three main ingredients of the new economic order that was taking shape around him: the pursuit of self-interest, the division of labor, and access to freedom of trade. He took a benign view of self-interest: in his most famous turn of phrase, he spoke of the "invisible hand" of individuals who tended to promote the good of society while pursing their personal economic goals.

While Smith was theorizing, some were already putting these new trade ideas into practice. Born in 1732, Richard Arkwright was the youngest of 13 children and was apprenticed to a wig maker, but his real passion was mechanics. In 1767 he began tinkering with a machine designed to spin cotton into thread. He hit on a working design within a few years, and began looking for a way to put it to practical use. He decided to build his "manufactory" at Cromford, Derbyshire, on the banks of Bonsall Brook, a quick-moving stream he could harness to power his machines.

By 1771 Cromford Mill was operational. Arkwright's "overshot" waterwheel, which fed water into the top of the giant wheel, provided much more power than the traditional "undershot" wheels, allowing him to power five floors of machines from a single source. Making thread had always been the job of skilled spinners working at a single spinning-wheel. One of Arkwright's looms could spin 128 threads simultaneously, and was simple enough for a child to work—and children as young as 10 years old were his favorite source of cheap labor. The mill operated 23 hours a day year-round, with workers living, working, and praying right in the mill complex. Arkwright was so successful that he doubled the size of the mill by 1776 and again in 1790, then built another factory complex at Masson Mill on the nearby River Derwent.

Steam Engine

Water-powered mills and similar factories sprang up all over the world, but steam power would take things up a notch. People sometimes talk about "steam engine time" to refer to the sense that a particular technology or advancement is waiting in the wings—that if one person doesn't invent it, another person will, because it's simply time for it. The late 18th century was time for the steam engine, and while a few men made slightly different engines at around the same time, history gives principal credit to James Watt.

The Scotsman Watt was hooked on inventing. A sickly youth, he took pleasure in tinkering with mechanics and mathematics. He ended up repairing mechanical devices in the collections of the University of Glasgow, where he was first introduced to a Newcomen steam engine. Thomas Newcomen had developed the engine around 1712, but it was flawed and difficult to operate. Watt began experimenting with the Newcomen machine and the properties of steam in general. He eventually designed an improved boiler and condenser; his final designs were five times more powerful than Newcomen's engine.

Reduced to poverty while developing his machine, Watt worked for some time as a surveyor until he could raise capital through the sale of some of his patent rights. He formed a partnership with a Birmingham industrialist named Matthew Boulton. The firm of Watt & Boulton had some success in selling the engines commercially, mostly to new industries like cotton mills, waterworks, and iron-

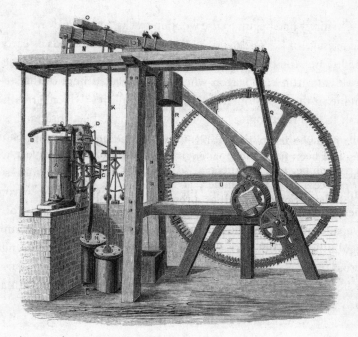

A rendering of James Watt's prototype steam engine.

works. Like most investors of the time, Watt's design was stolen, bastardized, and copied, forcing him to spend countless hours in court defending his patents. He made decent profits, but the real usefulness of steam engines would not become apparent until after his death, when it was applied to new forms of transportation like the locomotive and the steamship.

On February 22, 1804 the residents of the Abercynon Valley in Wales were privy to one of the key moments in transportation history: the moment when Richard Trevithick's new steam engine hauled 10 tons of iron, five wagons, and 70 men from Abercynon to Penydarren along the Merthyr Tydfil Tramway. They had plenty of time to take in the scene, since the "Puffing Devil" moved at a top speed of five miles per hour, with the whole 10-mile trip taking four hours and five minutes. It was an innovation a long time in coming.

Germany had begun to use wooden tracks, or wagonways, to ease the passage of horse-drawn vehicles over unpaved roads as early as 1550. Later these were improved to tramways, iron rails made to work with iron-clad wagon wheels. The development of the steam engine in the 1780s opened up new possibilities, which Trevithick took to the next logical step in 1803. "I have been branded with folly and madness for attempting what the world calls impossibilities, and even from the great engineer, the late Mr. James Watt, who said to an eminent scientific character still living that I deserved hanging for bringing into use the high-pressure engine," he wrote a friend. By 1821 Julius Griffiths had patented the passenger locomotive, and by 1825 the Stockton & Darlington Railroad was running regular routes with 21 passenger cars able to carry 450 passengers across the countryside at nine miles per hour. The railroad went on to become the dominant mode of transportation in the 19th and early 20th century.

Cotton Gin

When New Englander Eli Whitney arrived in Georgia in the early 1790s to take a job as a tutor on Catherine Littlefield Greene's plantation, he quickly learned that the local agricultural economy was in crisis. After more than 150 years, tobacco was beginning to play itself out as a profitable crop. Rice was limited to a few coastal areas. So, too, was cotton. Long-staple cotton, which only grew along the coasts, was the type most commonly grown at that time. Short-staple cotton would grow in a variety of environments, but was considered less profitable because of its load of tiny, sticky seeds inside each boll. These had to be laboriously picked out by hand—a process that cost countless hours of human labor.

Whitney had a mechanical mind, and set himself to the task of building a machine that would automate the process. After only 10 days, he had a working prototype. This cotton gin (short for engine) extracted the tiny seeds as the cotton fibers were pulled though a set of rollers over a fine mesh or set of fine wire teeth, with the whole thing operated by a simple hand crank. Once perfected, Whitney's gin could clean 55 pounds of cotton in a single day. He patented the machine in June 1793, and dreamed of the riches that would surely come. However litigation, patent violations, and production problems robbed him of significant profits, and he eventually turned to weapons manufacture instead.

Others profited greatly from Whitney's innovation. The development of the cotton gin revolutionized southern agriculture, pushing the annual production of raw cotton from 180,000 pounds in 1793, to six million pounds in 1795, to 93 million pounds in 1805. The fiber fueled textile production in the United States and Europe. As cotton production soared, so did the need for slave labor to tend the crops. Whitney's invention helped keep slavery alive and thriving for another three generations.

Textiles

The textile industry was so critical to the British economy by the 1780s that there was actually a law passed to prohibit the emigration of engineers, lest they smuggle out blueprints of the water-powered factories of the country's northwest. It was a legitimate concern. In 1789 a 21-year-old engineer who had spent seven years apprenticed to Arkwright disguised himself as a common laborer and boarded a ship for New England. Samuel Slater was well aware of the emigration law, so he was not carrying blueprints or drawings—at least not on paper. Instead he had memorized every aspect of Arkwright's design, with the hopes of recreating it in the United States. Just four years later he had done it, opening America's first water-driven textile mill near Pawtucket, Rhode Island, and becoming the young father of the Industrial Revolution in his adopted country.

Slater also embarked on an ambitious project in social engineering. His mill was the centerpiece of Slatersville, America's first company town. His employees—many of them small children, nimble and small enough to work in the dangerous spaces below and behind the clanging looms—lived in dormitories next to the mill. They were paid in script that could be used in the company store. They prayed at the company-built church. Neither Slater nor his cohorts saw anything negative in their actions, tending to view their strict control of workers' lives as benevolent, even philanthropic. Called the Rhode Island System, Slater's business model was copied countless times in the following decades. Slater eventually built 13 mills in New England, and died in 1835 a millionaire.

The Worker

Industry changed labor. It may seem too obvious to say that, but factories weren't like stores or businesses with a handful of workers, and they weren't like farms where the farmhands lived on or very near the property. Factory work was done by laborers who traveled to work (which encouraged the development of public and private transportation) and who were, in a sense, interchangeable—that is, in many cases a minimal amount of skill was sufficient to get the job done. The need for labor protection developed alongside industry.

In the annals of American legal history, *Commonwealth v. Pullis* is not a particularly well-known case. But it was one of the more chilling moments in the nation's long and violent labor movement. In 1794 a group of shoemakers in Philadelphia formed a union called the Federated Society of Journeymen Cordwainers. (Cordwainers were shoemakers who worked with a certain type of durable leather.)

The little union had managed to win wage increases in 1804, and voted to strike again in 1805. This time their employers were ready to take action. After a minor scuffle between strikers and nonunion laborers, eight union leaders found themselves under arrest for criminal conspiracy. George Pullis and his seven codefendants were tried before the mayor's court in early 1806. The prosecution—which was paid for by the city's anti-union forces—argued that Pullis and company were guilty of "conspiring" to increase their wages.

Under the prosecution's reading of common law, citizens had no right to decide their own economic value. For strikers to do so was a disruption of society as a whole. Even though the strike was essentially nonviolent, the strikers were viewed as terrorists. By the time the three-day trial was over, the court was inclined to agree.

The eight defendants were each found guilty and fined $8 plus court costs. The Pullis case set the precedent that trade unions were illegal conspiracies with no legitimacy in the eyes of the law. It clearly staked out the distance between workers and owners that would be the source of tremendous conflict over the next two centuries. Pullis was the law of the land until 1842, when it was finally overturned by a Massachusetts court in *Commonwealth v. Hunt*.

In Europe, meanwhile, labor interests and the changing social, economic, and political climate led to the formulation of Communism as a political-economic philosophy. *The Communist Manifesto* was a small book written to promote a small group of revolutionaries sitting on the fringes of the political and social movements that swept Europe in the mid-19th century. Philosophers Karl Marx and Freidrich Engels probably did not expect their slim volume to become one of the most important books ever written.

Marx defined the history of the world up to that point as "the history of class struggle," peasants exploited by their lords, employees exploited by their employers, with the capitalist system no better than its predecessors. While it was the bourgeoisie that had brought down feudalism, Marx maintained that they were sowing the seeds of their own destruction, because their unfair practices would inevitably cause the proletariat rise up against them.

American System of Manufacture

Through this time, the Industrial Revolution in America had been chugging along for more than a generation without impressing the older industrial states like England, that saw more imitation in the New World than innovation. This changed in 1851, when American industrialists attended the Crystal Palace exposition in Hyde Park in London. Organized by Queen Victoria's husband Prince Albert, the exposition was similar to later World's Fairs—like a science fair for adults, designed to gather the most modern technological advances in one place for examination by the general public. What America brought to the table was truly revolutionary.

Machine-tool manufacture—machines that made parts for other machines—may not sound exciting now, but in the late 1850s it was the next step in industrialization. A machine that could make endless copies of a clock had enormous profit potential, since one no longer needed to rely on a skilled craftsman to make it, only to assemble it.

This idea of interchangeable parts was not a new concept, but it had not caught on yet. The Americans seized the idea and made it their own. Gun manufacturer Samuel Colt was one of the exhibitors at the Crystal Palace, and to convince onlookers of the precision of his purpose-built machines, he had his workmen take apart 10 randomly-selected rifles, built over several years at Colt's armory in New England. The pieces were jumbled in a box. Then the workmen proceeded to rebuild the 10 rifles from the mixed-up parts. All 10 guns fired perfectly.

The American System of Manufacture was soon used for guns, plows, nails, sewing machines, even houses, and it jump-started the consumer era by providing the market with vast quantities of affordable, mass-produced products and goods.

Labor Strikes Back

With the start of the Long Depression of the 1890s, labor unrest in America reached new heights. Among the best-known was the Homestead Strike of 1892. Homestead, Pennsylvania was a company town belonging to one of Andrew Carnegie's largest steel manufacturing plants, with about 3,800 employees and their families living around the factories. Like most industries, by 1892, Homestead was beginning to feel the economic pinch, with the value of rolled steel dropping from $35 to $22 per gross ton. At this moment, general manager Henry Frick decided to try to break the local union, the Amalgamated Association of Iron and Steel Workers. After completing a large contract in June on 1892, Frick announced a series of pay cuts. When the union protested, he began a lockout of over 1,000 workers.

Over the next few days, Amalgamated leaders capitulated to all but one of Frick's demands—they refused to dissolve the union. At the start of the lockout, only 750 workers had belonged to the union, but Frick's high-handedness was too much for the majority of nonunion members, and over 3,000 voted to strike. The factories were surrounded by wire fencing—soon dubbed "Fort Frick" by the strikers—and nonunion strikebreakers were brought in to work. To protect the strikebreakers, Frick hired a small private army from the Pinkerton Detective Agency, who tried to sneak themselves into the plant by floating down the nearby Monongahela River under the cover of darkness. Strikers saw them and sounded the alarm. This began a 14-hour gun battle that left three Pinkertons and nine strikers dead; the governor had to send in the state militia to restore order. The lockout lasted four months, and by the end, the union was gone. The Homestead Strike left lasting scars on the company and its workers. "Nothing in all my life, before or since," wrote Andrew Carnegie, "wounded me so deeply."

Powering the Modern Age

For nearly six years in the late 19th century, two of the world's greatest inventors were locked in a bitter propaganda war, the outcome of which would determine how the modern age was powered. Nicola Tesla had once been an assistant in Thomas Edison's famed New Jersey laboratory, but had broken with the older man over differing scientific theories and personal styles.

By 1887, Tesla had perfected and patented a new electrical system based on his experiments into alternating current. Edison saw Tesla's system as a threat to his own electrical system, which was based on direct current, and was then growing in popularity as cities began to invest in electrical power for homes and industries. So Edison invested considerable time and energy raising doubt in Tesla's ideas.

Edison sponsored public exhibitions where dogs and horses were actually electrocuted on stage with alternating current. He and

George Westinghouse were also involved in the execution of convicted ax-murderer William Kimmler in New York's new electric chair, which was powered by alternating current. Westinghouse supported Kimmler's appeal that electrocution was cruel and unusual punishment, while Edison supported the state's pro-execution position, hoping to use the event as a new demonstration of alternating current's dangers. This worked better than Edison might have anticipated: the electrocution was badly botched, taking over eight minutes, and ending with Kimmler's body actually catching fire before he was declared dead.

Despite losing some public relations battles during the war of the currents, Tesla and Westinghouse won the war when they were granted the contract to light the Chicago World's Fair. On May 1, 1893 President Grover Cleveland hit a switch and sent 12 1,000-horsepower generators into action. Over 100,000 incandescent bulbs bathed the white buildings of the exposition grounds in brilliant light. The "White City" showed over 25 million visitors what Tesla could do. Within a few years—and ever since—over 80 percent of the power in the United States has traveled via alternating current. It's a shame that his subsequent plan for electricity failed: convinced that electricity could be transmitted wirelessly like radio waves in order to power devices from afar, the inventor pursued plans for broadcast power for years, with little success.

New Ideas

Just a decade later Henry Ford used a $28,000 investment to found the Ford Motor Company in Detroit, Michigan, and saw $1 million in profit in the company's first year. In 1913 in order to meet demand for his automobiles, Ford established the moving assembly line, pushing automobiles through the assembly process on a conveyor belt. This innovation dropped the time it took to build the Model T from 12.5 hours down to just one hour, 33 minutes, and increased production to over 200,000 cars per year. The price consequently dropped from $850 in 1910, to a highly-affordable $300 in

Detail of the headlight and grill from a 1914 Ford Model T.

1920. Putting the auto within financial reach of the common American family revolutionized transportation, turning the United States into a modern, mobile nation. The late 19th and early 20th century saw the adoption in various quarters of a number of intellectual and scientific ideas, from theories of evolution and the washing of surgeons' hands to prevent infection, to progressive reforms in government and religion.

Charles Darwin was a controversial figure because of his theories about the evolution of the human species, and although he didn't originate the idea of evolution, the label of Darwinism was usually used to describe it. Social Darwinism, by extension, developed as those scientific ideas became familiar to nonbiologists, particularly intellectuals in the social sciences like economics and politics.

In popular thought, the phrase "the survival of the fittest" has long been overwhelmingly associated with Charles Darwin's theory of evolution. In fact, Herbert Spencer coined the phrase in *Principles of Biology* (1864), before Darwin's work on evolution was published. Spencer put forth many of the ideas adopted by Social Darwinism—which should probably be called Social Spencerism for that reason. Spencer sought to apply the principle of evolutionary progress to all branches of knowledge. Like Marx, Spencer saw society as evolving toward a utopia—but unlike Marx, Spencer was a libertarian and envisioned an extreme form of laissez-faire capitalism. He believed that such a society would best maximize the happiness or well being of society. In his utopia, all members of society would be free to do what they desired, as long as they did not infringe on the happiness of others.

Limiting Government

From this, it followed that the powers of government must be limited. The proper role for government in Spencer's view is the establishment of a legal system to enforce private contracts and to punish acts that harm others, and the establishment of a military for defensive purposes. He rejected any form of government aid to the poor, because it interfered with the survival of the fittest. The goal of nature, he said, is to rid itself of "feeble elements," and to interfere with that was to encourage weakness. "It is the universal law of nature—a law that a creature not energetic enough to maintain itself must die."

Social Darwinist ideas, based on this general line of thinking—that government and society should act with an awareness of these laws of nature, and not interfere with them—became popular in the early 20th century. They were sometimes combined with eugenics, the study of the improvement of the human race through breeding—especially popular with racists who sought to argue for the innate inferiority of one race or another. Social Darwinists claimed that social existence was a competitive struggle among individuals possessing different natural capacities and traits. Those with better traits—the fittest—succeeded, becoming wealthy and powerful, while those who were unfit were condemned to poverty.

Social Darwinists believed government intervention in economic and social matters should be minimal. Improving the condition of the poor would only be useful to preserve bad traits: the only alternative to the survival of the fittest was the survival of the unfittest. There was no moral obligation to the poor, in Social Darwinism's view; protecting the poor constituted theft from the rich. While few would identify themselves as Social Darwinists today, their ideas survive in some political and economic arguments.

The Crash to Credit Cards

In October 1929 the New York Stock Exchange crashed—the first warning many Americans had that anything was amiss. Over the next three years, the economy went into free fall. The Great Depression had a worldwide reach, and in Europe contributed to bringing Adolf Hitler to power. At home, President Franklin D. Roosevelt adopted the far-reaching reforms and programs of the New Deal; since the end of the depression coincided with the increased military spending of World War II, it's hard to say exactly what ended the era.

Americans greeted the end of World War II with a mix of relief and trepidation. Wartime production helped to lift the country out of its decade-long depression, and there was naturally some concern that spending would fall with the war's end. These fears turned out to be exaggerated, and the United States quickly became an economic superpower—unlike much of Europe and Asia, the manufacturing infrastructure of the United States had survived the war. America could produce goods needed by a recovering world. The start of the Cold War kept the production of weapons and airplanes high, and helped stimulate research and development into new technologies, particularly electronics.

The U.S. government was an active player in restructuring the world economy, supporting the International Monetary Fund (IMF), the World Bank, and other organizations that promoted open, capitalist economies around the world. Most importantly, millions of returning servicemen were ready to come home, start families, buy

The first credit card was issued by Diner's Club in 1950.

homes, and purchase the material goods of modern, American middle-class life.

The GI Bill allowed tens of thousands of former soldiers to go to college, which in turn allowed more to find jobs in the newly-invigorated service industry. By 1956 there were more white-collar workers in the country than blue-collar workers, for the first time in U.S. history.

Until the late 20th century credit was not used for everyday purchases. This began to change in 1950, when the Diner's Club began issuing cards as a way for businessmen to pay for their meals at member restaurants, and then pay the accumulated charges in full at the end of a billing cycle. American Express began issuing cards in 1958, and BankAmericard (later Visa) began in 1959, again targeting the growing white-collar and middle-management workforce. In 1966 these and other companies banded together to create the InterBank Card Association as a way to speed payments between lenders. Realizing the profits they could make by promoting the use of credit cards to the average consumer, creditors began increasing the pool of cardholders in huge credit card drops, issuing millions of cards to anyone and everyone.

Communism to Globalism

Formed after the removal and execution of Czar Nicolas II during the Bolshevik Revolution of 1917, the Soviet Union seemed to transform itself into a model of a disciplined Communist state over the next decades. But in reality things were never all that smooth. More than 50 percent of all Soviets were not ethnically Russian, leading to repression and occasional violence whenever nationalism raised its head. The state was never able to apportion goods to the satisfaction of the people. By the 1980s the country was bogged down in a brutal war in Afghanistan, and spending heavily in an effort to keep up its superpower status in the ongoing Cold War with the United States.

When Mikhail Gorbachev took control in 1985, he established new policies of *glasnost* (free speech) and *perestroika* (economic reform) in an attempt to hold the fraying union together. But economic reforms did not pay off fast enough, and freedom of speech allowed people to vent their pent-up emotion against the government. The Baltics went first, with nationalism movements rising up in Estonia, Lithuania, and Latvia. Unrest quickly spread to the southern states. Finally in August 1991, Soviet hardliners kidnapped and deposed Gorbachev. He formally resigned on Christmas Day 1991. By the end of January 1992, the former Soviet Union had become the new Commonwealth of Independent States. The dissolution of the Communist state was seen as an overwhelming victory for democracy and free-market capitalism.

Around the same time that markets were opening in the former Soviet states, India was becoming a more visible player in the global economy, largely a result of workforce outsourcing. Outsourcing isn't a new concept—the practice of producing products where labor costs are cheaper dates back centuries. But the telecommunications revolutions of the late 20th century made it possible for businesses to outsource not just the production of material objects, but also routine office functions like data processing, billing, and customer support.

American companies began setting up shop in English-speaking countries in the 1980s to take advantage of the benefits of business process outsourcing. In 1990 a new Indian government began an ambitious policy of privatizing the nation's industries and opening up to foreign investment and trade. The Indian workforce was perfect for budget-conscious Western businesses: large, youthful, English-speaking, college-educated, tech-savvy, and willing to work for low wages.

Medical transcription companies began to outsource to India in the 1990s, followed by IT companies. This proved so successful that other industries set up call centers across the subcontinent. The call center workforce grew at a rate of 40 to 60 percent a year by the early 2000s, with at least 500,000 Indians working in the industry by 2006. The cost benefit to Western companies was tremendous: Indian call center workers earned $7,500 a year on average, compared with of $19,000 for comparable U.S. workers.

Internet Revolution

Computer technology advanced rapidly in the late 1960s and early 1970s, laying the groundwork for the later revolutions in personal computing. But during this period computers were bulky, expensive units used primarily by the government and research facilities. To facilitate communications between leading university research centers working on the development of Cold War technologies, the Department of Defense set up the Advanced Research Projects Agency Network, or ARPANET, in 1969.

At first the departments could only send files over the network, but in 1971 an engineer named Ray Tomlinson decided to develop a simple program to allow network users to send messages. There was no directive from above to create this program—it just seemed to him like a "neat idea." Within the first two years, email grew to 75 percent of all ARPANET traffic—a level that would be matched by the general public as personal computers and access to the Internet grew through the 1990s and early 2000s.

At the same time, Internet access was becoming common enough to give birth to a new industry—and an adjunct to existing industries. Ecommerce—the buying and selling of goods and services online—was the perfect industry for the growing information-hungry society. Backed by infusions of venture capital, these new dot-coms often operated at a loss in an attempt to build market share; only then would they start charging for their services. "Get large or get lost" was the motto of many of these new companies, and some spent millions on advertising to attain the trappings of success and make themselves appear to be a good investment.

In other cases, venture capitalists simply threw money at ideas that were popular, even if it wasn't clear how to turn that popularity into profit—a conundrum that the Internet made much more common. Plenty of low-level computer techs became overnight millionaires when their companies made their initial public offering on the stock market, and the value of their stock options went through the roof.

By 2000, however, it was clear to most that this was not a valid business model. For every Google or Ebay, there was a Webvan—an online grocery service that in 18 months went from nothing to $1.2 billion and then back to nothing, with the loss of over 2,000 jobs. Billions of investment dollars were lost by 2001. "The fact is that a bubble market had allowed the creation of bubble companies," said super-investor Warren Buffett at the height of the dot-com boom, "entities designed more with an eye to making money off investors, rather than for them."

Dominance

Capitalism became the dominant economic system worldwide in the 21st century. The Soviet Union crumbled and turned to market economies, while Communist stalwart China explored free market policies while retaining a strong Communist core for its government.

More and more the focus shifted to intangible or intellectual properties—whether in the form of record labels combating (or attempting to profit from) online music sharing, the movie industry's battle against pirated movies both domestically and in foreign markets, large corporations' lobbyists getting copyright extension legislation pushed in order to protect the profitability of well-known icons, or consumer concerns about privacy and identity theft.

The global economy weathered the Asian financial crisis, but the United States faces the repercussions of an oil crisis, the subprime mortgage crisis, the 2007–09 financial crisis, and the emergence of a global recession. Capitalism has spread quickly, but it faces big challenges.

Chapter 3

People Every Capitalist Should Know

Capitalism and individualism have grown up side-by-side. Hundreds of years ago, artists and composers didn't even sign their work, and property was granted by the crown or seized by one army or another as often as it was earned. Capitalism, democracy, and a concern for human rights all developed simultaneously as part of a growing concern for the well-being of the individual—as well as a growing accommodation of self-interest. When we talk about the great capitalists of history, we're not speaking of princes and princesses. They were achievers, people who played the game and won. It is not always a rags to riches story—even a computer genius's start-up is often funded by a generous uncle. But whatever they started with, the great capitalist figures achieved their success as a result of individual merit.

The individuals capitalists need to know about include the theorists as well as the practitioners. For every Elvis Presley, there's a Leiber & Stoller writing "Jailhouse Rock" so he has something to sing; for every movie star, there is someone writing the script. Capitalism has developed over time—often in response to changing technology or social conditions. Scholars have shaped, defended, or criticized capitalism every step of the way. Learning about these people will deepen an understanding of both the theory and practice of capitalism—the lyric sheets and the way the song's been sung before.

Throughout recent history, a stream of noted capitalists' philosophies, achievements, and ideas have changed daily life. From their successes and failures, and from what they have in common, we can learn valuable lessons in creating a financial destiny. From innovative entrepreneurs to classical economic philosophers to ruthless businessmen, these personal journeys comprise the crux of capitalism.

David Hume (1711–76)

Scottish philosopher David Hume's reputation grew steadily as he published works on metaphysics and human nature. Adam Smith considered him "as near to the idea of a perfectly wise and virtuous man, as perhaps the nature of human frailty will admit." Hume took the empirical techniques of the scientific revolution and applied them to the study of the social and moral world. Both Hume and Smith observed that individuals' actions can promote economic distribution and social harmony without deliberate coordination, a whole arising from the sum of its parts.

His early works were little-noticed by the public, and so he published two small volumes of essays that would be called popular nonfiction now, and which brought him better success through word of mouth. His *Political Discourses*, published in 1751, was his only work to gain financial success with its first printing. *Political Discourses* addressed money, the balance of trade, commerce, interest, taxes, and public credit, and supported a rejection of mercantilism as well as the argument that national wealth came not from gold, but agricultural surplus.

Adam Smith (1723–90)

Adam Smith's *Wealth of Nations* was so profoundly influential in its defense of capitalism and dismissal of the mercantile system that no other school of thought survived it. Classical economics are Smith's economics, plain and simple. He cut through the noise of the day, assembling and advocating existing ideas in a way that reached a wider audience than those who had come before him. Not just a historically important figure, he was also a bestseller in his day, and a household name. His most famous metaphor is the "invisible hand" of the market—the self-correcting nature of the free market that moves unguided by government (or by conscious effort), to produce the right amount and variety of goods.

Smith talks about this invisible hand the way earlier writers might have talked about God or fate, a force personified. He was determined to show that a person could promote the social good without setting out to do so—that acting selfishly could benefit everyone. Intentions weren't important to Smith—results were. An economy doesn't operate according to what people meant to do or want to happen, any more than gravity cares whether a person jumps or falls.

The benefits of self-interest are still controversial, and they are called into question any time economic interests come into conflict with someone's well-being. For Smith, individual liberty was not only compatible with national prosperity—the wealth of nations—it was necessary for that prosperity. For that reason, government and its interference with individual and business rights had to be limited.

Classical economics since Smith has focused on capital theory, international trade theory, the market as a system that regulates itself through price, and the idea that exchange creates wealth. Exchange is necessary for specialization—otherwise, those working in a pin factory all day would just walk home with a bucket full of pins and nothing else to show for it. By specializing labor, we can assign different people to different tasks, and each person can become better skilled by not having to worry about the rest of it. In time, this leads to shortcuts and other improvements that wouldn't have been noticed before when we were trying to do everything at once. It also allowed for the Industrial Revolution, where the assembly line, in which each worker does one small task and does it quickly and skillfully, was necessary.

Smith depicted the market as a self-organizing system where prices would naturally settle at a certain level. The natural price of a thing is the cost of bringing it to market—the cost of materials, labor—whatever is involved in starting with an empty spot on the shelf and filling it with a clock radio. The market price is the price for which it actually sells. If there aren't enough clock radios to go around, people will pay more and the market price goes up; when the market price goes up, more factories get into the clock radio business, but now there are so many that the price comes back down. Eventually, maybe after a little back and forth, supply equals demand and there's no incentive to change.

Capital is everything owned by a person or business that's been put aside to earn revenue—this includes the fixed capital of factories and equipment, and the circulating capital of the raw materials, money, and other goods. Dividing labor requires the build-up of some capital first, because of the delay between the time when you start producing something and the time when you're paid for it. Capital is needed not only to pay workers in the meantime, but to buy the materials and equipment they need to work with, especially since the division of labor so often involves the use of machinery and special equipment.

Smith differentiated between productive labor—like agriculture and manufacturing, which added value to the things being worked on—and unproductive labor, like the service industry. Because the rich use more of their wealth on unproductive labor—by hiring servants and having people do things for them—they don't accumulate capital the way they would if that wealth were going toward making something.

His argument for free international trade is made on the same basis as his argument for keeping government from interfering with domestic business. It permits international specialization—wine and cheese made in France, electronic parts in Japan and Silicon Valley, luxury automobiles in Germany—with all the same benefits as specialization at the domestic level.

Edmund Burke (1729–97)

Edmund Burke was England's most outspoken opponent of the French Revolution. His responses to this fundamental political challenge in his most famous work, *Reflections on the Revolution in France,* produced arguments about the ideal quality of social change that lie at the basis of conservative political thought in the West since the French Revolution.

Born in Ireland, Burke entered Parliament in 1765 as the secretary to a Whig MP, the Marquis of Rockingham, and subsequently served as MP representing the pocket borough of Wendover. In Parliament, Burke became known for his pragmatic and liberal views on free trade and the management of colonies, and opposition to national budget deficits and the investment on money interests in the public debt. He opposed British colonial policy in North America.

Burke was a contemporary and friend of Adam Smith, and evidence suggests that while Burke originally arrived at his economic views due to his education at the University of Dublin, and so independently of Smith, the two thinkers appreciated and influenced each other's subsequent work. The most important assumption of Burke's thought is his emphasis on the support of traditional order and the maintenance of social stability, two concepts that underlay all his works. This preoccupation has been related by various authors to Burke's loyalty to British hierarchical society, his inheritance of Aristotelian ideas and natural law thinking, his conviction that civilized society was the prerequisite for successful commerce (a contradiction to the views of the Scottish political economists, like Hume, that commerce led to civilized society), or his view that the origin of government lay in its prerogative to protect property.

On a political level, Burke argued that social change should occur slowly and organically, according to the inherited constitution of a country. Tradition, rather than metaphysical speculation, should govern the structure and content of politics. Although Burke's economic attitudes can be read throughout his works and underlie his complaints about the French Revolution. He thought, for instance, that the debt crisis that provoked the threatened government bankruptcy of 1789 could have been avoided if the government had been prevented from financing its debt the way it did. His most explicit economic text is *Thoughts and Details on Economic Scarcity*. In it, he equated the laws of commerce with natural and divine law, and coined the phrase "bite the hand that feeds them" in an argument against government food support for the poor.

The book is frequently used to support an understanding of Burke as champion of an unrestrained free-market economy, the interpretation of Burke's political economy adopted by utilitarians, against which Karl Marx reacted vituperously in *Capital*. But Burke's ideas should not be separated from their context. Intended as a persuasive memorandum to British Prime Minister Pitt in response to the Speenhamland famine, the book was published only after his death and is specifically a response to local circumstances. In 1795 after repeated famines, justices of the peace subsidized wages of workers whose earnings fell below subsistence, thereby negatively impacting the local wage market for both laborers and employers. The book should be read as an argument against government wage supports, not a justification of allowing the hungry to starve, for Burke supported private charitable efforts. This apparent disjunction might be attributed to a general philosophical emphasis in Burke's thought on prudence and pragmatism.

Alexander Hamilton (1755–1804)

Alexander Hamilton is both a character on the stage of American capitalism, and one of its main theorists. His tale is one of upward mobility: the son of a bankrupt family, he became one of the most influential politicians in his America. After early business success, he joined a patriot volunteer company during the American Revolution and became George Washington's personal secretary and aide.

After Independence, Hamilton left the military for politics, as delegate to the Constitutional Convention of 1787, the main author of the Federalist Papers, and the first secretary of the treasury from 1789 to 1795. While a beneficiary of American capitalism—virtually a character right out of Horatio Alger—Hamilton was also one of the system's main theorists, and is considered the father of the U.S. financial and banking system. As the first secretary of the treasury, Hamilton took advantage of the young, malleable nation and argued strongly for his interpretations of the Constitution, which favored a strong centralized government. While others established the new United States as a political presence, he made it an economic one, assuming the state debts at the federal level, creating the national debt and a national bank, and instituting a system of tariffs and taxes to pay for federal expenses. He emphasized trade both between states and between the United States and European nations, to keep the country economically healthy, and called for further exploration of the lands beyond the Mississippi, where the continent's vast natural resources offered untold opportunities.

In addition to the Federalist Papers, he authored four reports as Secretary of the treasury that were presented to Congress in 1790 and 1791. Each addressed a specific concern: Public Credit (the national debt), the Establishment of a Mint, the Establishment of a National Bank, and Manufactures. In these reports, Hamilton described the United States as a new empire, one in which the economy and the state were dependent on each other and the federal government would need to intervene in order to support American industry.

Protective tariffs would tax imports to make foreign goods more expensive than American ones; some foreign goods would be purchased anyway (especially if they had no competing domestic counterpart), which would generate income for the government. But the existence of the tariff would help the sales of domestic goods, encouraging Americans to buy American.

America was going to be more than a nation of farmers, and so these tariffs were especially aimed at encouraging the growth of American factories, when the Industrial Revolution had only just begun. Hamilton's call for high levels of government involvement in American business—in support of it, granted, but involvement all the same—put him in opposition not only with noted economist Adam Smith, whose theories guided the Founding Fathers and the building of the American economy, but also to Secretary of State Thomas Jefferson. A gentleman farmer himself, Jefferson was one of many who saw America as an agrarian, pastoral society.

The tensions between rural America and urban America have existed throughout much of American history, and even here—when there was very little "urban" America—Jefferson challenged Hamilton on the basis that rapid growth in manufacturing would threaten America's agrarian values. Factory workers were too liable to be controlled by their masters, Jefferson believed, while farmers were inherently independent. Events in the 19th century proved this wrong, as sharecropping made agricultural workers far more dependent on their employers than any factory workers were.

Karl Marx (1818–83)

A philosopher, economist, and sociologist, but perhaps most of all renowned as the founder of the so-called scientific socialism, Karl Marx made two great intellectual contributions to history: the *Communist Manifesto* (cowritten with Friedrich Engels in 1848) and a three-volume treatise on the political economy of capitalism, *Capital* (1867–95).

Marx settled in London in 1849, the year after writing the *Communist Manifesto* with Engels, whom he had met in Paris after several years of involvement in radical politics. Because of his politics and their influence on the world after his death, much of Marx's writing is relevant only to his followers, for whom he is the equivalent of Adam Smith—influential, but not the last word.

The biggest such contribution is the economic interpretation of history, one of the greatest achievements of sociology. The economic interpretation of history does not mean that people are motivated only or primarily by economic motives—it means that religions, philosophical concepts, schools of art, ethical ideas, and political movements are shaped by the economic conditions of their times, and that changes in the economic conditions account for their rise and fall.

Those changes (the development of the productive forces of a society) can be influenced by noneconomic factors but, in the end, the needs coming from the economic side will meld institutions for their continued development.

The economic interpretation of history is closely related to Marx's theory of social classes

and his understanding of the historic process as inherently driven by class struggle. Classes are defined in their relationship to material means of production (ownership of factors of production, in modern terminology).

The development of productive forces gradually changes the relative importance of factors of production, and that is translated into relative changes in their power. As the ascending class fights against the declining class, the social order and the whole political and ideological landscape undergo drastic changes, often by means of a violent revolution. This logic is applied to the past human history in the *Communist Manifesto*, and it is extended to predict the future, in which the takeover by the ascending class under the bourgeois system, the proletariat, will eventually result in a classless society and an unlimited potential for economic development.

Although the theory of class struggle is not accepted in its Marxist form by modern social sciences, many of its insights, including the role that competition for political influence plays in shaping institutions and government policies continue. Also, although the prediction of an imminent collapse of the capitalist system and the proletarian revolution has not materialized, some of the most forceful passages in the *Communist Manifesto* actually refer to the greatest achievements of the bourgeoisie class and to complete changes in the ways human history has been made after its ascendance to power (that is, after the advent of capitalism).

Marx can thus be credited as one of the first thinkers to recognize the fact (widely accepted today) that the capitalist, or free market system, represented the biggest breakthrough in human history since the dawn of civilization.

Horatio Alger, Jr. (1832–99)

Horatio Alger gained fame as a writer of children's fiction during the late 19th century. His rags-to-riches tales of young orphans and scrappy street kids who managed to triumph over their humble beginnings struck a chord with generations of young Americans. A highly prolific author, he produced well over 100 novels and numerous short stories, which remained in print well into the 20th century. When Alger sent a series of stories entitled "Ragged Dick, or, The Streets of New York" to a magazine aimed at young people, he found his calling. He was hired as a regular contributor, and the stories were eventually collected and published in book form. This work contained many elements that would recur in later Alger  novels. The protagonist was a poor boy who lived on the streets of New York, polishing boots. The boy's honesty and strength of character impresses a wealthy man, who takes Dick into his charge. By the end of the story, the hero has acquired an education and is starting a new job as a clerk, destined for great things.

Although Alger's critics charged that his stories were highly formulaic, young readers did not care any more than their great-grandchildren cared when the same criticisms were made of the Hardy Boys or Goosebumps. Novels with titles like *Strive and Succeed*, *Risen from the Ranks*, and *Julius, the Street Boy* were snapped up by the handful.

Over 250 million Alger books were sold around the world. In addition to fiction, he wrote biographies of figures who could also serve as inspiration for young boys. In Alger's hands, the life of President James Garfield became *From Canal Boy to President*.

Alger's work is often cited as a celebration of the possibilities of capitalism. He chose the modern city as the setting for his tales, and followed young newsboys and peddlers as they rose to achieve the "American Dream."

Alger's heroes succeed not only due to their own perseverance, but also because of the kindness of a wealthy benefactor. Many of the novels feature chance meetings that forever change the lives of the characters. Nevertheless, Alger's name has become synonymous with individualism and self-reliance.

Andrew Carnegie (1835–1919)

In a country in love with the idea of the self-made man, Andrew Carnegie was the real deal—one of the most powerful and successful men of a generation that excelled at power and success. Born in Scotland, he moved to the United States as a poor teenager and became a telegraph operator before working his way up in the Pennsylvania Railroad Company, all the while investing what money he could and amassing a small fortune. It would arguably be another century—until the dot-com age— before anyone would start with so little and turn it into so much.

His investments all reflected the times he lived in—railroads, sleeping cars, oil, the telegraph, bridges, and iron mills. His first company was the Keystone Bridge Company, a highly profitable construction company that took up the task of repairing the country in the wake of the Civil War. He founded the Carnegie Steel Company in his 30s, and made that small fortune enormous, thanks to his reliance on vertical integration. By buying up raw materials and transportation facilities, the entire process of steelmaking was under the control of one company, so that no profits escaped through the cracks the way they would have had he constantly been making deals with middlemen. He had taken the first step toward vertical integration while running the Keystone Bridge Company, when the amount of jobs that lay before the company threatened to deplete his iron supply and he responded by purchasing an iron mill—thus protecting himself from the possibility of rising costs in response to rising demand.

He was quick to invest in new manufacturing processes that improved efficiency or the quality of the product, and just as quick to kick an extra payment or two to the railroads to arrange cheaper shipping when needed. When the rival Duquesne Works developed a new steel-making process, Carnegie sent a letter to all of the railroads claiming that the new process produced inferior steel rails. Later, with Duquesne on the brink of bankruptcy, Carnegie bought the company and adopted the process himself. He was the steel baron of the Gilded Age, supplying rails to the rapidly-expanding railroads, and beams for the increasing number of skyscrapers and other modern buildings.

By the turn of the century Carnegie could have dictated the price of steel; he had no significant rivals in the steel industry, and had for 10 years been the largest manufacturer in the world. Maybe the criticisms against him began to sting, because as such a visible and successful businessman he certainly heard his share of them.

In 1889 he published a collection of essays, *The Gospel of Wealth*, in which he put forth a theory of philanthropy that he hoped his fellow industrialists like Jay Gould and J.P. Morgan would follow. The wealthy man, he said, had a duty to set an example—American wealth should not be displayed extravagantly like that of the European noble families, nor should American businessmen live in that kind of splendor or lead such idle lifestyles.

After accumulating wealth, the rich man should redistribute it—having demonstrated his competence already, he should then "do for them [the poor and less fortunate] better than they would or could do for themselves."

Carnegie donated money throughout the country to build libraries and universities. Carnegie Hall in New York City is one of the better-known cultural institutions he funded. He purchased a number of newspapers in his native Great Britain, instructing them to support American-style republican democracy and free-market capitalism over the outdated European monarchies. Carnegie Steel was eventually merged by J.P. Morgan into the U.S. Steel Corporation, but Carnegie's example as a success story never faded, and vertical integration remains important to corporate America today.

Jay Gould (1836–92)

Another 19th century tycoon, New Yorker Jay Gould built a reputation as one of the most ruthless financiers in American history. Beginning with $5,000 at age 21, Gould increased his capital by speculating on railroad securities, and joined James Fisk and Daniel Drew in their defeat of Cornelius Vanderbilt's bid for control of the Erie Railroad. He was named director of the railroad shortly after, and was accused of a number of  unscrupulous moves, from issuing false stock to bribing regulators.

Over time he came to control more than half of the railroad mileage in the Southwest, the Western Union Telegraph Company, and the elevated railroads of New York City. In 1869, along with Fisk, Gould manipulated and cornered the gold market, resulting in the Black Friday panic that ruined many investors. Due to public protest, Gould and his group were forced out of the Erie Railroad. Subsequently, Gould bought into the Union Pacific Railroad and other western lines, eventually gaining control of four major railroads. His intent was not to build and grow these rail lines, but to manipulate their stock for his personal profit. Leaving $77 million upon his death, Gould is best known in the annals of 19th-century capitalism as one of the robber barons.

J.P. Morgan (1837–1913)

The most powerful financial leader of the Progressive Era, Connecticut native J.P. Morgan is best known for preventing the 1895 collapse of the U.S. Treasury during a run on gold. Morgan helped develop the industrial might of the United States by organizing financing for railroad, steel, and agricultural machinery firms. As head of the Northern Securities Company, Morgan became the first victim of the Sherman Antitrust Act when the Supreme Court ruled against him in 1904.

The son of a merchant banker, Morgan worked for the New York merchant bank of Duncan, Sherman & Company for several years as a young man before founding the private wholesale bank of J.P. Morgan & Company, which shared the risk of underwriting new bonds or stocks (committing the bank to sell securities at a minimum price, and profiting only if the sale was made at a higher price) among several syndicates.

Morgan's banking skills fueled American expansion by providing funds necessary for the country's growth. The United States simply lacked the financial wherewithal to fund its developing industries, while European nations had capital surpluses that could be tapped to pay for massive American projects like railroad expansion. Morgan pried loose European money by reducing the risk associated with investment in American securities.

To attract investors, Morgan sought to guarantee that American companies would pay timely dividends on stocks and bonds. He hoped that the securities would appreciate in time, thereby providing him with a profit. While tycoons like Jay Gould and Jim Fisk got rich from colluding to fix rates, Morgan stood to gain more from fair play, and so clashed with both of them. In 1885 he set out to sea on his ship, the *Corsair*, with the heads of the New York Central and Pennsylvania Railroads, in order to end the rate wars. The Corsair Compact increased the value both of the eastern railroads, and Morgan's reputation.

The other major risk to investors at that time came from currency exchange. After 1873 the United States fixed the value of its dollar to the price of gold. Farmers and others in the Populist movement preferred a silver standard, because the fluctuating rate would reduce the amount of interest that they paid. Morgan worked to keep the United States on the gold standard because it minimized the risk of foreign investor losses through adverse currency exchange rates. Morgan's stands helped to maintain the inflow of European funds that were so necessary to American expansion, but also made him enemies among farmers. Morgan's dependence on gold led him to prop up the U.S. Treasury. In 1895 the government appeared ready to abandon the gold standard in the face of political pressures and a major depression that had caused a run on the metal. Morgan rushed to offer aid to President Grover Cleveland. The private pact formed at the White House provided for the purchase of more than $62 million in gold for the U.S. Treasury and saw Morgan guarantee the Treasury against gold withdrawals from February through the end of September 1895.

Morgan's enormous financial power frightened many Americans and, partly in response to concerns about the might of the banker, the Sherman Antitrust Act passed in 1890. The aim of the new law was to forbid combinations in restraint of trade, and Morgan became the first to be ensnared by it. In railroad reorganizations, Morgan had typically maintained control through selecting company presidents and by placing his men on the boards of directors. A hard-fought war with railroad barons over the Northern Pacific forced Morgan in 1901 into a new strategy of forming a holding company, Northern Securities, to control railroad stock.

The state of Minnesota brought suit and President Theodore Roosevelt ordered his attorney general to enter the case in an effort to curb the excesses of big business. In 1904 the U.S. Supreme Court ruled that the Northern Securities Company was in violation of the Sherman Antitrust Act and forced its dissolution. Morgan formed another trust, U.S. Steel in 1901, but kept prices high enough to foster competition. When the government attempted to shut down U.S. Steel, Morgan's competitors came to his defense.

John D. Rockefeller (1839–1937)

A philanthropist and industrialist so strongly associated with American wealth that his name has become synonymous with it, John D.

Rockefeller was an instrumental figure in American history both for his success in the oil business, and for the antitrust breakup of his company in 1911. Like Carnegie, he was a devoted philanthropist—as well as an avid churchgoer who abstained all his life from alcohol and tobacco, in an age when important men were accustomed to making their decisions over cigars and brandy.

Big Bill Rockefeller, John's father, was a travelling salesman who maintained a home in New York and was known more for his get-rich-quick schemes than his work ethic; John's mother Eliza was the primary caregiver for the family's six children, and the one who instilled in him a strong sense of the Baptist faith. When he took his first job at age 16, keeping the books for a produce company, he announced his intention—presumably encouraged by his mother or minister—to tithe one-tenth of his earnings to charity, a practice he maintained throughout his life. Working as a bookkeeper was a good introduction to the business, and eight years later he and a business partner built an oil refinery in Cleveland, Ohio, a city that during the Civil War years experienced significant industrial growth.

Two years later Rockefeller bought out three of his partners and formed the company that would eventually become the Standard Oil Company, after several "The firm of Rockefeller and..." name changes. Cleveland became one of the main refining centers in the United States, and Rockefeller's company became its biggest refinery. A deal with the railroads—Rockefeller backed a railroad cartel in exchange for high-volume shipping rebates—made Standard the country's leading shipper of petroleum products. By 1872 Standard had merged with or bought out nearly all of its local competition, and his biggest competitors in New York merged with

Standard, rather than go through the expense of fighting. Legend has it that many of Rockefeller's acquisitions were made bloodlessly and without resistance: all he had to do was show them Standard Oil's ledger, and once they realized how much money he had available, they knew they weren't competing in the same league.

The Standard Oil Trust was formed in 1882 as a holding company for locally-incorporated Standard Oil businesses. State regulations often complicated attempts to incorporate a business in one state while operating in another, an increasingly anachronistic problem in the industrial age, as more companies sought to operate nationally. This brought the company under attack by politicians and the press, because of its effective monopoly on American oil—and the accusations of the behavior this monopoly encouraged, especially as detailed in Ida Tarbell's 1904 book *The History of the Standard Oil Company*. Tarbell, who also published bestselling biographies of Napoleon and Lincoln, was the daughter of an oil man who had been driven out of business by Standard's growth, but insisted that she didn't object to the company's size or wealth. What bothered her was a lack of fair play.

Rockefeller was kept on his toes by shifting antitrust laws, having to reincorporate Standard Oil in New Jersey after Ohio's legislature forced Standard Oil of Ohio—the original Standard company—to separate from the trust. In 1911 the New Jersey–based company, which controlled almost two-thirds of the nation's oil, was found in violation of the Sherman Antitrust Act and broken up into 34 companies. Descendents of Standard include Exxon, Mobil, Amoco, and Conoco. Rockefeller by this time was no longer involved in the day-to-day activities of the company, and with the dissolution of the trust, he no longer held the honorary title of president.

By this time in Rockefeller's life, continuing his practice of tithing to charity involved such great sums of money that he had to do more than just drop an envelope in the Sunday collection plate. He hired advisers to guide his philanthropy, seeking out sensible situations in need of money, and arranging for practicalities. He helped found Spelman College, a college for African-American women that he named for his wife's family, who had been staunch abolitionists before the war. He put considerable amounts of money aside for medical research, which in his lifetime advanced from the leeches and bleeding of "heroic medicine" to the discovery of DNA and vaccines. Just as the extraordinary advances of the Industrial Revolution had needed money in order to act on the vast creative resources made available, so did those advances of the early 20th century's medical renaissance. The Rockefeller Institute for Medical Research, which today is known as Rockefeller University, was founded in New York in 1901.

The Rockefeller Foundation, founded a dozen years later, funded and founded a great many research and educational institutions, including the Johns Hopkins School of Hygiene and Public Health, a major resource in the study of disease.

George Westinghouse (1846–1914)

George Westinghouse, Jr. was one of the pre-eminent inventors during the late 19th century's Age of Invention. The son of a mechanic, young George tinkered with machines and dropped out of school at age 14, served in the Union Navy during the Civil War, and patented his first invention, a rotary steam engine, at the war's conclusion in 1865.

In 1869 Westinghouse witnessed a collision between two trains unable to stop quickly, and the idea for his most famous invention was born. Later that year he took out the first patent on an air-brake system for trains that allowed a single train engineer to apply the brakes on all the train's cars simultaneously. The system worked by transporting compressed air from a steam-powered pump to a network of pipes leading to the brake shoes of each car. At first he had trouble selling his idea to skeptical railroad companies; he had to fund his system's first demonstration and insure the trains involved in case of damage. But by the mid-1890s his brake system had been installed on over 400,000 cars and 27,000 engines, making Westinghouse extraordinarily wealthy, and greatly facilitating safe train travel.

Next he immersed himself in electrical invention. Westinghouse had been in the audience of inventors to whom Thomas Edison debuted his incandescent electrical lamp in 1878. But his electrical system employed direct current, which limited the distance electricity could be transmitted from a central power source.

Westinghouse thought he could do better, and in 1886 he devised an alternating current that transmitted electricity over a long distance. He and Edison became fierce competitors over whose system would electrify the United States. Westinghouse established the Westinghouse Electric Company and hired other inventors to assist him in perfecting his alternating current. Among them was Nikola Tesla, a Hungarian immigrant and former Edison employee, who invented an electrical motor that used alternating electricity to power mechanical devices.

By the 1890s Westinghouse's firm had proven the benefits of alternating current outweighed those of Edison's direct current. In 1893 a hydroelectric plant that employed Westinghouse and Tesla's inventions was constructed at Niagara Falls and transmitted electricity over a 22-mile distance. By the turn of the century power plants across the country running on alternating currents could send 30,000 volts of electricity up to 75 miles away.

By the time of his death in 1914, Westinghouse had patented over 400 inventions. Westinghouse's inventions helped fuel the larger process of industrial growth and economic development in the Gilded Age. His air brakes facilitated the era's transportation boom, which linked markets and aided the flow of goods and people across the country. His electrical innovations made cheap electricity widely available and greatly applicable as a source of power, revolutionizing leisure, work, and production.

Thomas Edison (1847–1931)

Thomas Edison sold his first invention when he was 23 years old. The young inventor had spent three years working on a new universal stock ticker for use in the New York financial markets, a tool that Western Union president Marshall Lefferts wanted to buy. Edison hoped to sell it for $5,000, and would have been quite happy with $3,000. When Lefferts offered him $40,000, Edison nearly fainted. Three days later Lefferts handed over a check for the full amount— the equivalent of over $500,000 today.

Edison took the check to the bank, but the teller refused to cash it, saying something the hard-of-hearing inventor couldn't under-

stand. Fearing he had been swindled, he went back to Lefferts and demanded to know what was going on. The president and his secretary roared with laughter: Edison didn't know he had to endorse the check. When the matter was cleared up, Edison gravely left the bank with a huge wad of small bills shoved in the pockets of his overcoat. He stayed up the whole night, afraid someone might rob him, and was talked into opening a savings account by the end of the week.

Edison went on to secure 1,093 U.S. patents and scores more in Europe, launching 13 companies, including General Electric, and revolutionized American life with inventions like the electric light, the phonograph, the motion-picture camera, the industrial research laboratory, and a host of other innovations. But he never lost the joy of invention or the satisfaction of bringing his ideas into the world. He was a uniquely even-tempered man. "I have not failed," he said of one project, which had indeed failed for the time being. "I've just found 10,000 ways that won't work."

Edison was profoundly interested in the practical application of his inventions. He had no interest in innovation for its own sake, only in finding new and useful things. He could be a ruthless business-man—as he showed in his long-running "war of the currents" with his former employee, Nikola Tesla. Edison relentlessly promoted his direct current electrical systems, while spreading propaganda about Tesla's alternating current system. The battle resulted in a rare Edi-son defeat, when Tesla won the contract to light up the 1893 World's Fair in Chicago. Within a few years, 80 percent of electrical systems and products used alternating current. Edison never fully conceded defeat, but he moved on to other inventions.

Thorstein Veblen (1857–1929)

An eccentric and nonconformist raised by Norwegian immigrants on an isolated farm in Wisconsin, Thorstein Veblen brought a new approach to economic analysis. Never a successful academic despite his graduate degrees from Yale and Cornell, his unconventional ideas and strange personality made it hard for him to fit in, but also led him to found the school of Institutionalism.

Veblen strove to offer a new way of thinking. He believed that a key assumption underlying economic thinking is that there is har-mony in the system. Smith's emphasis on the invisible hand implied the existence of natural laws that could be identified using economic analysis. Veblen argued that economic and social behavior evolved in response to existing institutions. Rather than assuming institutions as given, he intended to examine and explain the particular institu-tions of a culture in order to see the economic forces they created.

Veblen published his most widely read book, *The Theory of the Leisure Class*, in 1899. He set out to discover why and how the lei-sure class had evolved, and why members of this class garnered such respect and admiration from other members of society. Classical economists had not bothered with the question, maybe taking it for granted that those who found success would spend as little time working as possible. Veblen questioned the assumption that leisure was inherently more enjoyable than work.

Veblen considered the possibility that productive activities were as pleasant a way to pass the time as leisure activities. In some cultures, pride of workmanship drove men to try and outdo each other, and leisure wasn't esteemed like it was in the United States. Often a predatory class developed, whose members used force and cunning to take what they needed, instead of producing it.

Warriors, who were admired by their society but produced none of the things they needed, constituted the first members of the leisure class. In earlier stages, society couldn't afford to support a nonproductive class, but progress—and surplus resources, thanks to farmers who could harvest more crops than they needed for themselves, eventually allowed it, and man's natural aggression channeled that extra energy toward war. That's where Veblen saw the beginnings of the resentment of work.

Veblen grew up in the age of robber barons and the early captains of industry, when many people were coming to suspect the ethics of those who had especially prospered under capitalism, for very different reasons than they had once suspected those nobles who prospered from the labor of their ancestors. F. Scott Fitzgerald, chronicler of the 1920s and author of books like *The Great Gatsby*, was influenced by Veblen's model of the world, and both demonstrated that there's nothing especially rewarding about a life of leisure. Veblen introduced and used the terms *conspicuous consumption, conspicuous leisure, conspicuous waste, and pecuniary emulation* to describe why people did what they did in the modern society he sought to understand. Success only brings respect when it's seen and recognized by other members of society, so those who achieved it needed to put it on display somehow. Enjoying a good meal at a restaurant takes a basic need—food—and turns it into a display of power.

The Theory of the Business Enterprise was published in 1904, but was never embraced by intellectuals the way *Leisure Class* had been. Veblen argued that there was a conflict between making money and making goods; that the businessman wasn't the driving force behind production, but was actually sabotaging the whole system. He used a score of examples in which the quality of a product or service was irrelevant to a business's plan to dominate his industry, and that a lot of successes came from schemes to create profit from nothing.

Veblen's institutional approach emphasizes the need for economic analysis to be dynamic, and for economists to understand that human behavior evolves over time as social mores and habits of thought change. He would not advocate that modern economists simply devote themselves to finding new examples of conspicuous consumption or corporate misdeeds, but rather that they identify the next stage of evolution and explain what is happening and why. Probably the most important legacy of Veblen is the current emphasis on empirical research. Whether we realize it or not, we are responding to Veblen's demand to take a more open-minded approach, even if it is largely due to the enormous increase in computing power and data availability.

Henry Ford (1863–1947)

Always fascinated by engine design and application, Henry Ford experimented with gasoline-powered internal combustion engines throughout the 1890s. On June 4, 1896 Ford and a group of friends tested out their first automobile, comprised of two bicycles harnessed together and powered by a gas engine. After testing out a number of prototypes over the next three years, Ford and a group of investors established the Detroit Automobile Company in August 1899. The company lasted just over a year before closing, the fate of most of the thousands of automobile ventures that were started during the era.

Ford attracted new investors in the Henry Ford Motor Company after winning an auto race in Grosse Pointe, Michigan in October 1901. Ford left the company within a year after a series of arguments with its principal investors; under a new name, the Cadillac Corporation, the company eventually became the luxury division of Ford's chief rival, General Motors.

On June 16, 1903 Ford incorporated the Ford Motor Company with its principal assembly plant on Mack Avenue in Detroit. The Ford Model A—a moderately priced automobile featuring an innovative, vertically operating engine with cylinders that gave more power with less friction—was an instant success with 658 cars sold in its first season. In 1907, countering conventional wisdom in the industry, Ford decided to concentrate on lower-priced automobiles with the

Model N, starting at $700. The decision led Ford to $1 million-profit that year, with 8,243 Model N automobiles sold for gross revenues of over $4.7 million. Sales of the Model N increased to 10,000 in 1908. Despite refinements in his Mack Avenue assembly lines, Ford could not keep up with demand.

Ford's new factory in Highland Park, Michigan, opened in December 1909 as a state-of-the-art manufacturing facility. Each step in the production process was routinized through the intensive use of machinery that deskilled the labor process. The mechanization of production, standardization of the components, and constant planning and refining of the manufacturing process came to be known as Fordism. Yet Fordism went far beyond the factory-shop floor. In order to combat the high absenteeism and turnover that Highland Park's never-ending assembly lines produced—in 1913 10 percent of the plant's work force was absent on any given day—Ford announced an incentive pay plan in January 1914 heralded as a "Five-Dollar Day." In actuality, the plan retained the basic daily wage rate of $2.34 for an eight-hour day, with profit-sharing incentives making up the difference. As an essential part of Fordism, the higher wage rates recognized that mass-production workers were to be transformed into consumers of mass-production items, including automobiles.

The Ford Motor Company was the preeminent automobile manufacturer in the world during the first quarter of the 20th century: between 1908 and 1927 the Ford Motor Company sold over 15 million Model T automobiles. By 1930, however, General Motors had surpassed Ford by offering annual style updates and credit purchasing options on its cars, two actions that Henry Ford resisted. Ford's outside interests, including the sponsorship of a "Peace Ship" to negotiate an end to World War I, and his ownership of an openly anti-Semitic newspaper, the *Dearborn Independent*, added to the company's loss of dominance in its market. Ford was also plunged into controversy over the use of brutal and illegal tactics to keep labor unions out of his factories in the 1930s, including the infamous Battle of the Overpass outside of the company's River Rouge plant on May 26, 1937. Several union organizers were beaten, and the incident tarnished Ford's reputation as a down-to-earth man of integrity. Ford finally signed a collective bargaining agreement with the United Automobiles Workers union in June 1941, after all of the other major automobile manufacturers had done so.

Although the Ford Motor Company had declined somewhat since its heydays in the 1910s and 1920s, it remained the second-largest automobile maker in the world at the time of its founder's death. The production techniques and higher wages that Ford pioneered had also become standardized throughout the automotive sector, and in many other mass-production industries as well.

John Maynard Keynes (1883–1946)

The most influential economist of the 20th century was an Englishman born to a Cambridge economics professor and a social reformer. By age 11 John Maynard Keynes was winning prizes in mathematics, and he pursued his education through his late 20s, later declaring that a master economist should be a mathematician, historian, philosopher, and salesman. He hated World War I, during which he worked for the British Treasury and attended the Versailles Peace Conference.

After the war he resigned his post in protest over the British government's demands of reparations from Germany that he thought would damage the country too heavily. He spoke out against those reparations in his book *The Economics of The Peace*, and some historians blame the extent of those reparations and punitive damages for the political climate that brought Hitler to power and sparked World War II less than a generation after Versailles.

He fell out of favor with the government because of his political views, but continued to contribute major works of economic theory. By the 1930s, in the aftermath of the Great Depression, he had become convinced that an obligation of government was to take an active role in the economy in order to preserve stability. By this point he had become an influential figure, and so the rest of the 20th century saw a conflict between Keynesians and anti-Keynesians over this issue. Roosevelt's New Deal policies were distinctly

Keynesian, and even Ronald Reagan's economic policy was influenced by Keynesian Milton Friedman.

Keynes believed that economic cycles are constantly changing, and each cycle has a distinct impact on income, employment, prices, and output. Some people put their money in banks, while others choose to invest. They act from different motives, and expect different results. If people lost trust in the economic system, he argued, they would begin to hoard money, and the ripple effect would create high unemployment and economic crisis. Therefore, the government had a responsibility to increase its own spending and reduce taxes to stimulate the sluggish economy. If the government spends money on a construction project, for instance, new workers are employed who then spend more money, which improves the economy for everyone.

Before the United States entered World War II, John Maynard Keynes served as an advisor to the lend-lease deals whereby Franklin Roosevelt supported Great Britain's war effort with essential war materials. Keynes was finally honored for his contributions to Great Britain and named to the British peerage in 1942. In 1944 he served as a representative to the Bretton Woods Conference in Bretton Woods, New Hampshire, and was instrumental in establishing the International Monetary Fund (IMF) and the World Bank created by the conference, before dying of a heart attack two years later. His theories continued to dominate the economics discussions of the 20th century.

Friedrich August von Hayek (1899–1992)

Nobel laureate Vernon Smith called Friedrich August von Hayek "the leading economic thinker of the 20th century." Hayek was born in Vienna, and studied economics at the university there after fighting in World War I. After earning doctorates in law and political science, he became the director of the Austrian Institute for Business Cycle Research, and his analysis of business cycles led to his prediction of an impending economic crisis, one that would be felt hardest in the United States. The increase in the money supply sent misleading signals to the market, creating an unsustainable expansion that would have to be followed by a collapse, he said. Less than two years later, the Great Depression crashed like a tidal wave, every bit as bad as Hayek had warned. His fame led to a professorship at the London School of Economics, one of the premier institutions of its kind.

In 1944 Hayek published *The Road to Serfdom*, which became a surprise bestseller in England and the United States. He warned against the dangers of both fascism and socialism (against the backdrop of the ongoing war against Nazi Germany and the wary alliance between the Allied powers and Soviet Russia), arguing that state control over the economy led inexorably to totalitarianism, and concluding that "only capitalism makes democracy possible." According to Hayek, "Economic control is not merely control of a sector of human life which can be separated from the rest: It is the control of the means for all of our ends."

Hayek published "The Use of Knowledge in Society" in 1945, an article in which he described the price system of competitive markets as a "marvel" that allows society to use its resources efficiently. Market prices, he argued, act to coordinate the separate actions of many different people, providing them with information about how to respond best to economic changes. According to Hayek, "The mere fact that there is one price for any commodity… brings about the solution which … might have been arrived at by one single mind possessing all the information which is in fact dispersed among all the people involved in the process." He was eventually given the Nobel Prize for his work, and continued to lecture through his 80s.

John Kenneth Galbraith (1908–2006)

John Kenneth Galbraith originally intended his classic book, *The Affluent Society* (1958), to be a treatise on poverty. During the course of his research, he realized that affluence was much more critical to the understanding of postwar American capitalism, and scrapped his original outline in favor of what became a revolution in the philosophy of capitalism. The political economists before him had focused on scarcity and the belief that workers were doomed to starvation and misery. Galbraith saw that this model had to be thrown out to understand the world in the wake of the war.

He had been an active observer of modern capitalism, working for the Office of the Price Administration during the war, though he lost his job because of his incompatible views of regulation. In his first major work, 1952's *American Capitalism*, written and published while he was an economics professor at Harvard, he explained that smaller markets were disappearing, absorbed by a small number of corporations. Economists like Smith had believed competition would make sure no business would grow too strong, but Galbraith saw power concentrating in a smaller and smaller number of hands. The countervailing power of government regulation, labor unions, and consumer groups could check this corporate amassing of power.

He was one of the first economists to seriously treat the world of advertising and consumer culture. Corporations created "needs" in order to encourage consumption of goods, Galbraith said; consumer

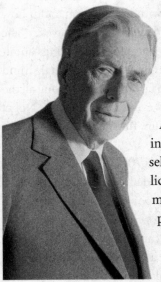

desire had to be inspired, contrived, or invented, in order to increase production. "Private opulence"—abundant consumer goods—existed alongside "public squalor," as public goods like schools, highways, and parks fell into disrepair. The concern over the state of American bridges in 2008 fits perfectly into what Galbraith warned against. A self-described liberal who believed public spending should address the needs the market failed to cover, Galbraith advised presidential candidate Adlai Stevenson before working for the Kennedy and Johnson administrations. In the 1960s he optimistically described the growing new class of white-collar employees, the "educational and scientific elite" who were given more and more control over the running of businesses, whether directly or in advisory capacities.

This optimism balanced itself against worries—not just about consumer culture, but more mundane things like inflation. Galbraith believed inflation was a new type of problem endemic to postwar economic prosperity. As wages went up within an "affluent society," corporations raised prices. This "wage-price spiral" was especially evident in the highly-unionized sector of the American economy. Though trained as a Keynesian economist, Galbraith broke with certain Keynesian tenets. He argued, "The preoccupation of Keynesian economics with depression has meant that inflation control has been handled by improvisation." Galbraith rejected the Keynesian tendency to shy away from direct regulation of the economy. Instead, Galbraith argued that a return to price control would probably be necessary to head off inflation, pointing out that when government stopped using price control mechanisms in the wake of World War II, inflation shot up. Against more conservative critics, Galbraith asserted that price control could be used much more flexibly than it was during the war. He also urged liberals to remain more open toward direct interventions in the economy in order to address inflation and other problems.

Milton Friedman (1912–2006)

The leader of the Chicago School of monetary economics, Milton Friedman for many years stressed the importance of quantity of money as an instrument of government policy and as a determinant of business cycles and inflation. Mixing economics with his social views, he supported public policy that favored the rights of man.

A Keynesian economist who supported New Deal policies and high taxes in the initial postwar years, he gradually moved away from his support of central control in favor of a more laissez-faire approach, which helped him to become prominent in the public arena. He served as economic adviser to presidential candidates Barry Goldwater,

Richard Nixon, and Ronald Reagan, and his theories were an important influence on the latter's economic policies. By that point Friedman occupied the more classically liberal position, advocating capitalism as the antidote to totalitarianism, arguing that political freedom followed as a natural consequence of economic freedom. This was a key point in the Reagan era's foreign policy as well, and one that was just as influential on Margaret Thatcher in the United Kingdom and Brian Mulroney in Canada.

The co-author of *A Monetary History of the United States*, Friedman revived interest in the study of the money supply and its link to inflation. In the 1960s and 1970s when he wrote, inflation was popularly believed to be the result of oil prices or wage increases, a belief against which he argued stridently. He considered his best work—which was in part responsible for his eventually being awarded the Nobel Prize—to be his permanent income hypothesis, which argued that individuals spend an amount of money proportional to what they perceive as their "permanent income." Neither windfalls nor tax reductions affected spending, because consumers didn't feel they affected their income, and believed they would be offset by later tax increases. This hypothesis had an enormous effect on fiscal policy.

Warren Buffett (1930–)

In the summer of 1942, 11-year old Warren Buffett made his first stock purchase: three shares of City Service Preferred at $38 per share. The value dropped to $27, and then went up to $40, at which point Buffett sold his stocks and netted a $5 profit after commission. Almost immediately after this sale was complete, City Service stock shot up to $200 a share, a painful lesson in patience for the budding entrepreneur.

Born in Omaha, Nebraska, Buffett was the son of a stockbroker and showed an early fascination with mathematics and investing. By the time he was 16, Buffet already had a net worth of over $6,000—an unheard-of sum for a teenager in the 1940s, and one earned entirely on his own effort. Like many boys, he wanted to skip college and go right into the business world; like many fathers, Buffett's father insisted he go to college anyway.

While studying at the University of Nebraska, Buffett read the work of Benjamin Graham, an investor and professional economist who touted "value investing," or finding undervalued stocks that have the potential for high yields down the line. Buffett later studied with Graham at Columbia University, and credits most of his business philosophy to his mentor. After graduate school, he worked for Graham for a time, then returned to Omaha and began to build his own investment partnerships. He was a millionaire by the age of 32. In 1965 he gained control of Berkshire Hathaway, a New England–based textile company, which he diversified into the insurance business, using the funds from policyholders to finance his investments. It was a successful plan: a person who invested $10,000 in Berkshire Hathaway in 1965 would be holding onto stock worth $50 million in 2008.

Buffett is a master of seeing the potential in undervalued stocks. Perhaps the best example is Coca-Cola. When Buffett began buying Coke stock in 1988, it was trading at $10.96 a share. Buffett saw its strong brand image and plans for global growth, and became a major Coca-Cola shareholder. By 1993 the stock had risen to $74.50

a share, and Buffett made a profit of $13 million. The "Oracle of Omaha" has always been a bit different. He prefers to buy and hold stocks. He does not have a computer at his desk, and he carries no cell phone. He has a personal net worth of around $60 billion dollars, but still lives in the modest Omaha home he purchased for $31,800 in 1958. His annual salary as the CEO of Berkshire Hathaway is only $100,000. He has been outspoken about ostentatious displays by other CEOs, so when he spent $9.7 million on a Gulfstream IV-SP, he named it "The Indefensible."

In 2006 he announced that most of his personal fortune would go to charity, with 85 percent of his Berkshire Hathaway stock—worth almost $40 billion—distributed to a number charitable foundations over a period of years, with a whopping 83 percent of it going to the Bill and Melinda Gates Foundation for educational and global health initiatives.

Bill Gates (1955–)

The richest private citizen in the world and one of the most successful entrepreneurs in history, Bill Gates dropped out of Harvard in the 1970s to found the Microsoft Corporation with his friend Paul Allen, and took sole control of the software company in 1982 when Allen was diagnosed with Hodgkin's disease. He became a billionaire by age 31, the youngest billionaire in history whose wealth had not been inherited.

At Microsoft, Gates is notorious for his focus, his total awareness of his products, and his confrontational management style. Gates insists workers argue with each other to fully examine ideas, and he has been known to verbally attack employees if he feels they are not properly prepared. In the early days of Microsoft, when it was still a reasonably small company, Gates insisted all decisions come through him; he preferred an open management style to bureaucracy (which became unavoidable in light of the company's enormous growth rate). Even today, Gates prefers informal management, and tries to keep the atmosphere at company headquarters informal.

After seven years of inquiry and discussion, the U.S. Department of Justice and 20 states brought an antitrust suit against Microsoft in May of 1998. The original question had been whether Microsoft's activities in the operating system market had been in violation of antitrust regulations. A 1994 settlement had resulted in Microsoft agreeing not to tie Microsoft products to the sale of Windows—to minimize Microsoft's ability to use virtually the only commercial PC operating system as a way to gain an unfair, anticompetitive advantage in the PC software market. The 1998 trial alleged that Microsoft's inclusion of Internet Explorer with its operating system, a product previously sold separately from Windows (as part of the Windows Plus! software bundle), was a violation of this settlement. Microsoft in turn argued that Internet Explorer was not a product but a feature, which the language of the settlement permitted.

In the course of the trial, it came to light that Microsoft had threatened to revoke manufacturers' licenses if they removed Internet Explorer from computers preparing for shipment, or removed its icon from the desktop. Microsoft originally claimed this was a matter of efficiency—that Windows ran slower without IE—a claim that it quickly retracted when it was proven false.

The judge ruled that Microsoft was guilty of attempting a monopoly, and must be split into two companies—one producing operating systems, the other producing software. When Microsoft appealed, the appellate court overturned the lower court's findings of law, but not findings of fact. In other words, they agreed that Microsoft was in violation, but disagreed with the remedy of creating babysofts, in part because the judge had discussed the ongoing case with the media, in violation of ethical requirements. In 2001 the Justice Department reached a settlement with Microsoft (with which nine of the original 20 states disagreed), requiring the company to share aspects of its code with third parties in order to encourage third-party development of Windows software. However no changes to Microsoft's business practices or Windows code were actually required.

Also in 1998 Bill Gates relinquished the titles of president and chief executive officer at Microsoft to Steve Ballmer, a friend of Gates from Harvard hired for his management prowess. Gates adopted the title of chief software architect; the change, Gates announced, allowed him to focus on Microsoft's products, and less on business operations.

Gates has always been an active philanthropist, and is particularly interested in lowering the price and raising the availability of prescription drugs and vaccines, one of the key goals of his charity foundation. In 2000 he and his wife founded the Bill & Melinda Gates Foundation with an initial $126 billion endowment. Globally, the foundation's primary funding targets are health care and poverty; in the United States, the foundation also devotes efforts to education.

Though the foundation's funding grew steadily, it did not come to prominent national attention until 2006, when Warren Buffett pledged $30 billion in stock share donations, doubling the foundation's size. Buffett attached a few conditions to the pledge, mainly that the foundation is required to actually spend the money he gives it, not simply let it sit in a bank being impressive. Legally, a charity is required to spend only 5 percent of its assets annually; Buffett's requirement is significantly greater.

Chapter 4

Capitalist Successes

Capitalism is sometimes seen as impersonal, despite its natural affinity for individualism. Modern capitalism wasn't born fully-grown in some mystical past—it has changed and developed over the course of history. Whether we're talking about a telegraph company becoming a digital communications giant, a computer nerd dropping out of Harvard to start the world's biggest software company, or Communist China adopting free-market initiatives in the 21st century, all success stories that take place on a long enough timeline are stories of change. All those changes are adopted for the same reason: to survive and to thrive. One of the successes of capitalism is a private sector in which success is passed on to entities that have to continue to work for that power—rather than Henry Ford's empire simply being handed to a nephew or grandson, as a Medieval land holding would have been. Corporations are run by groups who risk being removed from their positions of authority if they do a poor job—the system preserves the legacy of those founding individuals.

Another testament to the success of capitalism is the rise of the middle class. An entire class of people whose standards of living were higher than that of their parents is unheard of in world history prior to the 20th century, and capitalism gets the credit.

Coca-Cola

Remarkably, a soft drink has become synonymous with an international corporation—without a monopoly, and amid fierce competition from other soft drinks, some that taste nearly exactly like "the real thing." Coca-Cola is an American icon, to such a degree that in parts of the South, a "coke" is any sort of soda, and people all over the world would know what you meant if you said the color of a car was "Coca-Cola red."

According to the official story, the fizzy drink was cooked up by a small-town doctor in a three-legged kettle over an open fire in his Atlanta backyard. Dr. John Pemberton knew right away that he had something special, but it wasn't until the flavoring had been added to carbonated water that he realized he had created the perfect refreshing beverage. The rest was history, right?

The truth of Coca-Cola's history is more complicated and interesting. Pemberton had been selling patent medicines since graduating from medical school at 19. As much as patent medicines—nerve tonics, exotic elixirs, and their claims to cure whatever ails you—are mocked today, they were the alternative Pemberton chose over the other dominant medical trend of his generation, heroic medicine. Heroic medicine called for intentional blistering, bloodletting, and purging, all in an attempt to drive out illness. Pemberton's wares may have been questionable, but he was a member in good standing of the first pharmacist licensing board in Georgia, formed to scrutinize the industry and prevent spurious claims and injurious practices. Whether his medicines worked or not, he wasn't intentionally deceiving anyone.

Once in a while, one of these patent medicines actually tasted good—those exotic ingredients included things like cinnamon and vanilla. The widespread availability of refined sugar had a lot to do with this, too. Sugar remained expensive until the 19th century, which is why honey and molasses often appear in older cookbooks. Homemade root beer was a household staple, but as patent medicines became popular, they gave way to a commercial soda pop market. Pemberton's first foray into this world was Pemberton's French Wine Coca, which premiered in 1884. Cocawines were a small, but successful slice of the beverage market, a mixture of wine and cocaine that was advertised as a nerve tonic. Pemberton's contained kola nuts, and therefore caffeine, which made it a genuine

A late 19th century print bearing the slogan "Drink Coca-Cola 5 cents."

cure for many headaches. Cocaine was still used medicinally at the time, sometimes prescribed as an antidepressant. Pemberton's real success came because of temperance—when alcoholic drinks were restricted in Atlanta in 1885, he cooked up a nonalcoholic drink called Coca-Cola, which used soda water and extra sugar instead of wine. Carbonated drinks were becoming a popular alternative in areas where alcohol was outlawed.

Coca-Cola wasn't an overnight success. French Wine Coca still outsold it, and Coca-Cola's sales were impressive only compared to other carbonated drinks, which were still a small market at the time. Pemberton sold the rights to the drink twice, and his son kept on manufacturing his own version, making things confusing for awhile. Businessman Asa Candler saw the potential of the product, as well as the chaos these multiple rights-holders could cause, so he bought out all the invested parties and incorporated The Coca-Cola Company in 1892 to consolidate all claims on the product, name, and formula. He also changed Pemberton's formula, which hadn't been guarded very effectively. All the mystique surrounding Coca-Cola's original formula is Candler's doing; he made a couple of minor changes to Pemberton's formula, just enough to make a distinct product, and then limited access to the small number of people who absolutely needed to know the formula in order to do their jobs.

Further modifications came in 1903 when the company switched from cocaine to decocainized coca leaves. These days the company is large enough that it grows its own non-narcotic coca leaves, and has dropped the kola from its cola—there aren't enough kola nuts in the world to support the demand for cola drinks, and most of the beverage's flavor comes from spices and citrus fruit.

Convinced of Coca-Cola's potential, Candler offered free gallons of syrup—enough to make dozens of drinks—to various soda fountains and stores, gambling that customers would like the product enough to continue asking for it, encouraging the store to become a Coca-Cola customer. He was right; Coca-Cola's reputation as a hangover cure spread around the country, fueling weekend sales—given the combination of sugar and caffeine, the rumor may have been well-founded.

Consider the effect Coca-Cola had on the soft drink market. There may have been drinks with kola nuts, but there was no generic "cola" as we think of it today—Coca-Cola's distinctive flavor comes from the combination of kola flavor with citrus and spices, a pattern its imitators have followed. Unlike flavors like grape or cherry, cola isn't a self-evident flavor that would have arisen independently from many sources—the early cola drinks were all Coca-Cola imitators, following in Pemberton and Candler's footsteps, building little empires on the strength of a flavor. That is an American capitalist success: create a product so successful, so cheap to produce and easy to sell, that dozens of companies can imitate it and still fail to beat you at your own game.

If Coca-Cola was guilty of any anticompetitive practices, it was in going after companies using similar names. Candler believed strongly—more strongly than the modern company—in the importance of calling the company's product Coca-Cola, the full name, believing that shortening it could result in turning a proper name into a generic. He also discouraged soda fountains from adding flavors to Coca-Cola like vanilla or cherry—again, in the service of protecting distinctiveness. At the same time, the Coca-Cola Company launched a number of legal battles against companies producing colas with similar names, like Koke (a battle it won) and Pepsi-Cola (a battle it lost). Including "cola" in the name was not considered derivative enough of Coca-Cola's distinctive brand identity.

Advertising was a critical part of Coca-Cola's longevity and dominance over its competitors. The company affixed the logo to newspaper ads, pens, baseball cards, desk blotters, thermometers, metal signs, calendars, and virtually anything else it would fit on. In 1900 they were handing out a million of these branded giveaways a year; by 1913 the number had climbed to 100 million. Coca-Cola's importance to American advertising began with the use of pretty Coca-Cola Girls in print ads in the 1890s, and the popularization of Santa Claus as a jolly fat man in a Coca-Cola red suit in the early 20th century, and continued to the 1971 television ad jingle "I'd Like to Teach the World to Sing." It was soon the most advertised product in the world.

Pepsi Cola, the most successful Coca-Cola competitor nationally, survived Coca-Cola's lawsuits, and later its own economic struggles. But it grew to prominence during the Great Depression, when the 12-ounce bottle of Pepsi was introduced at the same 5-cent price as the 6-ounce Coca-Cola. Coca-Cola expanded its overseas efforts, including the creation of Fanta in German-occupied countries where imports of Coca-Cola concentrate were unreliable. Many of Europe's early Coca-Cola bottling plants were set up during World War II, while the company distributed free soda to soldiers.

Coca-Cola had penetrated the global market by the 1930s, and already had operations in 44 countries by the start of World War II. During the war it set up more than 60 special bottling plants to meet the needs of millions of American G.I.s, and those companies became the hub of it's postwar international expansion. In 2008, the international market brought in 70 percent of the company's annual profit.

The company boomed in the 1950s, as giant supermarket chains expanded across the country to serve a growing suburban, middle-class population. They began to produce larger sizes and in 1955, they debuted the aluminum can. In the 1960s and 1970s the company expanded their brand portfolio to include Tab, Fanta, Sprite, Fresca, Mr. Pibb, and Mello Yello. In the 1980s they introduced Diet Coke, Cherry Coke, and most controversially, New Coke—a new formulation of the original brand. Eventually, they brought back "Classic" Coke due to consumer demand. By 2008, the Coca-Cola Company was producing 400 different brands worldwide, many of them suited to the tastes of the regional markets of more 200 countries.

Toyota

Among the world's three largest automobile manufacturers, Toyota consistently produces a full line of models, from sedans to mini-vehicles to large trucks. Churning out products at a rate of more than 5.5 million vehicles annually, one every six seconds, the company sells them in 160 different countries and regions.

The king of Japanese inventors, Sakichi Toyoda, founded the Toyoda Automated Loom Works in 1926. Originally named for its founder, the company soon changed its name to Toyota Industries, changing the spelling of the name to something more auspicious. In Japanese, Toyota takes eight brushstrokes to write—a lucky number.

Essentially the Henry Ford of Japan—and heavily influenced by Ford's writings and methods—Toyoda integrated various approaches to manufacturing into the Toyota Production System (TPS). Japanese industry has become associated with efficiency and productivity, to which the TPS is a large contributor. The system was formulated to eliminate *muda* (waste and inefficiency) by designing manufacturing processes and procedures that would provide

トヨタ

The Japanese symbol for Toyota.

consistent products through smooth, efficient work. Seven kinds of *muda* are identified by TPS: overproduction, unnecessary motion (of the machine or its operator), unnecessary waiting (of the machine or its operator, especially when one is waiting for input from the other), conveyance, processing, waste of raw material, and errors. Legend has it the seeds of this efficiency-first system were sown in America, not by the assembly lines of the Ford factories, but by the restocking procedures used by the Piggly Wiggly supermarket chain in the 1920s. TPS, like Piggly Wiggly, emphasizes low inventory levels so that products aren't sitting around unused, taking up warehouse space, exposed to the possibility of damage or theft.

Jidoka is a Japanese term often heard in association with TPS, which enjoyed a surge of American interest in the 1980s when Americans saw Japan as their main economic rival in manufacturing and invention. It means roughly "automation guided by human intelligence," and refers to the goal of automating as many processes as possible, without doing so blindly, and without anyone mindlessly following instructions to the point that they fail to see problems that develop. Organizational learning is also stressed, in which the company constantly reflects upon itself, not only adapting to the market, but also looking for ways it can improve. There is nothing sacred about the procedures adopted, and they are always open to change. In practice, this involves convincing the right people of the need for that change.

Originally a machine company, Toyota Industries established an automobile department in 1933, the pet project of Kiichiro Toyoda, the son of Sakichi. Four years later the department was spun off into its own company, Toyota Motors. Other companies were created over the next 20-odd years, and in 1960 the Toyota Group consisted of 13 companies, most of them manufacturers. The worldwide economic calamities of the early 1930s led the Japanese government to encourage Toyota to produce automobiles to prevent Japanese dependence on foreign-made cars, and the trade imbalance that would result. (It's interesting to consider that the first major Japanese automobile manufacturer was thus making cars for Japanese consumption, when in later decades Americans would be encouraged to "Buy American" to reduce dependence on foreign cars.)

The early Toyota cars emulated the Chevrolet engine. After focusing on truck manufacture leading up to and during World War II, the company returned to automobiles in 1947, soon establishing the Toyota Motor Sales Company as its sales company, with a dealership chain following in 1956. By the end of the 1950s Toyota was exporting automobiles to the Americas for the first time, and opened large divisions in both the United States and Brazil. As the company expanded, it began operations in Australia and Southeast Asia, and it exported its one-millionth car at the end of the 1960s.

The presence of Japanese cars on American roads truly became entrenched in the 1970s, when stagflation and the oil crisis combined and made millions of Americans abandon their traditionally large American-made vehicles in favor of something cheaper and more fuel-efficient. Japanese cars had always been more fuel-efficient, not because of a shortage of oil, but because of the aims of the TPS and the premium placed on efficiency and pragmatism, ideals that luxury-loving, individualist Americans are not very good at living up to. Small American cars were typically not built to last, and certainly weren't built to the same standards as the larger cars that were considered the "keepers." This helped Japanese motor companies permanently establish their place in the American market, and a significant presence in Europe soon followed.

In large part because of these foreign markets, Toyota became one of the first Japanese car companies to put serious effort into developing distinctly un-Japanese vehicles. The Toyota Tundra full-size pickup truck; the luxury Lexus division that launched in 1989; the Camry Solara sports car—all of these expanded Toyota's market share. The Toyota Prius, launched in 1997, was not only the first mass-produced hybrid vehicle, but remained the best-selling in 2008, and was the most fuel-efficient car for sale in the United States, according to *Consumer Reports*.

Like other auto manufacturers, Toyota was hit hard by the credit crunch of 2008–09 and the resulting drop in auto sales. Toyota sales dropped 38 percent in November 2008 alone.

Boeing

A few years after the Wright brothers' first flight, William Boeing, a Yale-educated engineer, became entranced by aviation, and began to develop an airplane. The company formed to manufacture his plane would eventually dominate the American aviation manufacturing market.

Pacific Aero Products—soon renamed the Boeing Airplane Company—was founded in 1916 in Seattle. The Boeing Air Transport company, Boeing's airline, was founded separately in 1927 and was folded in with Boeing Airplane and the Pacific Air Transport airline to form the United Aircraft and Transport Corporation, in 1929. United rapidly acquired other small aviation companies, including Pratt & Whitney, an engine manufacturer; the Hamilton Standard propeller manufacturer; and the National Air Transport airline. The Boeing 247, the first aircraft to resemble modern passenger planes, was introduced by United in 1933. It had an autopilot, retractable landing gear, a metal construction, and cantilevered wings with wing flaps and deicing boots. Unlike previous twin-engine planes, it could safely fly with only one engine. Visually, the 247 looks very much like contemporary planes—30 years after the Wright brothers, the airplane had found its form.

United was both an airline and a manufacturer, and believed the Boeing 247 would revolutionize the industry—so it kept the first 60 of them for its airline,

A British Airways Boeing 777-200LR taking off from Heathrow Airport.

making competitors wait to own one. This was the early 1930s, in the wake of Roosevelt's Hundred Days and the strengthening of antitrust reforms; United soon found itself in a corner. The 1934 Air Mail Act prohibited corporations from both manufacturing planes and operating airlines, and United Aircraft was split into three companies: United Airlines, the United Aircraft Corporation, and the Boeing Airplane Company.

This freed the Boeing engineers to work with other companies, and by 1938 Boeing Airplanes had been contracted by Pan Am to build a "flying boat"—a seaplane that floats on its hull instead of using floats—capable of transoceanic flights. The resulting Boeing 314 was the largest passenger plane ever built, carrying up to 90 passengers, and regular passenger service was instituted in 1939.

Another innovation, the pressurized cabin, came in 1938, allowing Boeing planes to travel high enough in the atmosphere to fly over the weather—an idea that seemed as remarkable then as putting a man on the moon would 30 years later. The war saw Boeing turn to military production, with a predominantly female workforce building bombers to support their husbands who were fighting the war. Though massive numbers of workers were laid off when the war ended, and orders for bombers were canceled, the company had learned a great deal about aviation and other technologies, and new opportunities soon presented themselves in the Cold War. Guided short-range missiles guaranteed Boeing a place in the defense industry, competing with fellow aviation giants McDonnell-Douglas and Lockheed Martin.

Boeing remained consistently in the lead in aircraft, and has stayed there for the last 60 years. They introduced the 367-80, the first jet airliner, in the early 1950s, which led to the first commercial jet, the 707, in 1958. This was an important moment not only in innovation, but also in the economy of the Cold War industries: the 707 was a commercial application of a technology originally developed on a military contract. Boeing had managed a zipless double-dip. The famous 747, Boeing's most successful aircraft, was introduced in 1970. The research and development costs of $1 billion nearly bankrupted the company. Seating 450 passengers with an intercontinental range and an upper-deck, the 747 allowed the airline industry to grow enormously. Like their predecessor the 737, the 747s continue to be manufactured in large numbers, with new innovations added all the time.

McDonnell-Douglas, meanwhile, fell on hard times as a result of its failure to compete in the civil aircraft market. After permission was granted by antitrust commissions around the world, Boeing acquired M-D in 1997. Even before that acquisition, it had over half of the worldwide market share and a near-monopoly on intercontinental aircraft. The aircraft industry—and thus Boeing—have contributed significantly to the American balance of trade.

Airbus, a European consortium formed in 1970 with European Union (EU) subsidies, has emerged as a significant competitor to Boeing. Airbus began life in the short-to-medium range market, but now competes against Boeing directly in their large range market. There have been various trade disputes since the inception of Airbus, due to the subsidies that Boeing claims have violated the GATT and WTO's regulations. In 1992, Boeing and Airbus signed a bilateral agreement that limited the EU's direct R&D subsidies, and also the U.S. government's indirect aid (via military contracts).

After the 1997 merger with M-D, shareholders did not see the synergies that were expected, and Boeing recorded its worst performance for 50 years in 1997. This was due to losses in civil aircraft arising from the phasing out of M-D's airplanes, the relative neglect by Boeing's management of their civil business to focus on expanding the military side, escalating production costs and inefficiencies, as well as the increasing competition from Airbus.

As the crisis deepened, Boeing tried a comeback in 1998 by shaking up management and reorganizing. Boeing chose not to compete with Airbus's new super-jumbo jet, but instead to focus on short-haul flights. In the 21st century Boeing is the principal contractor for the International Space Station, and has been contracted for NASA's manned mission to Mars, but has lost ground to its competitors. Lockheed Martin won the contract for the U.S. Defense Department's Jet Strike Fighter project, and Airbus continues to gain market share in more markets. Boeing has returned to the arena in which it has never had a significant rival: long-range aircraft. The 777-200LR introduced in 2006 has the longest range of any commercial aircraft ever developed, and its fuel efficiency has made it a popular seller to airlines in an age of rapidly rising fuel costs.

British Petroleum

The largest energy companies in the world are the six supermajors—ExxonMobil, Royal Dutch Shell, BP, Chevron, ConocoPhilips, and Total S.A. The supermajors developed in the 1990s when existing oil companies began merging in response to the decline in oil prices. What elevates the supers is the vertical integration of petroleum products, oil exploration, and natural gas. All have revenues in the hundreds of billions of dollars.

British Petroleum, the third largest supermajor, began with the oil concession granted to William Knox D'Arcy in 1901, by Shah Qajar, the last Shah of Persia, before that country became known to the West as Iran. D'Arcy, already wealthy from land speculation and mines, found oil seven years later—the first large oil discovery in the Middle East. He founded the Anglo-Persian Oil Company—later the Anglo-Iranian Oil Company—to drill for and sell the oil. During World War I the British government took control of the company for strategic reasons. As the company became more prosperous—as the world's demand for oil increased in response to the ubiquity of automobiles, airplanes, and other petroleum consumers—the Iranian government sought to revise the terms of the agreement with the AIOC to give the Iranian people a bigger piece of the pie. In 1951, after the assassination of the previous prime minister, his replacement was a nationalist, considerably less friendly to the West.

The British and American governments collaborated to remove the nationalist Mossadeq from office, leaving the pro-West Shah

A BP station in Portsmouth, England, with prices in British pounds.

Mohammed Reza Pahlavi in charge. The British sought to protect their economic interests; the Americans were misled into believing Mossadeq was a Communist threat. Rookie President Eisenhower authorized the CIA's involvement, and the coup was carried out, with the Shah abolishing the constitution to preserve the power the British needed him to have. The AIOC reorganized as the British Petroleum Company, its name now emphasizing a single nation's interests (though Iran continued to benefit from BP).

We can't gloss over the effects of that coup in our BP history here, because its effects are so important to the history of the oil industry. The Shah was a Western ally, and took growing criticism from more nationalist and conservative Iranian factions. On the other hand, while Pahlavi was certainly liberal compared to many Middle Eastern leaders, the alliance was considered an embarrassment to the West because of how "backwards" many of his beliefs and practices were. When the Shah faced another coup, this time at the hands of nationalists and extremists who wanted a firm anti-Western stance, the West gave him the cold shoulder—offering no assistance, but allowing him to enter the United States for medical care. This fed directly into the oil crisis of the late 1970s, as well as providing the motivation for the seizure of American hostages by Iranian students.

Facing increasing public hostility in Iran, BP split its profits with Iran 50-50, provided the West retain control over the company. An international consortium was created for this purpose, involving BP and the major oil companies of the world. BP continued to expand, drilling for oil in Alaska and the North Sea in the 1960s and 1970s, and acquiring other smaller companies. In 1979 the regime of the Ayatollah Khomeini, which came to power with the Islamic Revolution, confiscated all of BP's assets in Iran without compensation.

The company was taken private again in the late 1980s, when the British government sold its controlling shares of stock—at which point the Kuwaiti government tried to buy up enough stock to take control, an attempt the British blocked. The corporation was soon restructured, and downsized its office staff while relocating its corporate headquarters. In 1998 BP merged with Amoco; while most Amoco filling stations have been rebranded to BP, many of them continue to sell Amoco-brand gasoline.

BP has major upstream oil exploration facilities in Alaska, the Gulf of Mexico, Colombia, and the North Sea, with production activities in 22 countries. BP is present in the exploration and production of crude oil and natural gas, refining, marketing, and the petrochemical industry. Currently BP is engaged in oil exploration in parts of the former Soviet Union, in the hopes of increasing its stores, and is recovering its image after a number of minor environmental disasters.

Royal Dutch Shell

An international partnership formed to compete with the American company Standard Oil, the Royal Dutch Shell Group was created in 1907. The Shell Transport and Trading Company was a British trading company founded in 1897 by brothers Sir Marcus and Sam Samuel, who had been instrumental in the industrialization of Japan. Shell's ships were among the first to be approved by the Suez Canal company, and so were used for transoceanic trade to and from Southeast Asia—transporting opium (then legal) in addition to oil. The company was named for their father's business, which had sold painted seashells to collectors in London.

The Royal Dutch Petroleum Company was an oil concern founded in 1890 by writ of royal charter issued by William III of the Netherlands and operated by Jean-Baptiste Kessler. The merger combined the oil production of Royal Dutch (which controlled 60 percent of the new company) with the ships and transport capabilities of Shell. It's one of the world's oldest joint ventures.

In the middle of the 20th century Shell was one of the Seven Sisters—seven oil companies that dominated oil production until the formation of OPEC and the increased influence of the Arab nations. The four Seven Sisters that haven't disappeared in mergers and buyouts are all among the six supermajor companies now (the other three are Chevron, ExxonMobil, and BP).

By the late 1970s leading firms in the global petroleum industry were facing strong competitive challenges, including the increasing power of individual nations, and the emergence of new rivals. Royal Dutch/Shell's performance began to deteriorate in the 1990s, and they also faced significant public relation problems. First, the proposed disposal of the Brent Spar oil platform in the North Atlantic aroused huge outcry from environmental groups, and forced Shell to change its plans. Then in late 1995 the Nigerian government executed a prominent activist author, Ken Saro-Wiwa, who had protested Shell's environmental record; critics felt that Shell did not handle the resulting fallout well.

While all energy companies face criticism on environmental grounds, Shell has been dealt a disproportionate amount of criticism on human rights issues because of its business operations in Africa, where Shell's business benefits the Nigerian government at the expense of tribal people and millions of people living in poverty. This public relations difficulty may play a role in Shell's public encouragement of whistle blowing to report ethical and legal violations by Shell employees and representatives—an opportunity that is available via an official website the company maintains, where anonymity is an option. Reports received on the website are examined by a case manager, who makes a recommendation as to what further investigation or actions should be taken.

In 1998 Shell undertook an ambitious restructuring program, moving from a geographically-based organizational structure to a more business-sector orientation in an attempt to shorten decision making, and improve flexibility and efficiency. Another restructuring came in 2004, in the wake of the discovery that Shell had been overreporting the levels of its oil reserves. Operations moved to The Hague in the Netherlands and were placed under the control of a new parent company, Royal Dutch Shell Plc.

ExxonMobil

The largest energy company in the world, ExxonMobil vies with Wal-Mart for the spot of largest corporation in the world by revenue. The company was founded in 1999 with the merger of Exxon and Mobil—both of which were descended from the 1911 breakup of Standard Oil.

Standard Oil was forced to split into 34 smaller companies, much like the more recent breakup of AT&T into the Baby Bells. Among the new companies were Standard Oil of New Jersey (which, though based in New Jersey, also operated in five other states and soon added five more) and Standard Oil Company of New York, or "Socony."

Standard of New Jersey used the Esso—"SO" for Standard Oil— brand for most of its filling stations. But in time other Standard companies objected, so the company rebranded itself as the Exxon Corporation in 1972. The Esso brand name remains in use in various parts of the world, both as a brand of gasoline, and as chains of filling stations. The 1972 renaming followed the restructuring through the 1960s, when Standard of New Jersey acquired the Humble Oil and Refining Company (which had introduced the "Put a Tiger in Your Tank" advertising campaign that would be used by Exxon). The various stations the corporation owned were rebranded as Exxon stations, with a uniform logo and presence. The "xx" in the name is there because the governor of Nebraska was named James Exon, and in the days of Big Oil and the energy crisis, it seemed a bad idea to name a gas station after a governor, even coincidentally.

In 1989 the *Exxon Valdez* oil tanker struck a reef in Alaska's Prince William Sound, resulting in the most extensive and expensive oil spill in history ,and prompting the passing of the Oil Pollution Act in 1990. Exxon was assessed $5 billion in punitive damages—an amount chosen because it was equal to the company's annual profits. Exxon appealed the case for 14 years before reaching the Supreme Court (at which point the Ninth Circuit Court of Appeals had reduced the punitive damages by half). The Supreme Court struck down the $2.5 billion punitive damages and sent the case back to a lower court, mandating that the punitive damages would be limited to the compensatory damages (about $500 million). Exxon's argument in its appeals was that the spill was an accident that it had already spent $3 billion to remedy.

Socony, meanwhile, merged with the Vacuum Oil Company, which had been founded before Standard, but in which Rockefeller purchased a controlling interest in 1879. In 1930 Vacuum acquired the Wadham Oil Company chain of filling stations in Wisconsin, before being acquired in turn by Socony. The new company was renamed Socony-Vacuum. The first post-1911 mutual involvement of the companies that would become ExxonMobil occurred shortly after the Vacuum acquisition, when Socony-Vacuum and Standard of New Jersey merged their Asian interests into a 50-50 joint venture called Stanvac (Standard-Vacuum). Stanvac operated in 50 countries, but was dissolved in 1962.

Socony-Vacuum went through a few names through the 20th century before becoming the Mobil Corporation in 1976. Mobil's marketing angle was the premium quality of its gasoline, which they advertised as the best gasoline for new cars, and old cars that wanted to run like them—the "Mobil Power Compound" blended into the gasoline was said to prevent the carburetor from gumming up and spark plugs from misfiring. More additives were added in the 1960s and 1970s, with ads describing Mobil as a "detergent" for the engine, one that would scrub away the dirt and residue left by other brands of gasoline. Cleanliness proved a useful marketing tool as consumers began to shift to using premium and unleaded gasoline.

In 1998 Exxon and Mobil agreed to the largest merger in American history, forming the world's largest private oil company. Of the companies formed in the wake of Standard Oil's breakup, ExxonMobil is the only reunion. It announced that due to the complications of rising crude oil costs, it will abandon the retail gasoline business and divest itself of its many filling stations—something it already did in California, where the Valero Energy Corporation owns the Exxon-branded stations. The 2,200 Exxon and Mobil branded stations will continue to exist under new ownership, with ExxonMobil licensing the use of the names.

Nestlé

Nestlé was founded by Henri Nestlé in 1867 in Vevey, Switzerland, where it is headquartered today. Henri Nestlé was a pharmacist searching for an alternative to breast milk for infants who were premature, or whose mothers could not breastfeed. The company began as a producer of infant formula/cereal. Since then Nestlé has become the largest food company in the world.

The current Nestlé company was created when Henri's company merged in 1905 with the Anglo-Swiss Milk Company (established 1866), soon opening factories across Europe and the United

States. The government contracts for canned and powdered milk for troops during World War I more than doubled Nestlé's production. Armistice ended the increased demand, but Nestlé was prepared, branching out into chocolate. Candy was fast becoming a major industry, thanks to the expansion of so many food companies and the development of better and cheaper transportation for shipping products.

Sales dipped during World War II, but the military became a steady customer for Nestlé's next major product: Nescafe, an instant coffee. Nestlé has since expanded beyond its primary milk-coffee-chocolate focus to encompass a far broader food product range, with products using either coffee or cocoa accounting for approximately 40 percent of profits. Nestlé is one of the world's oldest multinational enterprises, having first expanded beyond its national borders to produce in the UK and Germany by 1874, which was a necessity given the small market size of the Swiss market.

After World War II Nestlé began steadily acquiring other companies and brands. It merged with Swiss food company Maggi, a maker of soup and soup mixes, instant noodles, and bouillon cubes, following the war. British grocery company Crosse and Blackwell followed in 1950; Swedish frozen food producer Findus in 1963; American canned food manufacturer Libby's in 1971; frozen food giant Stouffer's in 1973; diversified American food producer Carnation in 1984; British candy company Rowntree Mackintosh (responsible for Kit Kats, the Willy Wonka brand, and Rolo) in 1988; American ice cream company Dreyer's in 2006, making Nestlé the world's leading ice cream producer; and Ovaltine and Gerber baby foods in 2007.

Nestlé also became the world leader in mineral water, by acquiring Vittel, Perrier, and San Pellgrino; it entered the cosmetics and pharmaceutical industries in the 1970s by purchasing a large stake of L'Oreal and acquiring Alcon Laboratories (and later the medical nutrition division of Novartis Pharmaceutical).

Along with Cadbury-Schweppes, Hershey, and Mars, Nestlé is considered part of "Big Chocolate"—the world's leading chocolate producers, processing an eighth of the world's cacao production and the bulk of the more affordable chocolate candies. Once a luxury product, the big chocolate companies have been instrumental in turning the commodity into a daily treat for people around the world.

Johnson & Johnson

Pharmaceutical giant Johnson & Johnson was founded in 1887 to provide doctors with prepackaged, sterile surgical dressings and wound care products. In 1867 cofounder Robert Wood Johnson had attended a speech given by British surgeon and antisepsis pioneer Joseph Lister, and quickly became a proponent of Lister's ideas on germs and their control. The process of sterilizing surgical instruments was already saving lives, though not everyone was convinced that it wasn't mere quackery.

Working with his brothers James Wood Johnson and Edward Mead Johnson, Robert set up shop in New Brunswick, New Jersey and began the painstaking process of research and development. The company produced its first goods in 1886 and incorporated in 1887. The company remained family-owned until it went public in 1944, and Robert Wood Johnson II served as chairman of the board until 1963.

In 1943, just before its public offering, board chairman (and son of the founder) Robert Wood Johnson created the company credo, a simple, one-page statement of corporate responsibility. Among the principles Wood laid out were a commitment to "the doctors, nurses and patients, to mothers and fathers and all others who use our products and services"; a desire to create a respectful, comfortable working environment for employees; a sense of responsibility to the wider community shown by "support(ing) good works and charity and bear(ing) our fair share of taxes"; and finally, an attention to shareholders through the running of a good, ethical business that would bring them dividends. "Research must be carried on, innovative programs developed, and mistakes paid for," the credo said.

Today, Johnson & Johnson is one of the world's largest pharmaceutical conglomerates, made up of more than 250 companies in 57 countries around the globe. Among the thousands of products made by the Johnson & Johnson family of companies are many of the items standard to virtually every American medicine cabinet: Band-Aids, Tylenol, Listerine, Rogaine, Sudafed, St. Joseph's baby aspirin, Pepcid, Nicoderm and Nicorette, and dozens of others. Sales increases have been posted every year since 1932.

Johnson & Johnson faced its greatest crisis in the fall of 1982, when seven people in the Chicago area were killed after taking Extra Strength Tylenol laced with potassium cyanide. When the link between the deaths and the Tylenol was established, the company immediately stopped production and advertising, pulled 31 million bottles off the shelves, and issued a $100,000 reward for the arrest and conviction of the perpetrator. An investigation quickly determined that the poison had not been injected during the production process, but had occurred when someone pulled the bottles off the shelves, added the cyanide, glued the packaging back together, and replaced them in stores. The "Tylenol Killer" was never found. Within a year, Johnson & Johnson had developed a new, tamper-proof gel cap pill, and repackaged the product in a triple-sealed, tamper-resistant package. It quickly regained its market share, and the security designs it instituted have since become the industry standard.

IBM

Founded by Thomas J. Watson, Sr., International Business Machines (IBM) grew into one of the world's largest companies. IBM manufactures and sells computer services, hardware, and software, as well as providing financial services.

Born in a tiny farming town in New York, Watson's family urged him to rise above his roots through education. He joined John Henry Patterson's National Cash Register Company (NCR), headquartered in Dayton, Ohio, then one of the world's most innovative companies.

An early IBM PC 5150 with floppy drives, running MS-DOS 5.0.

At NCR, Watson became the company's best salesman, but battles with the firm's volatile founder led to his dismissal in 1913. Watson took an executive position at Computing-Tabulating-Recording (CTR). CTR had been formed by the merger of four smaller companies in 1911: the Bundy Manufacturing Company (est. 1889), the Computing Scale Corporation (est. 1891), the Tabulating Machine Company (est. 1896), and the International Time Recording Company (est. 1900).

These four companies specialized in various means of measurement, such as precision scales and timepieces, and tabulating machines using punch cards. Willard Bundy, whose brother Harlow founded Bundy Manufacturing to mass-produce his invention, had built the first time clock, a mechanical device that kept track of the hours an employee worked. This kind of precision had been made very profitable by the Industrial Revolution—for a company putting out thousands of units, small differences per unit added up to a great deal of money. Timekeeping was also necessary for the operation of trains and other forms of transportation. Charles Flint organized the merger. He had previously merged various American rubber producers into U.S. Rubber, combined chewing gum companies into American Chicle, grouped wool producers into American Woolen, and negotiated the first overseas sale of a Wright Brothers aircraft. They called him the Father of Trusts, and he saw the common threads among these disparate, noncompeting machine companies and borrowed money from the Guaranty Trust Company to fund the new company. Watson approached Flint directly, even though he was then appealing a guilty conviction relating to antitrust violations while at NCR.

Because of the criminal conviction and possibility of losing him to the prison sentence (his appeal was eventually successful), Flint took Watson on only as general manager. In that job, Watson adopted the same emphatic workplace motto used at NCR: "THINK." Ten years later, in 1924, he took over as CEO. Watson's genius at CTR was pushing the development of tabulating machines, at the time the least profitable aspect of the business. Within a decade, the product would be Watson's top seller, securing his place in business history. His experience at NCR also helped him organize the large number of salesmen, a task overlooked in the wake of the merger.

CTR changed its name to IBM in 1924. Watson was a master at building a sales force and shaping a corporate culture that glorified the sales that would build IBM into one of the world's largest companies. He talked about his "competitive proposition," pitting salesmen against each other in competition for clients and commissions. Salesmen maintained relationships with their clients, not only for repeat sales, but also because the company rented out much of its equipment rather than selling it outright, and by doing so was able to attract many more clients.

The IBM name came to be associated with service, and with solid relationships between provider and purchaser. In the 1930s IBM supplied electric accounting machines to the federal government for use with the census and social security system. Profits rose from $1 million in 1921 to $9.4 million in 1940, despite the Great Depression. IBM's computing machines cut costs dramatically, which forced businesses into purchasing them to remain competitive. The 80-column punch card the company adopted in 1928 became a standard not just for its own machines, but across the industry, first for tabulating machines and later for computers.

During World War II, IBM was among the many manufacturers involved in the war effort, both directly and indirectly. Its machines were used by the increasingly modern military to help manage the extraordinarily large war, and by the Manhattan Project that developed the atomic bombs eventually used in Hiroshima and Nagasaki to end the Pacific war. The Harvard Mark I, completed in 1944, was the first large-scale digital computer built in the United States, using 60 sets of 24 switches and a 24-channel punched paper tape. IBM built it for the navy.

After the war IBM was awarded a hefty air force contract to develop computers for its defense systems, and as part of the contract, was given access to critical computer research at MIT that advanced the state of the nascent computer industry considerably. Thomas Watson, Jr. took control of IBM in 1956. After a decade of training at his father's side, Watson, Jr. pushed the company into computers. The gamble pitted father versus son, since Watson, Sr. did not see the vast potential computers held. The elder Watson is famously quoted as proclaiming in 1943 that "there is a market for maybe five computers." The computers he was envisioning, of course, were the ones that took up entire rooms and used massive amounts of resources to perform tasks no more complicated than what a wristwatch can do these days—he simply lacked the vision, as most did, to foresee developments like the microchip.

The younger Watson reinvented IBM in the 1950s and 1960s. Around the world, computers were known as "IBM machines," and people in the industry talked about "IBM and the Seven Dwarfs" because of IBM's two-thirds market share in a market with eight major producers (one of which was NCR, the elder Watson's former employer). The field narrowed even further in the 1970s, and the catchphrase became "IBM and the BUNCH": Burroughs, UNI-VAC, NCR, Control Data Corporation, and Honeywell. In 1970 IBM reached $7.5 billion in revenues and the company was worth more than $36 billion. A heart attack forced Watson to retire in 1971.

A key decision in the development of the computer industry was the 1969 unbundling of software and services. We take this for granted now, but in the early days of the industry, software was provided free with computers—which were more specialized, with fewer options and certainly no Minesweeper—and local IBM offices provided installation and computer training. IBM began selling its software as products, aside from the very basics necessary to run the computer. This had the side-effect of encouraging the "homebrew" software subindustry of hobbyists working on their own code—an arena from which many of the important figures in the computer industry of the 1970s, 1980s, and beyond would come.

Basic operating programs were written in assembly language. IBM helped to develop a number of higher-level programming languages that were instrumental in the course of the software industry. Fortran, SQL, and PL/S originated as IBM projects specifically; COBOL was a joint venture.

In the mid-1980s, with the arrival of the personal computer, IBM was slow to realize the wholesale changes the new systems would have on the business. IBM's decline was tied to its weakening hold on the computer industry, especially in big mainframe computers, and it could not make up for the loss in the highly-competitive personal computer and laptop marketplace. IBM's competitors were beating the company to the market with new products, and cutting prices in an effort to undersell the giant. IBM abandoned its previous tendency toward vertical integration, in favor of farming out aspects of its products to other companies: the development of its operating systems was sourced to Microsoft (first MS-DOS, and later Windows was launched from DOS, and then Windows 95 took over), while microprocessors were the purview of Intel.

After a decade of losing money, IBM hired Louis Gerstner as chairman and CEO, the first outsider to hold the position. Within two years Gerstner's strategic plans, combined with cost-cutting measures, transformed IBM into a competitor. In 1994 IBM posted a profit of over $3 billion, the first time in the decade that IBM was in the black. By 1997 the company would post revenues exceeding $78 billion, and stock price quadrupled.

Samuel Palmisano replaced Gerstner as chairman and CEO on January 1, 2003, capping a 30-year career with "Big Blue." IBM is now the world's largest information technology company, and has continued as one of the most recognizable brand names. In 2002 it implemented a multibillion dollar program to develop supercomputer resources that are available for business use on a metered basis—hearkening back to the early days of the computer industry when programmers and other researchers would rent computer time to test out their work. Research in other areas continues at an impressive rate: IBM received over 30,000 patents between 1993 and 2005, far more than any other company (nearly half as many as General Electric has been awarded in its entire lifespan). The corporation makes billions of dollars from intellectual property, and recent advertising campaigns have reemphasized this aspect of the company as a service and consultation provider for business solutions.

General Electric

General Electric (GE) is a diverse service and technology company, the only company listed on the Dow Jones Industrial Index of 1896 that is still listed today. GE's success and longevity have involved power generation, financial services, aircraft, plastics, television, and appliances, and it employed over 300,000 people in 100 different companies in 2008.

The GE Company traces its origins to Thomas Edison's 1878 Edison Electric Light Company, founded with a number of financial backers, including J.P. Morgan (who, after the War of the Currents, later backed Nikola Tesla's attempt at broadcast power). The first incandescent light bulb was demonstrated a year after the company's founding, and Edison declared his intention "to make electricity so cheap only the rich will burn candles." The Edison Electric Illuminating Company was founded in 1880, and power was distributed to Manhattan customers two years later.

Edison consolidated his various companies into the Edison General Electric Company, and in 1892, Morgan arranged a merger with the competing Thomson-Houston Electric Company, to form the General Electric Company, based in Schenectady, New York. Its early business came from electricity distribution, home electric lighting, and the provision of electric street lights to various cities—a booming industry in the increasingly urban end of the century.

GE's century of operation has brought two Nobel Prizes and over 67,000 patents. The company developed the tungsten filament used in electric lighting, the man-made diamond, the microwave oven, the first radio and television broadcasts, X-ray machines, and improved MRIs. The company founded the Radio Corporation of America (RCA) as a publicly held company in 1919, keeping a controlling interest. RCA used GE's alternator radio transmitters and other components from Westinghouse, while taking over the assets of American Marconi. RCA was a significant player in the new broadcast radio industry, founding the National Broadcasting Corporation (NBC) as a network of radio stations. In the 1930s it sold the first electric record player (yet another descendant of an Edison invention) and the first 33 1/3 records, which would become and remain the standard format for full-length vinyl records. It later became involved in television—developing the first test pattern and the industry standard for color television sets—along with radar and vacuum tubes, and had its only major misstep with its advocacy of the 8-track audio cassette over the compact cassette that outlived it. RCA was eventually reabsorbed by GE in 1986, at which point most of RCA's holdings were broken up. General Electric retains ownership of NBC (the television network; the radio network was sold to Westwood One), and has taken tenancy at RCA's old offices at 30 Rockefeller Plaza.

In the 1930s GE helped spread electric technology to the home by building power generation systems and home appliances that became standard after World War II. During the war GE pioneered the television station, the American jet engine, and jumpstarted the field of atmospheric science with forays into rainmaking, or cloud seeding. In the 1950s GE popularized its innovations in plastics and home appliances. In the 1960s GE played an integral role from products to service in placing the first human on the moon. During the 1970s GE power sources became the norm for most commercial aircraft. In the following decade GE developed fiber optics, and began to expand operations into new markets such as the launch of CNBC, the world's first cable news network.

GE continues to diversify today with offerings in insurance, finance, and entertainment to supplement its traditional business of power generation and electrical and plastics products. GE experiments in the world of super magnets and space age materials. In 2008 over half of GE's revenue came from its financial services, which offered everything from equipment leasing and vehicle fleet management to lines of credit, working with clients in 35 countries. The consumer unit is one of the world's largest issuers of store credit cards, including those of Amazon, J.C. Penney, PayPal, eBay, Chevron, and Texaco. GE's embrace of financial services hurt its operations during the credit crisis of 2007–09. In 2009, it had to shore up its financial services unit with cash from the parent company.

GE Healthcare, based in the United Kingdom, provides a variety of medical technologies, including ultrasound, electrocardiogram, incubators, and other technologies for clinicians. Its Global Diagnostic Imaging focuses on CT scans, MRIs, X-rays, and other imaging techniques, while Integrated IT Solutions provides both medical and financial software. Life Sciences deals with drug discovery and biopharmaceuticals. Medical Diagnostics manufactures imaging agents for medical scanning procedures.

GE Infrastructure was formed in 2005 after Jeff Immelt succeeded Jack Welch as CEO. Under the Infrastructure umbrella are such General Electric divisions as GE Aviation, GE Energy, GE Energy Financial Services, GE Oil and Gas, and GE Transportation.

The newest division, GE Enterprise Solutions, was founded in the summer of 2007 and subsumed much of what used to fall under GE Industrial—Plastics, Security, Sensing and Inspection Technologies. GE Industrial now includes Appliances, Electrical Distribution, and Lighting—the three things GE first brought to life.

Microsoft

The largest producer of consumer software in the world, Microsoft products include the most successful operating system (the various incarnations of Windows), the most successful Internet browser (Internet Explorer), and the most successful productivity suite (Office), each considered the industry standard. Microsoft ultimately has been credited with turning computers away from a mere toy of hobbyists and toward mass, popular acceptance, but the company has also been accused of bullying the industry and operating as a monopoly.

Microsoft was formed in 1975 by Bill Gates and Paul Allen, two childhood friends and, later, both Harvard College dropouts. Theirs is one of the great success stories of the early personal computer industry, a time when the barriers to entry were low, and computer expertise was a rare commodity—many colleges didn't yet have computer science programs, or only offered them in the engineering department.

Upon reading about the Altair 8080, the first computer designed for home use, available as an assembly kit, the two wrote a BASIC programming language program for the machine and began selling it to computer companies such as Radio Shack and Texas Instruments. They had initially demonstrated it to Micro Instrumentation and Telemetry Systems (MITS), offering the demonstration before they had even written the interpreter. They did this without even owning an Altair system, meaning their code had to be close to perfect.

It was, and MITS became the distributor of Altair BASIC. Gates and Allen moved to Albuquerque—where MITS was located—for a few years, registering Microsoft as their company name and trademark. The first international office—ASCII Microsoft, now Microsoft Japan—was opened in 1978. They relocated to Washington state months later, establishing company headquarters in Bellevue, near Seattle. Future CEO Steve Ballmer, another Harvard alumnus, joined the company in 1980, and the company was incorporated in 1981.

At a time when computer companies primarily focused on hardware and proprietary software, Microsoft only sold software that was compatible with a wide variety of hardware. Microsoft also licensed its software to hardware manufacturers at low rates, hoping to grow via a high quantity of business rather than high profit margins. It was a new business model, for a new industry that hadn't stopped changing long enough for anyone to know what normalcy would be.

These days Microsoft is known principally for operating systems, even among computer novices who aren't entirely sure what an operating system is. Its first OS was Xenix, a UNIX variant released in 1980 after being acquired from AT&T. Though it wasn't developed by Gates and his team, Xenix is notable because it was the platform on which the first version of Microsoft Word—one of the company's "killer apps"—operated. It was the first program to be distributed as a free diskette insert in a magazine, which would become a common way of distributing demos, especially in the days before high-speed Internet downloads.

Called Multi-Tool Word at the time, the word processor was the first example of Microsoft's core, industry-changing, design concept: WYSIWYG. What You See Is What You Get. In an era of green-on-black console displays and thermal printers that used endless spools of paper like a paper towel dispenser, the idea of taking what you see on the screen and reproducing it exactly on paper was not only ambitious, it was almost ridiculous. The WYSIWYG principle paved the way for desktop publishing.

Its first successful operating system was the result of IBM awarding Microsoft the contract to produce the operating system for the first line of IBM Personal Computers (PCs). Microsoft purchased a

CP/M clone from Seattle Computer Products, tailoring it to IBM's needs, and the resulting PC-DOS (Disk Operating System) became the standard for PCs. As the PC took off and the market filled up with PC clones (compatible computers using IBM's BIOS), Microsoft aggressively marketed its own MS-DOS, which was compatible with a wide variety of hardware. PC compatibles were cheap, by computer standards—cheaper than the brand name IBM PCs, and much cheaper than Apple's flagship Macintosh computer (which cost as much as a cheap car when it was introduced, was resistant to tinkering by hobbyists, and shipped with numerous problems). As a result, they caught on quickly in the new home computer market, and MS-DOS became the default operating system for most of the American home computing world. The Microsoft Mouse—a pointer device that would soon become commonplace—was introduced shortly thereafter, the company's first serious foray into peripherals.

In conjunction with IBM's development of the PS/2 system—intended as the next generation of personal computers, leapfrogging ahead of Apple's offerings—Microsoft developed the OS/2 operating system. Neither was a success, and they were gone from the market by the mid-1990s. Part of the reason for OS/2's failure, though, was Microsoft's 1991 announcement that they would focus their OS efforts exclusively on Windows. The first version of Microsoft Windows—a graphical user interface that extended MS-DOS—was released at the end of 1985. GUIs (Graphical User Interfaces) had first been developed in the late 1970s at Xerox's research lab, but the Macintosh popularized them, albeit in the form of a prohibitively expensive computer. Still, it was clear that in the near future, GUIs would be necessary to compete with Apple. Windows grew slowly at first, and was launched from the DOS command line; most PC users therefore remained command line users, until 1990, when Windows 3.0 came out (followed quickly by the 3.10 and 3.11 upgrades). The 3.x versions of Windows resembled Macintosh's interface much more than previous versions had, and Apple filed an unsuccessful infringement of copyright lawsuit.

Microsoft grew enormously in the 1990s. One of the company highlights in this decade was the release of the productivity suite Office, which combined spreadsheet, word-processing, and (among others) presentation software. Rather than simply bundling software together, Office attempted to integrate the component programs by having them look and operate in similar fashions, and by making data easy to move from one program to another.

Microsoft's first real stumble was in underestimating how quickly the Internet would become popular. Windows 95 shipped without a web browser, though browsers had by then been introduced. Because Windows 95 included a link to the company's fledgling Internet service Microsoft Network, America Online accused Microsoft of unethically using its position as producer of the leading operating system in an attempt to dominate the Internet market. When Microsoft bundled its Internet Explorer web browser with its next operating system update (Windows 98), the U.S. Justice Department (prompted by web browser rival Netscape) investigated Microsoft, and declared the company a monopoly. The eventual settlement was mostly in Microsoft's favor, however—few existing practices were required to be changed.

Microsoft has also bought entire companies to acquire a particular program; when Microsoft wanted to enter the web-page design software market in 1995, they bought Vermeer Technologies to take over their FrontPage program. These acquisitions have sometimes proven ruthless; when talking to America Online about a possible merger, Bill Gates told AOL executives, "I can buy 20 percent of you or I can buy all of you, or I can go into this business myself and bury you."

Subsequent Microsoft developments have included its unexpectedly successful entrance into the video game console market with the XBox, which has built its brand identity on games intended for older teenagers and adults. Though the manufacture of the console represented $1 billion loss in the early days, the system proved tenacious, and the next-generation XBox 360 was as widely anticipated as its competitor, the Sony Playstation 3.

Starbucks

When Jerry Baldwin, Zev Siegel, and Gordon Bowker were thinking about opening a coffee supply shop near Seattle's famed Pike Place market in 1971, there was the inevitable question of what to name it. Baldwin was an English teacher, Siegel a history teacher, and Bowker a writer, so it was perhaps inevitable that they turned to literature for inspiration. Bowker liked the name "Pequod," the ship in Herman Melville's novel *Moby Dick*. "No one's going to drink a cup of Pequod!" one partner protested. After more debate, they stuck with the *Moby Dick* theme, but chose a slightly more melodious name: Starbucks, after the *Pequod*'s first mate.

The original Starbucks did not sell coffee drinks: it sold equipment and coffee beans. The partners felt strongly that coffee was a personal thing to be enjoyed in the home. Eyeing expansion in 1982, they were joined by entrepreneur Howard Schultz, who not long after went on vacation to Milan, and came home convinced that there was a strong American market for an Italian-style coffeehouse. The partners were unmoved by his arguments, so in 1985 he opened the Il Giornale coffee

Lingering customers at a Starbucks location in Istanbul, Turkey.

bar chain on his own. It was so successful that in 1987, Starbucks sold itself to Il Giornale, which promptly rebranded itself as the Starbucks Coffee Company and began to expand across the country.

They built their brand around espresso, specialty coffee drinks, teas, pastries and light meals, roasted coffee beans, and merchandise. Over recent years, Starbucks has continued to expand through the acquisition of other companies, including Tazo Tea, Seattle's Best Coffee, Torrefazione Italia, Ethos Water, and the Hear Music label that is broadcast on XM Satellite Radio and in Starbucks stores.

Starbucks says it wants to be the "premium purveyor of the finest coffee in the world while maintaining our uncompromising principles as we grow." Its goal is to function as a small company, even as its international workforce passes the 170,000-employee mark. All Starbucks employees—"partners" in company parlance—have access to benefits and stock options. Through charity programs, workers have contributed over 380,000 volunteer hours for community projects.

Starbucks seeks to be a "third place" for customers, a bridge between home and work. The design of its full-service stores are meant to be warm and welcoming. Wireless Internet access is available in some markets. Music and lighting are also meant to encourage customers to linger and spend.

The Starbucks experience is not cheap: their most popular coffee drinks are $4 and above, and their snacks and sandwiches run $5 or more. Some personal finance experts call the amount of money spent at Starbucks the "latte factor," the amount of discretionary income spent on feeding a trendy coffee addiction, which, over the course of a year, can take $1,200 or more out of a person's budget. They urge the cash-strapped to forgo their daily visit to their local barista as the quickest, easiest way to attack their debt woes.

In 2008 Starbucks reached the point so few companies do: it decided it had become big enough. With nearly 17,000 locations around the world—more than half as many as McDonalds—Starbucks decided to contract. The period during which it became common to see a Starbucks across the street from another Starbucks had ended; underperforming stores were closed, planned expansions were cancelled, and the corporation focused its energies on existing locations.

Wal-Mart

Beginning with the first Wal-Mart discount department store in Rogers, Arkansas in 1962, Sam Walton built a chain of stores that ranked as the largest retailer in the United States when he died in 1992. Almost two decades since Walton's death, Wal-Mart continues to be the nation's biggest retailer and largest private employer in the world, with well over one million employees. The chain has faced criticism over its employment policies and business practices, but remains one of the few consistently profitable entities in the volatile retail sector.

Sam Walton was born in Kingfisher, Oklahoma on March 29, 1918. He learned frugality from his parents; the lessons were reinforced as he accompanied his father, a mortgage and insurance agent, to foreclose on farms across Missouri, where the family relocated during the Depression.

In 1943 he married Helen Robson, the daughter of a wealthy Oklahoma rancher, lawyer, and businessman. With his wife's family putting up a major stake, Walton bought a retail franchise from the Ben Franklin variety store chain in 1945 and opened his first store in Newport, Arkansas. He had an economics degree and a couple years experience at J.C. Penney—it must have seemed a big risk. He eventually held more than a dozen Ben Franklin franchises in the south-central United States, almost all of which were located in towns of fewer than 10,000 people.

Over the next decade Walton developed the competitive strategies that he would later implement in the Wal-Mart chain. Walton made a point of visiting other discount stores to take note of stock, prices, and displays. He bought directly from manufacturers and wholesalers instead of distributors, against the wishes of Ben Franklin executives. At the heart of Walton's retail philosophy was the strategy of selling goods at a high volume, with a small profit on each sale.

In June 1962 Walton opened the first store to bear the Wal-Mart name. By 1969 he had 18 Wal-Mart stores in Oklahoma, Missouri, and Arkansas. Walton located the stores in small towns with little retail competition, or in still-rural areas outside of major cities. The chain's sales volume and mostly rural- and small-town locations forced Walton to open his own warehouse and distribution system in 1969. Although he resisted making the investment, the company's control of its distribution eventually gave it an edge over its competitors, such as K-Mart, which were slower and had less flexibility in getting goods on the store shelves. In 1970 Wal-Mart became a publicly traded corporation, which allowed it to expand rapidly. By 1973 it had 55 stores in five south-central states, and in 1979 it passed the $1 billion mark in sales. Expanding even through economic downturns, Wal-Mart became the nation's largest retailer in 1991, and expanded its operations into Mexico and Europe.

After Sam Walton's death in 1992, his four children continued to be active in Wal-Mart's management. With 3,244 discount, supercenter, Sam's Club warehouse, and small neighborhood market stores in the United States, and 4,414 stores in Europe, Central and South America, Canada, and China, Wal-Mart's sales are in the hundreds of billions of dollars. The addition of grocery stores to many of its locations—branded as Supercenters and Neighborhood Markets—has given it a 20 percent share of the retail grocery business. The Supercenters have also been co-opted by Wal-Mart's attempt to attract a higher-income customer base. Some of its newer Supercenters are more attractively laid out, with sushi and coffee bars, and free Wi-Fi access. The retail sections stock premium brands, especially of consumables like beer and wine, and high-ticket items like home electronics.

In the 21st century Wal-Mart's international operations have become more significant, accounting for one-fifth to one-quarter of sales. The company is the largest private employer in Mexico (as well as the United States) and has a substantial presence of nearly 300 stores in Canada. In the United Kingdom, Wal-Mart owns ASDA, a grocery chain with a substantial amount of nonfood products for sale;

ASDA accounts for the largest share of Wal-Mart's international sales. It has also recently opened stores in India and taken control of chains in Brazil. It has majority ownership of subsidiaries in Japan, Mexico, Guatemala, El Salvador, Honduras, Nicaragua, and Costa Rica. Wal-Mart has come under criticism for its labor practices, such as low pay and skimpy health insurance policies. Consumer boycotts of Wal-Mart have resulted.

eBay

The first item ever sold on eBay was a broken laser pointer. Programmer Pierre Omidyar had purchased it on a whim, and used it for a couple of weeks to torture his cat with the little red light. Then it stopped working, and he set it aside. A few months later, on another whim, he posted it as an item for sale on the new "AuctionWeb" online auction he had programmed and placed on his personal website. It sold for $14.83. Concerned, Omidyar emailed the buyer to make sure he understood this was a broken laser pointer. The buyer wrote back and assured him he did understand, and it was okay: he collected broken laser pointers.

Four years later, Pierre Omidyar was worth $4 billion.

The French-Iranian programmer didn't start out to be a online auction mogul, but after conceiving and designing the AuctionWeb program in 1995 and making those few early sales, he began to think of it as "the perfect marketplace." An early adopter of the Internet and its ability to bring together people of similar interests in a community that existed only through computer networks, he saw the potential of eBay to level the consumer playing field, and secured $5 million in venture capital from Benchmark Capital. eBay (named for Omidyar's consulting firm Echo Bay—the echobay domain name was already taken by a gold miner) brought together buyers and sellers who otherwise would have no way to connect.

The auction format was the purest form of capitalism: people would end up paying what the market would bear, because the buyers and sellers were setting the prices. eBay would make its profit by charging modest listing fees, which ensured a profit for eBay even if the item didn't sell, as well as a percentage of the final sale price. It turned out to be a winning philosophy. In its first year eBay had 41,000 registered users, and traded $7.2 million in merchandise. A year later it had 340,000 users, and traded $95 million in goods. A decade after its launch it had 222 million users, and traded $52.5 billion in goods. By the early 2000s at least 100,000 people were making a full-time living as eBay sellers, and the bookshelf of titles promising show readers how to become the next eBay millionaire "powerseller" grew by the year.

Despite Omidyar's contention that most people in the world are basically good and the online environment fosters a sense of community and fair play, eBay has not been immune from controversy. The famed jeweler Tiffany & Company released a report in 2006 saying that 70 percent of eBay items listed as originating from Tiffany were fake. Tiffany has further pursued an intellectual property lawsuit against eBay, on the grounds that because eBay profits from those counterfeits, it profits from an infringement of Tiffany's intellectual copyright. The case has not yet been resolved, but it has the potential to set important precedent.

Other studies have shown that 67 percent of "antiquities" and 25 percent of "ancient" coins listed on the site are also fraudulent. Many other collectors' items for which fine differentiation of quality grades is important—vintage photographs, rare books, comic books, and other periodicals—are misrepresented in auctions, often unintentionally by sellers ill-equipped to fairly represent the item's quality. The online nature of the interaction makes it impossible for a buyer to closely inspect the item, and photographs (that are optional) only convey so much (and furthermore cost the seller money even if the auction fails). Deceptive language is used by some sellers, particularly if there are two similar or similarly-named items, and one is significantly more sought-after than the other. There's also a booming trade conducted in bootlegged videos and music—some of them recordings of things that are not commercially available (old TV shows recorded to tape), and others are outright piracies. Such recordings are forbidden by eBay's policies, but can be difficult to identify, and a successful buyer is rarely motivated to report the seller.

Over the years the company has had to develop a conflict-resolution system to deal with disputes between buyers and sellers. There are frequent complaints about eBay's listing fees, and their policy of turning over customer records to law enforcement on request and without a warrant. While the company tries to keep illicit items off their listings—prohibited items include most live animals, counterfeit money, downloadable media, tobacco products, ammunition, and government documents—it takes time to get tasteless, weird, or inappropriate materials off the site. The text field of the feedback form is virtually useless when the feedback is positive—buyers and sellers both conventionally use overblown hyperbole, describing every transaction as "AA++++ BEST EVER." Negative feedback tends to be more specific, reading more like a complaint form, but it is difficult to look at positive feedback and gauge between the acceptable and the extraordinary.

Tales of eBay auctions have become legendary, and many sites chronicle the stranger ones, many of which are covered in the human-interest segments of the nightly news. There's the 10-year-old grilled cheese sandwich with the image of the Virgin Mary, sold for $28,000 in 2004, or the town in California sold in 2002. Like Google, the brand has become a household name among even the most casual Internet users, while earning billions in revenues.

FedEx

Long before the ubiquity of computers, Fred W. Smith saw it coming. As a Yale undergrad in 1965, he wrote an economics paper theorizing that the growing importance of computers in the business world "…was going to change a lot of things, and in particular it was going to change the way things had to distributed and move to support those automated devices." Six years later, after Yale and two tours of duty with the Marine Corps in Vietnam, Smith launched his air courier service, Federal Express.

A FedEx jet readies for take-off for overnight package delivery.

As he had anticipated, computers changed the pace of business life. Smith's father, the founder of the Dixie Greyhound Bus Line, had died when Fred was just four years old, leaving him a substantial inheritance. He used this money to buy controlling interest in an aircraft company. He spent hundreds of hours in the air, flying cargoes of empty boxes from point to point, just to find the best routes. He operated at a loss for the first two years, and once even flew to Vegas to hit the blackjack tables, risking his own money to keep the company going. He won $27,000, which he wired to the offices in Memphis.

The company may not have found instant success, but enough people were interested in his idea of basing the service around "hubs and spokes" to help him secure $80 million in venture capital. In April 1973 he purchased 14 Dassault Falcon 20 cargo planes and began shipping to 25 U.S. cities. The deregulation of the airline industry in 1978 helped the company expand, and by the mid-1980s more and more customers were turning to Federal Express when, as their ads said, it "absolutely, positively has to get there overnight."

Formally renamed FedEx in June 1994, Smith's company is now one of the world's largest shipping companies. It maintains hubs in Memphis, Indianapolis, Fort Worth, Oakland, Newark, Anchorage, Miami, Toronto, and Subic Bay in the Philippines. With the Asian market undergoing rapid expansion, in 2008 FedEx completed work on their new "super hub" at Guangzhou Baiyun International Airport in southern China, phasing out the overloaded Subic Bay facility in the Philippines.

Google

The world's most popular search engine got its start as an academic project by Stanford computer science doctoral student Larry Page and his friend Sergey Brin. With the number of web pages growing exponentially, the ability of search engines to sift through data was increasingly important. Page and Brin wanted to find a better way to do it than the relatively simple keyword programs used by companies like Yahoo and AOL. In 1996 they released BackRub, a program designed to analyze the backlinks that tied Web pages together.

By 1998 it was apparent that BackRub (which would eventually be renamed PageRank) was sleeker and more efficient than any existing search engine. The partners dropped their Ph.D plans and began to look around for venture capital to bring the product out of the lab and into the real world. Naming the company Google—a misspelling of the mathematical term "googol," which is the number 1 followed by 100 zeroes—they began approaching venture capital groups and Silicon Valley heavyweights. They eventually raised $1 million in start-up capital and went to work. In 1999 they purchased the "Googleplex," an office complex in Mountain View, California.

From the beginning Google had a reputation for doing things differently. Rather than use gigantic, costly servers, Google used hundreds, maybe thousands, of low-end, off-the-shelf PCs linked in a network, which kept maintenance costs low. There were no cubicles in the Googleplex, but there were regular roller hockey games in the company parking lot. The company invested in ergonomic chairs and provided free meals for employees, prepared by a chef who used to work for the Grateful Dead.

To monetize the company, Google adopted AdWords, a simple advertising system where small advertisements tied to keyword searches were presented alongside search results. Advertisers paid a small fee every time a user clicked on the link. The "pay-per-click" model was cheap enough for millions of advertisers to adopt, and was implemented with minimal user complaint.

Google went public in August 2004 through a Dutch auction. Most IPOs are structured in such a way as to make it very hard for the average investor to buy into a company during its launch. The Dutch auction meant that almost 20 million Google shares were open to anyone who cared to bid. The IPO brought in $1.67 billion, and made some Google employees overnight millionaires. Two years later the verb "to google" was added to the *Oxford English Dictionary* and the *Merriam-Webster Collegiate Dictionary*.

In its effort to corner their market, Google has acquired or launched an impressive array of Web-based tools: Gmail, Google Calendar, Google Documents, Google News, Blogger, the Google Toolbar, and YouTube. They have launched Google Books, which in partnership with some of the world's largest university libraries, plans to digitize millions of rare and out-of-print books over the coming decade in an attempt to make these titles available to anyone with an Internet connection. The company's tendency to do things differently has become a distinctive brand identity. Hundreds of thousands of email users gladly switched to Gmail when it became available, and it was the most quickly-adopted email service since the initial boom of such services. New features continue to be added to Google's services at such a rate that they often aren't even announced, they merely appear on the page, suddenly available. In addition to the features developed in-house, recent acquisitions have included the software that forms the backbone of Google Reader (a cross-platform, web-based aggregator) and Google Groups, various advertising companies, and image-organizing, spreadsheet, and blogging software.

Like the battle between virus-writers and antivirus software, there is a sort of arms war that continues between Google's attempts to keep its results useful and accurate, and programmers' and copywriters' attempts to optimize their sites to earn a better, but undeserved, ranking. The popularity and power of Google has created a niche industry within the copywriting field: SEO (Search Engine Optimization), which has its own seminars, pep talks, celebrities, books, and get-rich-quick schemes.

The Middle Class

Sometime in the 11th century a new class began to rise to prominence in the walled cities of France. Mostly artisans and craftsmen, they were men and women who did not fit the neat social categories that had long dominated Europe. Neither peasants, nor landlords, nor clergy, these people eventually became known as the bourgeoisie, from the Old French word *burgeis*, meaning citizen of a town. Consigned with the peasant class to the Third Estate, they were habitually overtaxed and underrepresented, and there was certainly no indication that their descendents would ever amount to much.

Instead the bourgeoisie went on to become one of the most driving, fluid forces in history. What constitutes the middle class has shifted continually over the generations, with the much-maligned workers of one generation becoming the economic powerhouses of the next. In the 1850s Charles Dickens created Bob Cratchit, Ebenezer Scrooge's lowly, put-upon clerk, as an object of pity who could barely feed his family. By 1950 a character like Bob Cratchit would have been the perfect "organization man," dedicated to his job and family and earning enough money for a house in the suburbs, with a barbecue out back and a car in the driveway.

Fueled by capitalism, the middle class steadily expanded to encompass an increasingly wide segment of the population, particularly in America, which by the mid-20th century was predominantly a middle-class nation. Some look down on the American middle class as narrow-minded and materialistic, but it has nevertheless become the most a potent social and economic force in American life.

Most historians set the rise of the middle class in America at the decade or two before the Civil War, when the Industrial Revolution was in full swing and the economy had matured to the point where a broad merchant and professional class of clerks, operators, and low-level managers was needed. But the outlines of the middle class had begun in the decades before the Revolutionary War, in the mid-18th century. A small class of professional men from modest social backgrounds, among them John Adams and Benjamin Franklin, adopted the same social values that would be familiar to their great-grandsons, generations down the line. Diaries and letters from the period show an emphasis on deportment and proper social behavior, and between 1750–1900 many bestselling books on the market were etiquette guides, designed to help the rising middle class establish new social norms.

The American and French revolutions can be interpreted as middle-class movements, as the merchant class tried to throw off rule by royal birthright in favor of democratic systems more attuned to the needs of businessmen. The middle class quickly established a symbiotic relationship with both government and commerce, becoming active participants in the processes of government and business.

A stable government was crucial to the development of industry, and through that, the growth of the middle class. Government opened new farmlands in the early republic, built roads and harbors used to move products to market, and passed and enforced laws that helped American industry compete in a world market. Over time national and state governments passed laws regulating workforce hours and safety conditions. As social conditions changed, it was government that passed laws removing African-American men and young children—traditionally America's cheapest forms of labor—from the workforce, opening the field primarily to white males who, as family breadwinners, could command at least slightly higher wages.

Because the American middle class was as much a mindset as a socioeconomic designation, those who aspired to the middle-class lifestyle were voracious consumers by the end of the 19th century. The middle class was identified by its adherence to rules of etiquette, dress, hygiene, civic standing, and religious participation, but most of all by the accumulation of material objects that filled their homes.

The rise of capitalism led to a rise in the middle class.

Possessions became visual clues that defined a person's class. In 1902 the phrase "standard of living" was coined to describe the way a person must live to be part of the group, and though what constitutes an appropriate middle-class standard of living has changed over the years, the desire to reach it has not.

But the biggest change wrought by the growth of the middle class is the shift in attitudes toward time. For centuries workers had largely controlled their own time. People worked hard, but they did not work by the clock. Farmers followed seasonal rhythms. Artisans could close up shop for a mid-afternoon nap if so inclined. Wealthy middle-class merchants or professionals could make a year-long trip to Europe. The concept of a two-week vacation or holiday was alien.

All this changed with the start of the Industrial Revolution. To be profitable, a factory had to be steady and productive, which meant compelling workers to follow set hours and set days. In the earliest years, this often meant 12- to 16-hour days, six days a week, and the history of the 19th century labor movement was largely dedicated to trying to win an eight-hour, five-day week at living wages. Over the years this rigorous attention to the clock filtered throughout society, and time became split between work and leisure. Some social historians see this as a great triumph of capitalism: promoting productivity, while giving people a sense of order and routine in their lives. But in an era of cellphones and e-mail and steadily shrinking vacations, many middle-class Americans now view time as an enemy, as the lines between work and home life become increasingly blurred.

Chapter 5

Disasters in Capitalism

Many have heard the old saw about the ideogram for "crisis" being a combination of the characters for "danger" and "opportunity." Whether it is true or not, the notion is solid. A crisis puts things in perspective and forces a person to bring their best resources to the table in dealing with it. When the repercussions are severe, every error in judgment, every problem in procedure, is clearly outlined—the way the cracks and gaps in a house are revealed by the winter's wind. In the words of Warren Buffett, "It's only when the tide goes out that you can see who's swimming naked."

Modern capitalism would not exist in its current form if not for the massive disasters of the past, and the modern study of economics owes much of its shape to those men and women who turned their attention to the state of the economy in the aftermath of the Great Depression. Just as heavy weather strengthens architecture and construction, economic crises have strengthened economic theory and practice, and will continue to do so. These lessons are perhaps even more apt considering the crises in the world economy in 2007–09; historians and economists have yet to judge.

The Long Depression

A generation before the Great Depression of the 1930s came the Long Depression, a period marked by economic stagnation, high unemployment, rocketing farm foreclosure, violent labor protests, and political unrest. The first signs of the Long Depression came in the 1870s, reaching its apex in 1893. The worst was over by 1896, though in some regions the impact would continue to be felt through the following decade.

The Long Depression came toward the end of the expansionistic, urbanizing, and mostly prosperous period that followed Reconstruction. The United States hadn't wholly healed from the Civil War. But the nation had recovered enough to make a living again, and to devote its energies to the industrialization of its cities, the urbanization of its towns, and the settling of its frontiers.

American agriculture thrived. The number of American farms leapt over the course of a generation from 2.66 million to 5.74 million. Their combined size shot from about 400 million acres to nearly 850 million acres. Much of this expansion took place in the Great Plains, where the 50,000 farms in the Dakotas, Kansas, and Nebraska ballooned to 400,000 by 1900. That was part of that gradual taming of the continent, as the age of the wild frontier came to a close.

While the rural population fanned out, the urban population tripled, as did the number of cities with 50,000 or more people. That may not sound like many people by today's standards—barely a "city"—but this was before skyscrapers increased population density, and before the automobile and subway allowed people to work farther from home. In 1870 cities with populations greater than 50,000 included Indianapolis, Charleston, Providence, and Syracuse.

It took years for the rural South to adapt to a new labor system after slavery ended, and what developed was the system of sharecropping. Under sharecropping, the landowner paid the laborer with a share of the crop. The basic principle was not all that different from salesmen working on commission, and landowners during and after Reconstruction were cash-poor. Most sharecroppers purchased or rented their equipment, draft animals, seed, and fertilizer from the landowner if he could not provide them himself—and few could. If a sharecropper could not cover his costs with cash, he reduced his eventual share of the crop, or went into debt to his employer. Since the sharecropper would receive neither his portion of the crop nor his profit from selling it until harvest under this arrangement, he went further into debt to clothe and feed his family.

Debt or no debt, being a sharecropper meant steady work, and employers couldn't cheat everyone, nor deny them everything. It was not a life anyone would choose, except to avoid the uncertainty of seasonal work, or the slavery that had preceded the Civil War. For many, it was the best available option. It was a system from which there was little chance to exit. Sharecroppers could not earn enough to purchase their own land and equipment, and after paying off the debts they had run up, they rarely had enough cash to do more than pay their taxes and other basic expenses.

Sharecropping was used across rural America, but the crop-lien system was common principally in the south. The war and Reconstruction had left southern landowners and small farmers in debt, and they found themselves relying on credit to a greater degree than before to purchase goods they needed from local merchants, who in turn had often purchased them on credit from wholesalers in northern cities. Since slaves were no longer available as collateral, southern merchants let farmers—and share tenants, and sharecroppers in less frequent cases—promise a portion of their crop, which the merchant then sold at harvest, using the proceeds to pay off the debt and interest.

The goods the merchants were selling were already marked up in price because they had bought them on credit themselves, and the northern wholesalers were not exactly generous with credit terms. On top of that mark-up, the interest the merchants charged farmers and tenants ran as high as 60 percent, and was rarely less than 33 percent. These were often condemned as usurious at the time, but landowners kept entering into the agreements because they felt they had no choice. The crop-lien system also affected what the landowners chose to plant—cash crops were virtually all that made sense, in order to maximize the chance of having money left over after paying off debt at the end of the harvest.

Urban Americans were much more satisfied with their lot, and few realized that America had become a little too successful. All those farms and factories were producing too much for the world to consume. Backlogged inventories of manufactured goods led to a slowdown in production and shrinking payrolls. The prices of staple crops dropped as the market became glutted with unsold corn, wheat, cotton, and other goods, which in turn led to increasing farm foreclosures as farmers found themselves unable to meet their mortgages. The housing market peaked in 1892, resulting in a subsequent fall in construction. Railroad construction also declined, which caused a slowdown in steel manufacturing. At the same time the European economy was slowing, leading to less consumer activity overseas, and contraction in the international credit markets.

There had been stumbles along the way. The Panic of 1873—in the 19th century depressions were more often called panics—was the result of a number of factors. An epidemic of horse flu had dealt a severe blow to the transportation industry, as there were simply not enough horses to go around, forcing laborers to drag wagons around town, and the army had to fight the Apache on foot.

The 1873 Coinage Act had moved the United States to a gold standard instead of a gold and silver standard, to the horror of many. Not only did the value of silver plummet, hurting the mining industry that had become a significant part of the economy, but the money supply dropped as well. The debate over "bimetallism" (the old way of doing things) became a key issue in American politics for the rest of the century, fueling the careers of William Jennings Bryan and William McKinley.

In addition, the railroad boom following the interruption caused by the Civil War had been funded in no small part by speculators, and when President Grant reined in the money supply, the expansion jerked to a sudden stop, as there simply wasn't enough money left to fund it. A quarter of American railroads went out of business, and public opinion favored the Democrats in the next congressional elections, blaming the Republicans for the policies that had led to the crisis.

Economic Crises Persist

The 1873 Panic was severe, but short-lived compared to other American economic crises. The 1880s saw a return to expansion and apparent prosperity, and soon enough the railroads were again the subject of rampant speculation, a new technology with what seemed to be near-limitless profit potential—much like the dot-com boom of a century later. The Panic of 1893 occurred for many of the same reasons as that of 1873; the 1880s can be seen as a temporary interruption of the same ongoing economic crisis. Various rail companies sacrificed their own financial stability to take over their smaller rivals, overextending themselves even more than before, and when the Philadelphia and Reading Railroad went bankrupt, people started to panic.

Foreign investors demanded gold in payment in case the American currency was devalued, which soon resulted in the Treasury's gold being depleted to its legally mandated minimum—the point at which it was allowed to give out no more gold, leaving people unable to turn their notes in for hard currency. As in a lot of economic panics, every little disaster made people more worried, and worried people are more likely to cause a run on the banks or call in their loans—and the more people do that, the bigger the disasters get. Banks began to go out of business. The price of silver dropped again. Railroads and other companies drew up stakes and vanished.

In urban areas, unemployment hovered between 20 and 25 percent, and averaged between 12 and 14 percent nationwide. Evictions spiked sharply in all major cities. Arrests for vagrancy also rose: 40 percent in Baltimore, and 29 percent in New York City. Part of this rise was due to the strengthening of antivagrancy laws, as people became fearful of anarchy among the poor and unemployed. Remember how rapidly America had urbanized over the last generation—some of that was due to immigration and birth rates, but much of it was because people who had grown up in the country were moving to the city. The new city-dwellers were often uncomfortable with the established urban- ites, just as city-dwellers might fear the new arrivals would turn to crime in hard times. There was a racial element here, too—following the Civil War and Reconstruction, large numbers of African Ameri- cans migrated from the South to northern industrial cities.

The national economy began to show signs of recovery beginning with the election of William McKinley in 1896. Not surprisingly, the 1896 campaign between the McKinley and Democratic chal- lenger William Jennings Bryan focused mainly on the bimetallism question. Bryan argued that switching to silver would make money cheaper, putting more currency in circulation and making it easier for struggling farmers to pay their debts and improve their property. McKinley argued that gold was more secure and stable than silver, and enhanced the national economy over the long run. In the end, Americans preferred McKinley's conservative economic policy to Bryan's riskier plans, and he won the election, 51 percent to 47. It turned out to be the correct choice. Under McKinley the country began a 10-year period of growth and expansion that turned around the losses of the 1890s.

The United States wasn't the only country affected by the Long Depression, which in Europe had roots in the Vienna Stock Exchange collapse of 1873 and the economic toll of the Franco-Prussian War. European countries abandoned the use of silver as the basis of legal tender at around the same time as the United States, with similar results. Many European governments restricted free trade in response, reviving or enacting high tariffs on various goods.

While American expansion—both leading up to and in response to the panics—took place across the still sparsely-settled parts of the continent, the European analogue was the "scramble for Africa." With the Americas now largely made up of independent former colonies, Africa was the most available target for European imperialist aims. Britain, France, and Germany were particularly active in taking control of African markets through either economic means or colonization. Belgium, Italy, Spain, and Portugal all played their roles as well. This would be the last gasp of old-school European imperialism before World War I changed the nature of international politics.

The Panic of 1907

The Panic of 1907 was the last in a series of financial shocks that hit the U.S. economy between the 1870s and 1914. While the 1907 panic was felt primarily in the New York banking and trust community and did not impact the average American as severely as other panics, the implications of a financial catastrophe sufficiently spooked the government into action, and ultimately led to an overhaul of the national banking system.

Like the panics that occurred during the Long Depression, the 1907 panic arose from several different events occurring over a long period of time. In March the New York Stock Exchange experienced one of its first crashes. It rebounded, but credit remained tight and the banking community remained jittery through the summer and fall. In early October F. Augustus Heinze, head of New York's Knickerbocker Bank, attempted to seize control of the United Copper Company to corner the American copper market. Heinze's play failed, but his brazen move uncovered an intricate web of associations between Heinze and other key figures in the city's many banks and trusts. As members of the wider banking community began to look into the situation, they lost faith in the soundness of Heinze's bank, and by October 21, the important National Bank of Commerce announced they would no longer honor checks drawn on accounts held at the Knickerbocker Bank. Heinze quickly resigned, but not soon enough to prevent his bank from collapse.

In an era when bank deposits were unsecured, the personality of a bank owner or operator was a clue to the soundness of the bank as a whole. A scandal involving a banker could lead to a run on that bank, as individual depositors rushed to pull their currency out in the fear that if an owner was corrupt, so was his business. Because no bank holds 100 percent cash reserves, once the on-hand cash was exhausted, the doors closed, perhaps never to reopen. If you were the 221st person in line at a floundering bank, and the cash reserves ran out after the 220th person, all the money you had in that bank— maybe all you had in the world—was gone.

As the Heinze scandal unfolded, the crisis built into what historians Robert Bruner and Sean Carr called "the market's perfect storm," an event where multiple weaknesses in the New York financial and currency structures were exposed at once, leading to the threat of total meltdown. In the weeks following October 21 various groups and individuals moved to try to avert disaster. Among the most important players were the New York Clearing House, an association of bankers who worked together to clear checks between city banks, and also served as an informal watchdog group empowered to decide on the solvency of individual banks. Financier J.P. Morgan and Secretary of the Treasury George Cortelyou led this group. Together, they managed to weed out failing banks and pump enough money into the markets to keep the system afloat. Confidence was restored by February 1908.

The consensus was that the market had come a little too close to failure, and in May of that year Congress passed the Aldrich-Vreeland Act, establishing the National Monetary Commission. Over the next three years, this body looked into every aspect of American and foreign banking, including history and laws, and issued 30 reports that formed the nucleus of what became known as the Aldrich Plan, after commission chairman Nelson Aldrich of Rhode Island.

In 1912 Aldrich submitted a list of 59 recommendations to Congress. The core of the Aldrich Plan was the creation of 12 regional national reserve associations made up of representatives of private banks, that would be empowered to make emergency loans and create money to produce liquidity. Over the next two years, Congress would tinker with these ideas, trying to come up with a better mix of control between the private bankers and the federal government. In the end, they created the Federal Reserve, with the membership of Aldrich's 12 regional boards appointed by the Executive Branch, empowered to monitor the flow of U.S. currency between banks. All national banks were required to join the system, with independent and state banks free to opt in if they chose. It was passed into law by both houses of Congress on December 22, 1913, and signed by President Woodrow Wilson the same day. The creation of the Federal Reserve modernized U.S. financial markets and brought stability to the markets, bringing an end to the wave of panics.

The Great Depression

Until the 1930s, when people said "the Great Depression," they meant what we now call the Long Depression, just like when they said "the World War," they meant the first one. The Great Depression II was not a name that sat well with anyone, so the old depression took on a new label, because there was no denying that the Great Depression of the 1930s was far greater than that which had plagued the end of the 19th century. The most severe and lasting financial disaster in American history, the Great Depression strained the resources of every institution in the country. Countless businesses and banks failed, the nature of the federal government itself changed, and lifestyles changed. People continued to talk about it and memorialize it for several generations.

Most historians date the start of the Great Depression to the stock market crash of October 1929, but this is somewhat misleading. The collapse of stock prices certainly didn't help, but it was just one link in a much more complex chain of events, the particulars of which are still the subject of debate.

It was some combination of a global economic slowdown, the fall of stock values after almost a decade of rampant growth, underlying weaknesses in the U.S. monetary system, and overall poor financial policy of the part of the government; all of which came to a head at the end of 1929.

Wall Street during the October 1929 stock market crash.

Rumors were rampant that President Herbert Hoover was not going to veto the Smoot-Hawley Tariff Bill, which indeed he didn't— it was signed into law the following summer. Sponsored by Senator Reed Smoot of Utah and Representative Willis Hawley of Oregon, both Republicans, the bill raised to record levels federal tariffs on imported goods. Hoover was advised by economists and industrialists like Henry Ford to veto the bill, but to no avail.

The United States was overproducing again, and some thought that putting a prohibitive tariff on foreign goods—basically making foreign-made products too expensive to be worth buying—would force people to buy American. For a variety of reasons, it was not that simple, not least because not all goods had an American counterpart of equal quality, and foreign countries soon enacted retaliatory tariffs on American products. International trade shrunk in ways it had never experienced during peacetime.

The market crash came on Black Thursday, October 24, 1929. After five years of huge growth, the Dow Jones Industrial Average had finally begun its decline in September. Worried investors began to pull out of the market. On Black Thursday, a record 12 million shares were traded thanks to panicking shareholders. Bankers banded together to bid on blue chips to stimulate a recovery, like in 1907, and the slide seemed to halt the next day.

Over the weekend, though, the media covered the crash, and when the markets opened on Monday, everyone decided to get out while they still could. Both the drop (13 percent) and the number of trades beat Thursday's records, and over the course of the week the market lost $30 billion—at a time when the government's annual budget was a tenth of that amount.

One of the problems with masses of investors taking their money out of the stock market arose from the fact that many of them had borrowed money in the first place. This will seem a familiar pattern now: a boom of speculation led to overextension, and when the time came to pay the bills, the money was not always there. As with the later dot-com bubble, a lot of the rising perceived value of stocks came from the amount of borrowed money or credit used to purchase them—they became valuable because people were willing to pay a lot for them, which did not necessarily correlate strongly to the real value and strength of the companies that had issued the shares. There is a lot of debate—and probably always will be—about the extent to which the stock market crash was responsible for the Depression. Although the popular imagination links the two strongly, many economists believe that later actions, like the Smoot-Hawley Act and the Federal Reserve's contraction of the money supply, prolonged an event that could have been a briefer-lived economic panic.

The prosperity of the 1920s had seen the continued and permanent urbanization of the United States and the first generation of Americans who were more urban than exurban. Immigration had been enormously high in the first decades of the 20th century, and most of those immigrants settled in the cities, while southern African Americans continued their migration to industrial cities to take factory jobs that were open to all comers. But urban growth couldn't continue forever, and a few years before the stock market crash, the construction industry in many urban centers crumbled and collapsed, as the firms that had formed to deal with the urgent need for housing and commercial buildings downsized, or went bankrupt once those needs were met.

After the market crash, industry followed construction's nosedive. Steel towns, coal towns, and automobile centers like Detroit took it the worst, but across the board, the country simply wasn't making as much as it had been 10 years earlier, or even two years earlier. The Hoover administration encouraged public works at the local and state level, to take the edge off of soaring unemployment levels. The success of those public works programs was used to get the similar federal policies of the New Deal approved. Hoover-era urban relief programs also provided food and coal (for heating) to poor families, but were generally poorly organized.

There was one type of city that actually prospered during the Great Depression: the center of political service. Berlin, London, Washington, D.C., and other seats of national government all thrived from the amount of government activity. This was especially true of Washington, D.C., since unlike its European counterparts, it did not have an existence that preceded its purpose as a government city, and thus a larger proportion of its citizens were employed by the federal government or in service industries. (The greater London and Berlin areas still engaged in manufacturing, trade, and service jobs.)

There was considerable debate among average Americans as to whether or not there even was a depression, in the first couple years. Some saw only an economic decline affecting some cities or industries—others believed that an end to the boom times was being mistaken for a depression by people with short memories. There was no denying the severity of the stock market crash, but most Americans didn't own stock, and those who didn't put enough of their money into the market to risk ruin. What hit so many Americans was when the banks went out of business, they took their customers' savings with them. About 10,000 banks failed during the Depression, with more than 5,000 closing in the first three years of the crisis. Unemployment skyrocketed between 1930 and 1932, jumping from 3.2 to 24.9 percent nationwide.

It was much more severe depending in some regions or economic sectors—for example, automotive centers in the Midwest were among the hardest hit, with some areas seeing 75 to 90 percent unemployment rates. Even the Americans who held on to their jobs saw their hours and wages cut, as businesses struggled to stay afloat. Discretionary spending all but stopped. In the cities, charities and churches set up soup kitchens to feed the growing ranks of the poor.

Life After the Crash

Crude shantytowns—dubbed Hoovervilles after President Herbert Hoover—began to form. Hoover's name was lent to other makeshift items, too. Hoover leather was a piece of cardboard you stuck in your shoe when you'd worn a hole through the sole. Flying your Hoover flag meant you'd turned your empty pockets inside out. Hoover blankets were newspapers under which people huddled to stay warm, and when you got in your Hoover wagon, you were in an automobile dragged by horses because you couldn't afford repairs or gasoline. Shelters in Hoovervilles were made of whatever was available—tents, shacks, empty crates, and cardboard boxes. They cropped up all over the country, wherever large numbers of people were unable to pay their rents or mortgages, and had been evicted. In Brooklyn, Hoover City stretched for blocks.

Life wasn't much better on the farm. Not only were farmers struggling with falling commodity prices on the world markets, but a severe drought settled over the region in 1931 and lasted through the next several years. An endless stream of windstorms swept the dried-out croplands between 1931 and 1938, picking up three to four inches of topsoil and carrying it 10,000 feet up in the air, often redepositing it on the East Coast. These fearsome "black blizzards" were terrifying and dangerous; thousands died of respiratory diseases caused by the inhalation of fine dust. The environmental and economic disaster of the Dust Bowl left 500,000 Plains residents homeless, and at least 2.5 million people left the region between 1930 and 1940, including about 15 percent of the population of Oklahoma.

For the first three years of the crisis, the federal government took few steps to counter the impact of the faltering economy. President Hoover was not a proponent of the laissez-faire economic philosophy of his fellow Republicans, but neither did he come up with a bold plan to stop the bleeding. Disappointment and anger at Hoover's failings helped propel Democratic nominee Franklin Delano Roosevelt into office in 1932.

A New Deal

Promising "a new deal for the American people," Roosevelt entered office with a lot of energy, but few concrete plans. New Deal programs were loosely grouped around a general program of the "Three Rs": relief, recovery, and reform. The first goal was to help those most in need, the second to stimulate the economy to grow, and the third to reform the system to protect average Americans from economic catastrophe in the future.

First up was an overhaul of the banking and monetary systems. The day after his inauguration in March 1933, Roosevelt called for a four-day bank holiday, ordering all U.S. banks to close. He did this under an old World War I law, and when he was informed that he had acted outside the scope of the law, he quickly created the Emergency Banking Relief Act and pushed it through the Congress with such haste that most of the legislators didn't get a chance to read it before voting. Under the act, banks had to prove their solvency, and those who proved insolvent were not allowed to reopen. As the banks slowly started activity in the spring of 1933, the fact that they had proven their soundness helped consumers feel more confidence with the institutions, and they began making deposits once again. The country was taken off the gold standard and billions of dollars in cash were recalled in exchange for new currency, backed with silver. Later bills created the Federal Deposit Insurance Corporation (FDIC), insuring all bank deposits from loss in the event of a bank failure, and the Securities and Exchange Commission (SEC), set up to oversee companies issuing stock to the public and the investment companies that sold stocks.

The National Recovery Administration was established in 1933 as part of the National Industrial Recovery Act. Though later in the decade business and Roosevelt would seem to be on opposite sides, the NRA was strongly supported by both large and small business owners, and its two most important supporters were the president of the U.S. Chamber of Commerce and the head of General Electric. One significant opponent was Henry Ford, but his opposition wasn't voiced until after the act had gone into effect. The NRA sought, among other things, to reduce the economic ills caused by competition in the marketplace. For instance it instituted minimum wages so that businesses couldn't take advantage of the unemployment situation and exploit workers who would take underpaying jobs just to survive. Underpaying workers may benefit a specific company in the short-term, but if everyone pays their workers less and less to cut costs and cut prices to sell more goods, it creates a population with too little spending money to keep the economy afloat.

Certain price and labor codes were established too, in cooperation with various industries. The NRA's regulation of the poultry industry led to the Supreme Court case, *Schechter Poultry Corp v. United States*, that ruled the NRA unconstitutional in 1935. Because Schechter—which had been found by the federal government to be in 60 counts of violation of federal regulation—conducted its business intrastate, the court ruled that the NRA had overstepped its jurisdiction and assumed powers that constitutionally belonged to the states. In essence, this ended what historians call the First New Deal.

The Second New Deal was more focused than the first, in which Roosevelt had put into action almost any idea that found congressional support, in hopes of finding something that would work. The Second New Deal was more explicitly pro-labor and anti-big-business, and in general was focused on employment issues. Collective bargaining was given stronger protections, which helped to create more powerful labor unions.

An unemployment remedy was nationalized with the Works Progress Administration, a federal agency designed to create jobs, especially blue-collar and unskilled jobs that anyone could do if they were willing to work. That was seen as the great tragedy by many people: that there were so many men who were able to work, wanted to work, would have worked cheaply, but simply could not find a job.

The WPA was the largest New Deal agency, and in time employed millions of Americans, in every part of the country, urban and rural. Most jobs paid hourly, up to 30 hours a week, and included a great many construction jobs, road crews, and beautification projects. The WPA was often criticized for inefficiency and for not pushing its workers to work fast enough, but its principal mandate, after all, was to create work opportunities.

The most important New Deal program was the Social Security Act, part of the Second New Deal. Unemployment insurance (for those who had been employed at a certain level for a certain period of time) and retirement pensions were provided on a national level. Social Security has been controversial since its enactment, but was probably an inevitable development in some form even if there had been no Great Depression. The combination of modern medical advances—even those that cost nothing, like an awareness of proper nutrition—and changes in the American family meant that more and more people reached retirement age with a great deal of life ahead of them.

Unemployment stayed high despite the New Deal reforms, but other economic indicators had returned to 1920s levels. But in 1937 everything started to fall again, especially manufacturing output, while the national unemployment level rose from 14 to 19 percent. The 1937 recession provided the opportunity for a serious debate about the causes of and solutions to the Great Depression. The Roosevelt administration argued that the depression had been caused largely by the excesses of big business; the detrimental effects of businesses that were too large or exploitative on the economy and the American people had been a common thread in American politics for 50 years. Those business interests, though, argued that the New Deal's restrictions on business activity had been responsible for the 1937 recession. (Both sides could be correct, and neither position needs to disprove the other.)

In Congress, some who opposed Roosevelt's policies formed the Conservative Coalition, an informal group that lasted through the 1980s, though it had dwindled in the 1960s. The coalition managed to block nearly all major liberal legislation up through 1964, and was bipartisan (most of the Democrats involved were southern Dixiecrats). Its informal leader in the early days was Senator Robert Taft, the famously intelligent son of former president William Taft.

Worldwide Repercussions

The Great Depression had effects around the world. Europe's economy had suffered throughout the 1920s thanks to the ravages of World War I, and in Britain, industry had remained in recession throughout the decade. When the combination of the 1929 crash and the Smoot-Hawley tariffs and retaliatory tariffs hit, British industry was decimated as demand dried up. Unemployment doubled in a year, while exports halved.

Chancellor Neville Chamberlain cut government wages and aid to the poor while raising income taxes, which kept the government functioning, but worsened both unemployment and national purchasing power. As one of the first countries to adopt national healthcare, the cost of the poor was greater on the British government than on many others, resulting in a push and pull as every attempt to spend less on the poor seemed to create more people in need.

In the Netherlands, the effects of the Depression were more gradual. But like Britain, the country had spent the previous decade struggling, and it suffered greatly when countries around the world began to abandon the gold standard backing their currencies (throughout the early 1930s). The government of the Netherlands did not raise its tariffs as much as other countries did, believing that the international trade situation that developed after the stock market crash and the Smoot-Hawley tariffs would resolve itself. It was wrong; with no prohibitive tariff, foreign goods were cheap enough for Dutch citizens to cause a severe trade imbalance, sending the economy spiraling downward.

The government was greatly reluctant to put forth an economic policy that went beyond its usual mandate of balancing the budget—that just hadn't been the sort of thing the Dutch government did, and so every time it spent money throughout the 1930s in order to address these economic crises, it subsequently reduced spending in some other area, or raised taxes to an unreasonable level.

France never had the unemployment problems suffered by Britain and the United States, for a particularly tragic reason: so many French men had died in World War I that the new generation of young men was small. There simply weren't enough men to go around for unemployment to be a real concern. But because it was a less industrialized country than the United States or the rest of Western Europe, it had difficulty competing, and couldn't attract enough foreign investment to thrive when international trade contracted.

The part of Europe most affected by the Great Depression was Central Europe—Germany, Austria, and Poland, which helped set up the conditions for World War II. Unemployment soared to 20 percent across the region, production plummeted, and financial assistance from the American government dried up at the same time as the contraction of international trade, thus reducing or eliminating two major sources of national income.

The countries hit hardest by the Depression, though, were in Latin America—specifically Chile, Bolivia, and Peru, whose economies depended heavily on foreign investment and exports to the United States. The economic ills of the depression and the contraction of the money supply put an end to that investment; the Smoot-Hawley tariffs reduced the profitability of exports. The popularity of fascism throughout Latin America in the 1930s is due directly to fascist parties' appeals to nationalist sentiment in the wake of these countries' dependence on foreign money.

It is hard to say what would have happened if not for World War II. Beginning in 1940, when the economy was already taking another upswing after the recession, the federal government began massive military spending. When war broke out, the boon to manufacturing was unprecedented. In the early 1940s, when Americans could not buy something, it was not a lack of money they blamed—it was wartime rationing, and that served a patriotic purpose. Despite the men being away from home for so long, the war was the best possible thing for American morale and employment.

Unemployment was as low as two percent by 1943, thanks in part to government subsidies for wages of certain kinds of workers, as well as for on-the-job training. A whole generation of unskilled labor was turned into skilled labor, which there wouldn't have been time for if America's military involvement had been shorter-lived, as was the case in World War I.

The Savings & Loan Crisis

The Savings & Loan (S&L) crisis of the 1980s and early 1990s, at the end of the generally prosperous era that had prevailed since World War II, was the biggest U.S. economic disaster since the Great Depression. By the time it was over, some 1,600 institutions had failed and $150 billion had been lost by the banking system. The federal government's bailout cost $125 billion, accounting for the budget deficits of the early 1990s.

Savings & loan institutions, also known as thrifts, had been a part of the American banking scene since at least the mid-19th century. Thrifts were not full-service banks. They were organizations that used low-interest savings accounts to fund home mortgages. This could be a very safe arrangement for depositors, borrowers, and bankers, because they were based on the idea of long-term, low-risk transactions and community-level interactions between customers and mortgage managers. Savings accounts were insured (after the New Deal banking reforms), and mortgage rates were tightly controlled by the government.

By the late 1970s the thrift industry was chafing at the restrictions imposed on it by the state and federal governments. S&Ls were hit hard by the stagflation in the mid-1970s, as savings deposits fell off for a time. They were therefore unable to capitalize on the housing boom that began by the last years of the decade.

Stagflation, the combination of a stagnant economy (rising unemployment and falling economic growth) with inflation (rising prices) would probably have been the number one headline-grabber throughout the decade if not for the Vietnam War at the beginning and the taking of American hostages in Iran at the end. Economists and the Federal Reserve have linked stagflation to sudden increases in oil prices (or decreases in supply), which raises the price of goods while reducing their profitability. In the 1970s OPEC reduced the available supply of oil in order to dictate a price more to its liking, and enacted an embargo against the United States; the crisis is best remembered for the lines at the gas pumps and subsequent gasoline rationing, but the effects were much more widespread.

There is still considerable debate about which presidents, if any, deserve credit for pulling the country out of stagflation—Nixon, Ford, Carter, and Reagan all put plans into effect that could have been responsible. The problem with so many remedies being put into effect, of course, is that all the fixes take a while to work, and any of them can be considered responsible. But there was a sense at the time that the economy needed to be freed up more, and so the malaise of the 1970s helped to bring laissez-faire capitalist Ronald Reagan into office, and the country in general began to lean more in his direction even before he took the oath.

In 1980 the S&L industry was finally deregulated, and the scramble for profits began. New laws chartered more and more S&Ls and allowed them to borrow from the Federal Reserve, which they hadn't previously been able to do, and to issue credit cards at a time when credit was becoming especially big business. However to raise the capital to fund these expanded services and to pay back their loans, the thrifts had to pursue increasingly risky investments and practices. These strategies opened the door to spectacular profits, but also to the risk of spectacular losses. The people calling the shots weren't always qualified to assess risk, and like amateur investors, or lottery ticket holders, they were too often swayed by the prospect of winning, and did not consider seriously enough the repercussions of losing.

That is not to say that most, or even many, S&Ls were incompetent—only that not enough of them were competent enough. The losses piled up quickly. In 1980 the net profit of American S&Ls was $780 billion; by 1982 it had fallen to negative $4 billion. Insolvent banks began to collapse with alarming speed, despite the fact that regulations allowed insolvent S&Ls to remain in business longer than another lending institution would have. By 1983 the struggling institutions had actually bankrupted the Federal Savings and Loan Insurance Corporation (FSLIC), the organization that guaranteed the safety of deposits. The string of bank failures continued throughout the 1980s, with at least 1,600 banks—about one-half of all S&L banks in the United States—closing their doors for good.

Deposit brokerage was certainly part of the problem. Deposit brokers acted as intermediaries between consumers and the issuers of certificates of deposit, taking a fee from the transaction like a realtor. Regulations had limited five percent of a bank's deposits to brokered CDs, but those regulations were soon lifted, and S&Ls could increase their deposits—and their available assets—by offering a high rate of return, making their CD the best choice for the deposit broker. Supporting that high rate required more profitable investments, and of course the investments that promise the highest returns are always the ones carrying a higher risk of loss. Even worse, the brokerage system was abused by some S&Ls that would make deals whereby CD customers would be steered toward a particular S&L by a broker, and that S&L would then invest some of that money in investments the broker arranged.

As Congress groped for a solution to the S&L crisis, it became clear that some of their own membership was involved in obstructing federal regulators from investigating the activities of at least one bank. Charles Keating, president of the Lincoln Savings & Loan Association, gave $300,000 in total campaign contributions to five key U.S. senators: Alan Cranston (D-CA), John Glenn (D-OH), Donald Riegle (D-MI), Dennis DeConcini (D-AZ) and future presidential candidate John McCain (R-AZ). Quickly dubbed the "Keating Five," a congressional ethics investigation found that Cranston, Riegle, and DeConcini had worked to prevent the Federal Home Loan Bank Board (FHLBB) from probing Keating's business practices. Glenn and McCain were only minimally involved, and emerged from the ethics probe largely unscathed.

In August 1989 Congress passed the Financial Institutions Reform and Recovery Enforcement Act (FIRREA). This sweeping reform bill dissolved the FHLBB and replaced it with the Office of Thrift Supervision. With the FSLIC out of money, clean-up operations fell to the newly created Resolution Trust Corporation (RTC), which spent the next several years straightening up the books, liquidating the assets, and otherwise untangling the mess. By the mid-1990s the RTC had closed or resolved almost 750 failing banks.

Most individual depositors were able to recoup their losses through either the FSLIC or the FDIC. The remaining savings & loans survived, and launched a public relations blitz to reestablish customer faith in their institutions. The big losers were the American taxpayers, who ended up footing the bill for about $125 billion. The cumulative effect of the banking crisis was a major factor in the recession of the early 1990s, and the economy did not rebound until the second half of the decade, thanks in part to the dot-com boom.

The Asian Financial Crisis

Not every capitalist disaster begins in the United States. Two recurring themes in the coverage of economic disasters in the capitalist world are the increasingly intertwined economies of the world's capitalist-industrial nations. Consider the impact of the Smoot-Hawley tariffs on Europe and Latin America, for example. While Americans once called crises "panics"—describing the problem in terms of human response—the word fell out of use after the Great Depression, even though incidents would have fit the definition of a panic had they occurred earlier.

The Great Depression caused a great divide among economists—there's still no consensus about all of its causes or the effects of its remedies, and the forced boom of World War II clouds the issue. But there's no denying that it was a disaster representing much more than the overreaction of the public to money worries—after all, the stock market crash and Smoot-Hawley tariffs had long-lasting global consequences. Depression and recession became the terms of economic parlance, describing effects and conditions, rather than the emotional state that "panic" connotes. More recently, "crisis" has become even more common—a term so neutral and nonspecific that it may as well be called "the Asian financial bad thing."

Financial crises often refer to currency crises (also called balance of payments crises) during which a country's central bank loses international reserves and is eventually forced to allow the depreciation of the domestic currency. Countries with exchange rates that are pegged to other currencies—also known as managed currencies—are particularly prone to currency crises. While first-generation (canonical) currency-crises models support the view that deteriorating country fundamentals are at the core of such crises, second-generation (self-fulfilling) currency-crises models suggest that currency crises may occur despite strong fundamentals.

The Asian financial crisis occurred in 1997, when falling currencies struck several Asian countries and raised fears of a global disaster amid discussion of financial contagion. Financial contagion is a global economics term—it refers to the effects felt on one country's economy when another country's suffers. The terminology conjures up images of a global economy that works like the weather, with disastrous storms in one part of the world persisting long enough to be felt at least as a heavy shower weeks later and thousands of miles away. It's a good image and an instructive way to think of things. As with the weather, phenomena change as they travel—a thunderstorm in Vancouver won't always mean a thunderstorm in Boston, but it will mean something, somewhere. Those cities don't exist in enclosed bubbles; they breathe the same air, their waterways feed into the same world's rivers and oceans. The challenge is in studying these complex systems to learn how they all affect one another.

The Four Asian Tigers

At the point of the crisis, about half of the foreign investments made in developing countries went to Asia. Developing Asian nations had been experiencing healthy growth for years—since the 1960s in some cases, thanks to rapid industrialization. The healthiest, most dependable of these nations are known as the Four Asian Tigers—or in Chinese, the Four Little Dragons: Hong Kong, Singapore, South Korea, and Taiwan (all four have been under the Chinese sphere of cultural influence at some point).

The Tigers all built their economies on exports to industrialized nations—"Made in Taiwan," in particular, is a phrase that is associated with all manner of plastic goods. Education was improved in the Tiger nations as a long-term investment in productivity and the economy, with the United States and Japan standing as obvious examples of educated workers being effective workers. Unusual for many developing countries—especially in the 1960s and 1970s— high school education is compulsory in the Tiger nations. Tariffs help to retain a trade surplus, and laws guarantee a great degree of economic freedom—Hong Kong and Singapore rank the highest in the world—to attract lucrative foreign investments. As the Tigers developed, other Asian nations began to follow in their footsteps:

The Thai bhat, one of the Asian currencies that suffered in 1997.

Malaysia, Indonesia, Thailand, and the Philippines, for instance, all experienced healthy growth in the 1980s. The economies of the first three developed into bubbles fueled by short-term capital aimed at quick profits. The money sunk into those economies was often not as evenly distributed or well thought-out as in the Tigers, and leadership was not always up to the task of managing a rapidly-changing economy to everyone's benefit, rather than exploiting it to help out cronies and special interests. Most of these Asian nations pegged their currencies to the U.S. dollar.

For 10 years Thailand's economy was the fastest-growing in the world, but all that ended in 1997 when the Thai baht lost half its value. The Thai government had been unable to defend the baht against foreign currency speculators and the construction, real estate, and finance industries in Thailand imploded with layoffs. Foreign confidence in developing Asian nations was shaken. U.S. interest rates were rising as the American recession that followed the S&L crisis ended, and the dollar became more valuable, making Asian exports more expensive. At the same time, many Western manufacturers were shifting their concerns to China, a source of cheap labor.

The basic first-generation currency crisis model explains the cause of currency crises, based on the coexistence of a pegged exchange-rate regime and expansionary fiscal and monetary policies. However before the financial crisis struck, Asian countries successfully stabilized inflation by maintaining fiscal and monetary discipline under pegged exchange-rate regimes. Therefore researchers working with first-generation currency crisis models have used a different set of fundamentals to discuss the cause of the Asian financial crisis. Increasing foreign liabilities of the commercial banking system, maturity mismatches, and asset price bubbles are assumed to have made the financial systems in some Asian countries vulnerable to capital inflows of substantial magnitudes.

Some argue that financial liberalization precedes banking and currency crises. As financial liberalization allows a country to enjoy the inflow of foreign investors, the outflow may be substantial and speedy, which leads to a boom-bust cycle. This particular point has been made with respect to the Asian financial crisis. Financial liberalization may have led to the maturity mismatch between assets and liabilities of the banking system because of overlending and excessive risk, especially in short-term external debt. International investors may have become wary and expected financial problems in the future. Therefore based on the first-generation currency crisis model, systemic banking problems lay at the roots of the substantial devaluation of the Thai baht, Korean won, and Indonesian rupiah in 1997.

Researchers focusing on the self-fulfilling nature of the Asian financial crisis argue that markets' reaction to news demonstrate the possibility of currency crisis despite strong fundamentals. Some argue that the largest daily swings in financial markets in Asia during the crisis period cannot be explained by any apparently relevant economic or political news. Empirical studies indicate that news releases that contribute to significant movements in financial markets are releases that are about agreements with the international community and about announcements by credit-rating agencies.

Some also suggest that news releases about monetary and fiscal policies do not affect financial markets in a predictable fashion. In some instances, tight policies may contribute to financial market rallies, or lead to a slowdown in financial markets. There is also evidence that investors react more strongly to bad news than to good news. Generally speaking, investors' reactions to information have been used to argue that bad news in crisis episodes may increase uncertainty, which may lead to group behavior.

Financial Contagion

Some researchers suggest the possibility that a country may experience a currency crisis as a result of financial contagion. Contagion is exactly what the rest of the world worried about as those formerly miraculous Asian economies quietly collapsed. More so than at any other point in time, the health of Asia affected the health of the world. Recent developments with tainted foods arriving on Western shores from Asia underline what economists in 1997 already knew: everything is connected, none of us are in bubbles. Though Asia was well-aware of the severity of these problems—the foreign ministers of the Association of Southeast Asian Nations met in July to discuss their options—it was not long before the rest of the world intervened, and the nature and appropriateness of that intervention is still controversial more than a decade later.

There were hundreds of billions, maybe as much as a trillion dollars, at risk in the crisis, and the word "contagion" reflects the thinking about these phenomena: by healing the sick, others can protect the healthy who have not yet been infected.

While in the past financial assistance to other countries has been a sort of enlightened self-interest—shoring up a country in need to help them pay you back, while creating an ally in the process—helping out the critical Asian nations seemed to be in the best interest of the world regardless of any future rewards reaped from such benevolence.

The International Monetary Fund (IMF), a multinational organization founded at the Bretton Woods Conference in 1944 that includes nearly every United Nations (UN) member state, created a number of these rescue-and-reform packages for the nations affected by the Asian financial crisis. Notable UN members who are not part of the IMF include the communist countries of North Korea and Cuba. Providing financial assistance is its main purpose, and the countries that receive such assistance are generally required to reform their laws and practices in order to reflect the "Washington Consensus" (the IMF is headquartered in Washington, D.C.). The Washington Consensus calls generally for deregulation, privatization, low tariffs and a liberalization of trade, tax reform, and economic policies that are suited for participation in the global capitalist economy.

The IMF required that the Asian nations reduce budget deficits, raise interest rates, change banking-related regulations and policies, and abide by other reforms designed to protect the value of the nation's currency and reassure investors. Government oversight was set up to insure that the money provided by the IMF would go where it was supposed to, rather than to special interests or cronies, as had often happened earlier. In essence, these Asian economies had to be Westernized in order to receive their bailouts. Supporters of this plan argue that there is nothing wrong with this—that nothing of Asia's cultural heritage is lost by a conversion to Western-style capitalism, particularly if these countries want to participate in a larger economy in which that's the dominant mode.

However, after the decades of the Cold War, in which so many developing countries—not only in Southeast Asia but in eastern Europe, Africa, and Latin America—were fought over by Communist and capitalist ideologues, onlookers are naturally sensitive to any policies that appear to arrange the dominos like that again. And transitions are hard, even when they are necessary—in the United States, the South took decades to recover from Reconstruction. The IMF's required restructuring resulted in rampant unemployment, bankrupt companies, industry collapses, and a bust in Asian real estate—not to mention the resentment on the part of much of the citizenry and officials. Many, after all, blamed the crisis on the desire to participate in the world capitalist economy.

The American economy was affected by the Asian collapse, but not as badly as had been feared. Perhaps because of the IMF's bailout, perhaps not—when speaking of something that occurred little more than a decade ago, we can't assume that it's truly over. There may be repercussions not yet felt, in much the same way that the Asian crisis itself was connected to the S&L crisis. In any case, the Dow Jones plunged over seven percent on October 27, 1997, some 98 years after the week-long crash that precipitated the Great Depression. It was the third-worst loss in the Dow's history in terms of total points, though not as a percentage. Controversially, the New York Stock Exchange closed the market early in order to stop the crash in its tracks. Earlier in the day, the NYSE had halted trading from 2:36 to 3:06 P.M. When trading resumed and the Dow continued to slide, the market was closed at 3:35, just under a half-hour early.

A rally started the middle of the next morning, and over the course of October 28th, more than a billion shares were traded on the NYSE for the first time. Some 61 percent of the previous day's loss was recovered, enough perhaps to justify the early closing of the market.

In the United States and around the world, investors became more reluctant to deal with developing nations regardless of their current state of health—they were perceived to be more vulnerable to crisis than the established developed nations, and their governments perhaps less responsible. The shock caused a dip in the price of oil and other raw commodities that led to Russia's 1998 financial crisis, since 80 percent of the country's exports were directly affected by the reduced prices. Latin American crises followed, and worries continued of a global collapse, with conventional wisdom crediting Federal Reserve chairman Alan Greenspan with preventing, by coordinating bailouts.

In the years since, the Asian economies have largely recovered, though they do not experience the growth they did in the decade leading up to the crisis. China and India now represent a bigger competitive threat for those economies, with their vast resources of cheap labor.

The Economic Crisis of 2007–09

As this book goes to print, an ongoing economic crisis has come to a head. In the coming months, it may peak and head toward recovery; or the situations that seem most disastrous now may in hindsight turn out to be minor compared to other calamities.

Like all financial crises, the economic crisis that began in 2007 has roots that go back as far as you might care to look, but its most immediate beginnings are with the subprime mortgage crisis. The American housing boom of the new century came to a halt in many regions in 2005, and by 2006 many experts were confident that the market correction would result in a critical drop. Exacerbating the usual pattern of peaks and valleys in any market was the recent popularity of "house flipping"—the purchase and quick resale (sometimes after remodeling) of a home for a fast profit; only 60 percent of homes purchased 2005–06 were bought as primary residences. Some economists, including Nobel Prize winner Joseph Stiglitz, warned of the possibility of an American recession as a result of plummeting house prices. A month later, in October 2006, Fed chairman Benjamin Bernanke confirmed that the housing market was undergoing a "substantial correction" and predicted a drag on economic growth for the next year.

In the following quarter, the subprime mortgage industry collapsed. Subprime mortgages are lent to borrowers who don't qualify for market interest rates, usually because of credit history or insufficient income. Rather than denying them a mortgage entirely, they are simply given a significantly higher interest rate. The same practice is common in credit cards, but the debt load there is substantially lighter. The potential profit to the lender is much higher than a prime mortgage, so more and more subprime mortgages were offered, including loans to borrowers without means of repayment (so-called "ninja" loans, for No Income, No Job, and no Assets). In the last few years, the number of delinquencies and foreclosures of subprime mortgages has steadily risen to the point that while such mortgages represent only about seven percent of the total loans in the country, they represented 43 percent of the foreclosures in the third quarter of 2007. By mid-2008, more than 2 million homes purchased with subprime loans had entered foreclosure.

These days banks often pass on the credit risk incurred by their loans, by pooling mortgages and other debts into mortgage-backed securities (MBSs) and collateralized debt obligations (CDOs) which are then traded. At the same time, this practice made banks much more willing to take risks in their lending practices, since those risks would then be distributed through securitization; critics have blamed the combination of high-risk loans and securitization for the current economic crisis.

Financial institutions that had made significant MBS and CDO investments began to falter and fail. The value of these securities dropped as housing prices dropped; as this book goes to press, losses from the subprime mortgage crisis alone have exceeded $1 trillion. Banks began to fail, as the value of their holdings fell, erasing their capital. The crisis began to panic investors, who withdrew from risky mortgage-based investments.

Concurrent with and tied-up in all of this is the worldwide commodities crisis. After a long period of reasonably cheap energy, the price of crude oil skyrocketed, and in 2008 reached an all-time (inflation-adjusted) high, the sorts of prices not seen on crude oil since the Civil War, with refined products like gasoline costing more than they had since Henry Ford's assembly line started churning out Model Ts. At the same time, the cost of food goods rose worldwide, as a result of crops being diverted for the production of biofuel, an increased demand for resource-intensive food that has lead to shortages of basic (less profitable) foods like rice, trade imbalances caused by short-sighted regulations (such as the WTO's requirement that Japan, which produces as much rice as it can consume, is required to import still more rice, which is then left to rot in warehouses), the loss of croplands to soil erosion and drought, climate-related shortages, and food stockpiles coming up short. In early 2008 the price of wheat hit an all-time high, rice hit a 10-year high, and soy and corn skyrocketed. In some parts of the world, milk and meat—the products of a livestock industry that depends on those basic crops for feed—more than doubled in price, and all dairy products saw a significant jump in the United States. Other foods like citrus fruit had already seen a price hike the previous year, while the global demand for chocolate forced big chocolate companies like Hershey to rejigger their American market products to use chocolate-flavored coatings in place of actual chocolate whenever possible.

Although commodity prices fell sharply in late 2008, the food, oil, and mortgage problems were all related. Investors pulling their money out of MBSs often reinvested in food speculation, driving prices up. The oil crisis not only increased the demand for biofuel (which is subsidized in both the United States and the European Union, meaning that businesses have increased motivation to grow corn and sugar cane for fuel instead of food), it increased the cost of transporting food, which is significant. While New York once received most of its food from its neighboring "Garden State," New Jersey, it now imports much of it from California on the other side of the country. Where it once took one calorie of energy to make three calories of food, it now takes 10 calories of energy to put one calorie of food on a supermarket shelf. The mathematics underlying our modern food industry are dependent on the assumption that energy is inherently cheap—an assumption that no longer proves true. One short-term result has been renewed interest in locally-grown foods; victory gardens may be next.

The collapse of the subprime mortgage industry tipped a domino that landed on investment banking. Wall Street investment banks Bear Stearns, Goldman Sachs, Lehman Brothers, Merrill Lynch,

October 9, 2008:the Dow Jones industrials closed below 8,600.

and Morgan Stanley all found themselves in peril as a result of their heavy MBS investments. On July 11, 2008 IndyMac Bank—one of the largest mortgage lenders in the country—failed, the fourth largest bank failure in American history. It was put into conservatorship by the FDIC; this is an American legal procedure (called "nationalizing" in other countries) that puts an entity under control of the federal government. This caused speculation as to whether the government would also seize control of Fannie Mae and Freddie Mac, government-sponsored enterprises that help finance mortgages for individual homebuyers. It did in early September when the market continued to spiral out of control.

Fannie Mae and Freddie Mac—or the Federal National Mortgage Association and the Federal Home Loan Mortgage Corporation—were formed at the end of the 1960s to help keep the costs of mortgages low. But on September 7 their finances crumbling, and they were placed in conservatorship by the Federal Housing Finance Agency, with the support of the Treasury Department and the Fed. The goal of placing them into conservatorship was to keep them solvent and operating; the Treasury made $200 billion available to extend credit through 2009 in order to keep the companies from collapsing.

Later in September, both Lehman Brothers and Washington Mutual (the largest savings and loan) collapsed. Morgan Stanley and Goldman Sachs announced they would become traditional bank holding companies, leaving investment banking—the dominant force on Wall Street since the New Deal—behind. September was marked by extreme instability in financial markets worldwide, as these developments shook a climate already made unsteady by the commodities crisis. The Dow fell, and fell again, nearing 8,000 after a historic high of 14,000 less than a year earlier.

Against a highly politicized backdrop, the Emergency Economic Stabilization Act of 2008 (H.R. 1424; Division A of Public Law 110-343 after passage) proposed in Congress was dismissed by many as a bailout plan to subsidize Wall Street with the tax dollars of Main Street. Lawmakers running for reelection were reluctant to support a bill many Americans saw as rewarding bad behavior, while both incumbent President George W. Bush and the larger part of the Democratic Party argued in favor of a plan that would reduce the impact on the economy, foreseeing the possibility of a prolonged economic collapse like that of the Great Depression.

After some negotiation and rewriting, the act eventually passed and was signed into law on October 3, less than two weeks after its proposal. The act created the Troubled Assets Relief Program, which has $250 billion available immediately, and up to $450 billion more dependent on presidential and congressional approval. The money is to be used to buy the distressed assets of failing institutions—mortgages and debt securitizations—in order to prevent the collapse of those firms, and with the goal of making that money back when the markets eventually recover. But shortly after the law was passed, Henry Paulson, the Treasury Secretary, changed the program into one that purchased stock in troubled institutions to shore up their capital base. This shift in plans did little to enhance Mr. Paulson's reputation.

As the crisis continued to unfold, the Federal Reserve opened its lending window to a wide array of institutions, and created facilities to ease locked credit markets. But financial markets around the world remained skittish and with predictions of more than $2 trillion in total losses, the crisis of 2007–09 promised to have a lasting impact on the world economy.

Chapter 6

Capitalism Around the World

M ost of our discussion so far has been slanted toward the United States, where capitalism has thrived since the nation's inception, and where its greatest disaster—the Great Depression—impelled the world's economists to hone their science. But capitalism in various forms has been adopted around the world, and doing business today means doing business internationally. A capitalist needs to be aware of the rest of the world, not least of all because the economy is so much like the weather—a storm system may start far away, but that does not mean it won't reach you eventually.

International Institutions

The World Bank

Founded in 1944, the World Bank's charter spells out its aim: "to assist in the reconstruction and development of territories of members by facilitating the investment of capital for productive purposes, to promote private foreign investment by means of guarantees or participation in loans, to supplement private investment by providing, on suitable conditions, finance for productive purposes out of its own capital." It's one of the world's largest sources of economic assistance to developing countries, providing technical assistance, policy advice, and supervision for the implementation of free-market reforms. The bank plays a major role in overseeing economic policy, the reformation of public institutions within developing nations, and in shaping global macroeconomic agendas.

Loans are granted only to member nations, and only for the financing of specific projects. Prior to issuing a loan, bank advisors and experts determine if the country can meet the bank's conditions, most of which are designed to ensure the loan's productive use and repayment. The borrower must be unable to secure a loan from any other source, and the borrower must show that the project is technically feasible and economically sound. Repayment is ensured, via member countries guaranteeing loans made to private concerns within their territories. Subsequent to the loan being granted, periodic reports regarding the loan's use and the project's progress are required from both the borrower and the bank's own observers.

World Trade Organization

A multinational organization that defines rules for international trade, adjudicates disputes, and punishes countries that violate its rules, the World Trade Organization (WTO) imposes legal obligations on its members. Each member is required to submit schedules for improving the openness of its markets for international trade, and must abide by WTO rules governing issues such as goods, services, industrial policy, and intellectual property. Though these moves benefit the international trading system, they are not without drawbacks. In the United States, for example, the WTO has been criticized for ruling that U.S. anti-pollution laws violate international trade rules because some foreign gasoline products fail to meet U.S. environmental standards. Similar concerns have been raised in countries where taxes are lower and regulations less onerous: will countries be free to decide on tax and regulatory policy, or will officials of the WTO usurp those decisions?

The WTO is quite small compared to other international organizations, its budget a fraction of those enjoyed by the World Bank, the Organization for Economic Cooperation and Development (OECD, an international organization of 30 countries that accepts representative democracy and free-market economy), and the International Monetary Fund (IMF, a global financial oversight system and lender of last resort). Troubling questions remain about the relation between the WTO's authority to rule on trade issues and the sovereignty of member nations. Nonetheless, the WTO's work continues to open new markets and win gradual acceptance of international trade rules by countries that previously demurred. In the 21st century, the WTO will be an important force in global commerce.

OPEC

The Organization of Petroleum Exporting Countries is a group of oil-exporting countries that have banded together to set uniform output and price goals in the international petroleum market. It consists of 11 countries: Algeria, Indonesia, Iran, Iraq, Kuwait, Libya, Nigeria, Qatar, Saudi Arabia, the United Arab Emirates, and Venezuela. Member countries contain roughly 75 percent of the world's proven crude oil reserves, and supply about 40 percent of the world's output.

In the contemporary world economy, OPEC has the potential to wield a significant influence due its large reserves and market share, and the reluctance of many oil-dependent industrialized countries to develop alternative energy sources and implement serious oil conservation strategies. Some observers believe, however, that the emergence of non-OPEC competitors in the late 20th century, such as several post-Soviet states, has limited OPEC's ability to influence global oil markets. The Saudi political alliances being forged with the United States gives added weight to incentives not to restrict oil output to raise prices.

OPEC is vulnerable to the ups and downs of global economic activity. For some OPEC countries, oil is the most significant, or the only significant export commodity. These countries face the challenge of keeping their economies alive when there are economic slowdowns, and especially when the oil reserves run out. If they build infrastructure, invest in communications and computer technology, and diversify their economies to produce goods and services other than oil, their economies might not suffer much in the long run.

Islamic Banking

The accumulation of vast reservoirs of cash in the Arab Muslim nations as a result of rising oil prices led to the revival of Islamic banking as a religiously sanctioned, socially-responsible capitalist (interest-based) system. The basic principle of Islamic banking is the religious prohibition of usury, or high interest rates. Innovations were developed to circumvent the paying of interest, including various profit-sharing arrangements. A particular rate of return is sometimes guaranteed, though some religious officials argue that this is just interest by another name.

Foreign transactions are generally allowed on an interest-rate basis to keep complications to a minimum. The opponents of this mode of banking propose a different interpretation of religious law that distinguishes between interest and usury, sanction usury but leave the institution of interest intact. However another reading of the injunction is that interest is unearned income, and hence leads to a fundamental introduction of injustice in the community.

Money is not fecund in its own right; it does not create value by itself. Interest is a social mechanism to transfer value from those who create it through purposive human endeavor, to those who have control over money—an apparent case of exploitation. Since the spirit of *Shariat* in Islam is governed by a strong sense of social justice, fraternity, equality, and cooperation, it is possible to argue the logic of inadmissibility in Islamic social schema of a mechanism like interest.

The Vatican Bank

Little public information is available about the organization and finances of the Vatican Bank. This is due to the dual nature of the

The Vatican Bank's depositors are religious orders and organizations.

Vatican, which, as the home of the papacy, is the spiritual center of the Roman Catholic Church, yet is also a temporal institution. Vatican City is a sovereign state with its own laws, currency, diplomats, and so on. The Vatican Bank functions as both a temporal bank for Vatican financial assets, and an institution serving the spiritual works of the church.

The bank serves the officials and citizens of Vatican City and Roman Catholic institutions worldwide. In 1990, in response to scandals and suspicions about the bank's activities, the bank took on a more transparent governing structure. A lay director is appointed by a supervisory council of five banking experts, who are selected by five cardinals, all of whom are commissioned by the Pope to oversee the bank's activities.

As an institution with both secular and spiritual aspects, it has been the scene of scandal. The most famous involved its relations in the 1970s and 1980s with the Banco Ambrosiano, which collapsed in 1982. Other allegations include money laundering, bribery, and the concealment of assets seized from concentration camp victims in World War II. The Vatican's unique institutional reach across national boundaries enhances the bank's notoriety, at the same time that the bank remains a valuable institution for maintaining Catholic religious orders, charities, and other organizations around the world.

The following sections in the rest of this chapter deal with various countries and regions around the world—it is not all-inclusive, but gives a good overall picture of how capitalism has spread throughout the globe.

Asia and the Pacific

Asian Developmental States

Asian developmental states emerged during the Cold War in Japan, South Korea, Taiwan, and Singapore as a controversial hybrid of Soviet Union–style central planning and American free-market capitalism. Governments promoted industries considered strategic in enhancing overall economic growth, while nonstrategic sectors were left to market forces.

The industries chosen for promotion reflected the developmental states' nationalist orientation to economic activity. In contrast to internationalist ideas of comparative advantage and mutual gains from trade across national boundaries, developmental states viewed trade as a national struggle with clear winners and losers. Producers of technologically-sophisticated products became rich, while countries that concentrated on light manufacturing and commodities remained poor. Developmental states, therefore, raised their country's living standard by promoting industries with their high-paying jobs, such as automobiles, computers, shipbuilding, and petrochemicals.

Close business-government relations clearly favored large business conglomerates over smaller firms. Governments needed trustworthy companies to carry out development plans, and the firms were happy to receive government subsidies and windfall profits from these new businesses. The Korean government's cooperation with the gigantic Hyundai Group to promote shipbuilding in the 1970s and 1980s is a good example. The government subsidized Hyundai with lucrative contracts for ships, infrastructure at Hyundai facilities, and financial guarantees to foreign investors and Hyundai's early customers. With this support from the government, Hyundai grew into one of the world's largest shipbuilders by the late 1980s.

Government subsidy of new industries required a redistribution of resources within society. Big companies and their urban employees generally prospered. Farmers, small businesses, and laborers were less fortunate. To maintain political stability, Asian developmental states developed authoritarian political systems dominated by a single party like the Liberal Democratic Party in Japan, the Kuomintang in Taiwan, and the People's Action Party in Singapore.

With their systematic intervention in markets, close relations with big business, and authoritarian politics, developmental states have drawn substantial criticism. Some economists believe that developmental states' importance in promoting economic development has been exaggerated. Growth rates might have been even higher had entrepreneurs devoted all of their resources to innovation, rather than soliciting political favors.

China
GDP: $7.043 trillion; GDP per capita: $5,300

In 1966 Chairman Mao Zedong launched the Cultural Revolution. This was a mass campaign aimed at getting rid of all party officials who had supported capitalist development, and at eradicating "nonproletarian ideology" in society. Nonproletarian ideology was loosely defined, and all were encouraged to identify people who showed or harbored such ideology. Violent conflicts happened among different political factions. Party officials at all levels, managers and supervisors, former landowners, former business owners, and intellectuals were targets of the mass campaign. Existing government apparatus at all levels were destroyed, and new ones were put into place. Mao was deified and regarded as the embodiment of truth.

The Cultural Revolution caused economic stagnation and popular discontent. Mao died in 1976, and the revolution came to an end. A comprehensive program of reforms was adopted in its wake. A market economy was introduced, first in specially designated zones, and eventually in the whole country. In today's China, there are state-owned businesses, private businesses, businesses jointly owned by Chinese and foreign capitalists, businesses owned solely by foreign capitalists, and businesses owned by shareholders.

The political process is becoming more and more open. Efforts are being made to strengthen and perfect the legal system. Citizens in China elect representatives, who form people's congresses at the city, county, province, and national levels. These people's congresses in turn make laws and elect and dismiss government officials. At the local level, residents directly elect and dismiss officials of village and town governments.

In 1997 and 1999, China respectively recovered its sovereign control over Hong Kong and Macao, territories cut off from Britain and Portugal. According to China's Basic Laws, Hong Kong and Macao are special administrative regions, which continue to practice capitalism. China is a member of the UN Security Council, and has recently joined the World Trade Organization.

Singapore
GDP: $222.7 billion; GDP per capita: $48,900

After becoming a self-governing part of the British Commonwealth in 1959, the Singapore government actively promoted the growth of technologically-sophisticated export industries to attract multinational corporate interest, and to reduce Singapore's regional dependence. The government gave tax incentives and access to inexpensive capital to favored industries, and kept labor costs low by shifting a large share of the responsibility for worker welfare to the state.

The government also promoted the growth of Singapore's financial services industry. The Monetary Authority of Singapore established a system for offshore banking that encouraged nonresidents to deposit funds in Singapore to be invested in Southeast Asia. The Stock Exchange of Singapore was established in 1973, and in 1983, funds held by nonresidents and invested outside Singapore were granted tax exemption. Today Singapore is the region's leading provider of financial services.

Malaysia
GDP: $357.9 billion; GDP per capita: $14,400

Since the early 1970s Malaysia has transformed itself from a producer of raw materials into one of the fastest-growing economies in Southeast Asia. While primary production is important, Malaysia has focused on export-oriented manufacturing (particularly electronics) to drive its economic growth. This emphasis on manufacturing has led to the development of a variety of heavy industries, including steelmaking and automobile assembly.

The Malaysian government has implemented a social and economic restructuring plan, initially known as the New Economic Policy (NEP), which attempts to strike a balance between the goals of economic growth and the redistribution of wealth. The government has also encouraged the private sector to take a greater role in restructuring, leading to the privatization of many public-sector activities, including the national railway, airline, and telecommunications company. Malaysia's economic growth has created a demand for labor, which has tended to increase wages. However there has been a limited flow of workers from east to peninsular Malaysia, thus prompting the recruitment of foreign workers.

Indonesia
GDP: $845.6 billion; GDP per capita: $3,400

The island nation of Indonesia consists of eight major islands and over 17,000 smaller ones in the Indian Ocean between Asia and Australia.

Sometimes called the Spice Islands, Indonesia was fought over by the British, Portuguese, and ultimately victorious Dutch in the 16th century. Dutch interests dominated the Indonesian economy from that point until its independence in 1949.

In the 20th century the Indonesian economy benefited from the presence of rich oil and gas reserves. Possession of such strategic commodities was less helpful during World War II, when it made the islands a frequent target for bombing raids, but the two fuels constitute the bulk of Indonesian export income to the present day. The other major export, timber, is in increasing jeopardy because of deforestation. Since World War II, the Indonesian economy has had periods of prosperity, but faces serious problems in the form of chronic political instability, corruption, and massive debt.

The Philippines
GDP: $298.9 billion; GDP per capita: $3,300

In the late 1990s the Philippine economy deteriorated as a result of contagion from the Asian financial crisis and extremely poor weather conditions. The Phillippines's poverty level is a dismal 40 percent, but an encouraging sign is that the island's labor force has risen slightly since 1999—from 30 million to 32 million people.

At the beginning of the 21st century the Phillippines government promised to continue its economic reforms to help its people dig out of poverty to match the pace of development in the newly-industrialized countries of East Asia. The strategy includes improving the infrastructure, bolstering government revenues, moving toward further deregulation and privatization of the economy, and increasing trade integration.

Hong Kong
GDP: $293.4 billion; GDP per capita: $42,000

Hong Kong's free-market economy is improving. Very dependent on international trade, its natural resources are limited enough that major foodstuffs and raw materials must be imported. Hong Kong

Hong Kong's modern skyline reflects capitalist ambitions.

reverted to Chinese administration in 1997. While it is argued that the economy of pre-China Hong Kong was more stable, Chinese counterparts have demonstrated a competitive nature just as strong, if not more aggressive, than their British rivals. China dominates Hong Kong's trade in merchandise, with 40 percent of the total. China's share in Hong Kong's export of foreign goods is higher, at approximately 90 percent. Behind Japan and the United States, Hong Kong is China's third largest trading partner. The Chinese government's basic policy of minimum intervention and maximum support for business is responsible for much of the good that is occurring on the economic home front. China's policies for Hong Kong businesses include low taxation, free and fair market competition, an orthodox legal and financial framework, a fully convertible and secure currency, an efficient network of transport and communication, a skilled workforce (that includes an enterprising spirit), a large degree of internationalization, and cultural openness.

South Korea
GDP: $1.206 trillion; GDP per capita: $24,600
Between the early 1960s and 1990s South Korea's economy grew at an average rate of nine percent, its Gross National Product more than doubled, and its per capita income increased more than one hundredfold. South Korea, along with Singapore, Hong Kong, and Taiwan, is now considered one of East Asia's "Four Tigers." However it was not always this way.

To maintain control over industrial development, the government gave most of its support to giant-sized conglomerates, known as *chaebols*, that were emerging. The result was that smaller, privately managed industries had difficulty finding financing, and became dependent on the *chaebols* for survival. At the expense of consumer goods, the government promoted the import of raw materials and technology, and encouraged savings and investment over consumption. By 1980 the government was gradually removing itself from direct involvement in industry and these anticonsumer policies began to be reversed. In the 1980s labor unions gained significant wage increases, which contributed to the growth in consumer consumption.

Japan
GDP: $4.417 trillion; GDP per capita: $33,800
A common perception of the post–World War II Japanese economic miracle is that it happened as a result of very close cooperation between the government and business, with the leading role in

establishing what is often called "Japan, Inc." played by MITI (the Ministry of International Trade and Industry). In reality, the story is much more complicated.

In some cases, coordination by the government did play an important role, such as in helping Japanese construction equipment manufacturers and computer producers become internationally competitive. But the main driving force for the Japanese economic success from the 1950s to the early 1970s, just as almost a century before that, came from private initiative and spurring technological innovation based on entrepreneurial spirit and high human capital. Japan was also helped by the overall favorable business conditions in the world economy, low energy prices, expanding international trade, as well as by the fact that it didn't have to spend almost anything on military build-up.

Japan remains the world's second most powerful economy, and its potential of human capital is as strong as ever. It has also proven more than once in its history that it is capable of rebounding from failures.

Vietnam
GDP: $222.5 billion: GDP per capita: $2,600

Vietnam negotiated an end to the United States' postwar economic embargo in 1994, and restored diplomatic relations the following year. From 1993 to 1997, GDP growth rates averaged around 9 percent per year. The 1997 Asian financial crisis prompted the government to reassess the dangers of an unbridled market economy and to slow the pace of reform. The 2001 United States-Vietnam Bilateral Trade Agreement is expected to improve Vietnam's exports to the United States, and to bring further legal and structural reform to Vietnam.

Thailand
GDP: $519.9 billion; GDP per capita: $8,000

Thailand is a southeast Asian nation known for extremely high levels of economic growth in the 1980s and 1990s, before weakness in its financial system contributed to the Asian financial crisis of 1997. With the American military withdrawal from Southeast Asia in the early 1970s, the Thai government shifted its policy focus to promoting exports. Consequently, the GDP growth rate declined somewhat, but was maintained at an average of 7.2 percent in the 1970s. Between 1985 and 1995 Thailand's average growth rate climbed to 9 percent, the highest in the world. Speculative pressure undermined the country's financial and monetary system and triggered the 1997 crisis.

India
GDP: $2.965 trillion; GDP per capita: $2,700

India's population is frugal, saving over 22 percent of the rupees they earn, but unreliable rainfall forces many of India's 700 million rural inhabitants to borrow money at high rates of interest to buy food. The state government tries to remedy the situation, but is hampered by high inflation and poor transportation. Additionally, the privatization of state run businesses (by selling them off or trying to make them competitive by encouraging joint foreign ventures), has led to foreign-owned, but Indian administered industry that seeks profitable global markets, rather than developing Indian markets.

Although a stock market and banking system has existed in India since the days of the Dutch and British East Indies companies, government debt, public poverty, and distrust of foreign corruption has led to an increasing reliance on a strong central bank and regional stock markets for funding growth. Since 1986 the Mumbai Stock Exchange helped fund this growth, but foreign corruption scandals hurt the Indian banks and stock exchanges in 2001. India's economy and stock market have attracted foreign investors, and a corporate and entrepreneurial class has emerged.

Australia
GDP: $766.8 billion; GDP per capita: $37,500

Per capita GDP in Australia is on a level with the major West European economies, and a strong domestic economy has enabled Australia to be resilient in dealing with the international economic downturn. However, Australia's economy lags behind the United States by about six months, and thus may begin to show some weakness, especially if its trade situation worsens.

New Zealand
GDP: $112.6 billion; GDP per capita: $27,300

Though New Zealand's per capita incomes have been rising, they remain below the level of the Economic Union's four largest economies. Since New Zealand is still heavily dependent on trade to drive growth, it has been affected by the global economic slowdown and the slump in commodity prices. Thus far the New Zealand economy has been relatively resilient, but the New Zealand business cycle, like that of Australia, tends to lag the U.S. cycle by about six months.

Africa and the Middle East

South Africa
GDP: $467.6 billion; GDP per capita: $10,600

South Africa is a middle-income developing country with abundant resources and well developed financial, legal, communications, energy, and transport sectors. Its stock exchange ranks among the 10 largest in the world, accompanied by a wide infrastructure supporting ongoing major shipments exported to all major markets of the globe.

Fighting poverty has been a long, hard battle. In 1996 the government issued the four-year-long Growth, Employment and Redistribution plan, better known as GEAR, committing to open markets, privatization, and an investment climate that brought a greater discipline to the economy. Some success was evident, but by 2000 it became clear that GEAR failed in two of its chief objectives: to boost employment and empower the black population with more middle-class mobility.

Afghanistan
GDP: $35 billion; GDP per capita: $1,000

Afghanistan has not experienced an industrial revolution, thanks to its rugged terrain and near-constant state of war. The major industries in Afghanistan remain nearly unchanged since the country's founding in 1774. The major industries are textiles and rugs, fruits and nuts, wool, cotton, fertilizer, soap, fossil fuels, and gemstones. Exports include opium, fruits and nuts, hand-woven carpets, wool, cotton, hides and pelts, and precious and semi-precious gems.

In 2002 $4.5 billion was collected at the Tokyo Donors Conference for Afghan Reconstruction to be distributed to the newly formed Afghan Interim Authority. Funding went to building infrastructure for the war-torn Afghanistan, including education, health and sanitation facilities, and rebuilding of roads.

Pakistan
GDP: $446.1 billion; GDP per capita: $2,600

Poverty, healthcare, education, and basic infrastructure problems plague 40 percent of the population in Pakistan. Agriculture employs about half of the 38 million workers, producing cotton, rice, wheat, and sugar cane. Textiles are a key export; implementation of (*Sharia*) Islamic law prohibiting the charging of interest for loans began in July 2001 for the State Bank of Pakistan in Karachi, but money market rates remain high at 10 percent. However consistent import-export trade with the United States, Japan, Germany, and the United Kingdom indicate that Pakistan can participate in the global market if it is self-sufficient. Currently it imports 30 percent of its energy, but has significant hydrocarbon reserves that are being developed with foreign companies.

Iran
GDP: $852.6 billion; GDP per capita: $12,300

The lion's share of the country's budget goes to state organizations. Most private businesses are located in the non-oil sector, and are likely tied to the black market. Banking and stock exchange systems are state-controlled, and foreign investment is limited to partnerships with state energy development projects. During the 20th century, decades of capitalistic growth were followed by revolutions, wars, and Middle East strife, leaving Iran with few capitalist ventures. The strict enforcement of conservative Muslim beliefs allows for only a small internal consumer population. Its estimated labor force of 18 million is connected mainly to the oil industry with the global economy. Until state control of the oil economy becomes privatized, capitalism will be restricted to only about 10–20 percent of the GDP. State-sponsored privatizing attempts in industry have had little impact to date.

Saudi Arabia
GDP: $572.2 billion; GDP per capita: $20,700

A number of factors suggest that the Saudi economy will not become fully privatized or capitalist. These are: the small size of the Saudi population, the nature of the global oil industry, the large desert area it controls, the limited water supply, and Islamic beliefs. While Saudi Arabia can be self-sufficient and reasonably comfortable fiscally, these factors work against a traditional capitalism economy of varied surplus production for both domestic and international consumers.

Europe

The Euro

Since January 1999 the world has witnessed one of the most profound and far-reaching economic events of modern history. The European Union launched the final stage of Economic and Monetary Union (EMU), creating a new trans-European currency—the euro, which was adopted by 11 member states. The euro became a physical reality across Europe on January 1, 2002, enacting the biggest monetary changeover in history. Britain and Denmark chose not to participate. Sweden was not eligible because it had not been part of the European Monetary System.

The euro's core economic benefits are: eliminating the need to exchange currencies of EMU members, saving billions of dollars a year; reducing volatility among EMU currencies; rapid economic and financial integration among EMU members; a European Central Bank that may conduct a more expansionary monetary policy than the generally restrictive one practically imposed in the past; and greater economic discipline for countries such as Italy and Greece, that seem unwilling or unable to put their houses in order.

The most serious unresolved problem that the establishment of an ECB and the euro may create is how an EMU member state will respond to asymmetric economic shocks. It is almost inevitable that a large and diverse single-currency area such as the euro area will face periodic disturbances that will affect various member nations differently, and drive their economies out of alignment. In such a case, there is practically nothing that a nation so adversely affected can do. The nation cannot use monetary policy to overcome its particular problem, and fiscal discipline will also prevent it from using this policy to deal with the problem.

United Kingdom
GDP: $2.147 trillion; GDP per capita: $35,300

In the 1960s the UK's traditionally strong economy was beset by the "British disease": low productivity, stop-go macroeconomic policy, and trade union militancy. When Margaret Thatcher became Prime Minister in 1979, she took office with the goal of reversing that malaise—making her, in this as well as other respects, the British counterpart to Ronald Reagan, who was elected president of the United States the following year. Thatcher's Conservative party succeeded in freeing up the British market, reducing stagnating government regulations, and encouraging a new era of entrepreneurialism.

Since 1997 the UK has been governed by a Labour administration led by Tony Blair and (since 2007) Gordon Brown. Preaching a "Third Way" between capitalism and socialism, Labour has taken a cautious approach marked by a distinct preference for free market principles in its management of the British economy. It has also successfully declined to participate in the European currency, mindful of deep divisions within British society over European issues generally.

While the UK's condition certainly appears healthier than in the past, persistent systemic problems remain. Many of the new jobs created since the early 1990s are part-time, short-term, and poorly-paid, leading to suggestions that Britain is resigning itself to becoming the principal low-wage economy of Western Europe. Manufacturing has barely recovered from earlier traumas, and as in the past suffers from underinvestment and low productivity. Growing pressures of globalization will challenge the United Kingdom and its leaders.

France
GDP: $2.067 trillion; GDP per capita: $33,800

Unemployment has been stubbornly high in France since the 1980s, and the French economic system remains one in which the benefits of growth are concentrated in particular areas, while other regions are in long-term decline. A progressive system of taxation solves some problems, but there is a sense that the postwar French state and economy has nevertheless concentrated its benefits and growth on the middle and upper-classes. As France has become more integrated into a European and global economy, it has also become clear that French government has much less latitude in imposing its own solutions to economic problems. This became abundantly clear in the early 1980s when François Mitterrand was forced by global markets to abandon his program of nationalization and state intervention; and in fact reversed this strategy, becoming the socialist president who introduced privatization to France.

Spain
GDP: $1.362 trillion; GDP per capita: $33,700

A flood of products and a host of well-conceived governmental programs have made Spain one of the four leading Western European economies. Its economy ranks it fifth in overall Europe, and tenth among the world's industrialized nations.

The local administration historically supports privatization of the economy, as well as liberalization and deregulation. Some tax reforms have helped the economy, but the country continues to battle unemployment. While Spain's unemployment stands at 14 percent—the highest of the EU countries—the rate is falling.

Portugal
GDP: $232 billion; GDP per capita: $21,800

One of the smallest European countries, Portugal nevertheless stands tall in the eyes of global economic forecasters. Its GDP is high, its unemployment low (four percent) and its government possesses a practical view of what it takes to keep a country like Portugal growing. Portugal's economy is service based. The parliamentarian government has privatized many state-controlled entities. Over the last decade, except for a brief recession in the 2001–02 season, economic growth has surpassed the EU average, despite a poor education system that has hampered productivity.

Italy
GDP: $1.8 trillion; GDP per capita: $31,000

Italian capitalism remains an anomaly, and is negatively influenced by several factors: the low standard of living of the middle and working classes, the social and economic impasse of the southern regions of the country, the ambiguous role of the government in industrial production, and the inefficiency of the state bureaucracy. Still, the Italian capitalist system is nonetheless considered capable of assuring one of the most sustained economic developments within industrialized countries.

Until privatization started during the 1990s, 40 percent of the Italian manufacturing industry was controlled by the state, as was 80 percent of all banking operations. Such a massive presence of the state in the national economy had both positive and negative effects. In the 1950s and 1960s state intervention played a major role in creating the material conditions of the so-called "Italian economic miracle." The state succeeded in establishing several new chemical, engineering, and energy industries in which private Italian companies had been unwilling to invest. Yet the vast intervention of the state in the national economy also resulted in considerable corruption. The governing parties, especially the Christian Democrats and, in the 1980s, the Socialists, took direct hold of the public sector and supplied jobs in exchange for votes.

Germany
GDP: $2.833 trillion; GDP per capita: $34,400

Germany, which headed the efforts to unite Europe economically, still suffers from the effects of World War II and the treatment of other groups in Europe. Charges of political extremism are still common, and scars remain from reunification with East Germany.

The German economy is often described as a social market economy based on industry and the service sector. Free enterprise is sometimes subordinate to political goals, and exports are key for the long-term. The emerging East German market has increased imports, and may help to increase domestic consumption as its citizens transition to capitalism. A new generation and economy will have to grow out of the two older economies of the pre-unification era.

Switzerland
GDP: $300.9 billion; GDP per capita: $39,800

The Swiss economy is one of the most prosperous and aggressive economies on the globe, ranking among the top 20 states in the world. Its per capita income, virtually the highest in the world, is matched by its wage scale, which is the envy of workers everywhere. With a highly successful market-based economy founded on international trade and banking, Switzerland's standard of living, worker productivity, quality of education, and health care serve as models of a near-utopian society. Inflation is low, but some unemployment exists.

Russia

GDP: $2.076 trillion; GDP per capita: $14,600

Since 1999 the Russian economy has been recovering from a post-Soviet contraction. This recovery, besides starting from a very low base, is also very much dependent on the rising prices of natural resources. Structural reforms continue to lag, and the industrial base is increasingly dilapidated and must be replaced or modernized if the country is to achieve sustainable economic growth. Other well-known problems include widespread corruption, and lack of a strong legal system.

The inefficiencies of the new Russian capitalism were clearly manifested in a spectacular failure of its privatization program, once hailed as one of the most successful among the economies in transition. Privatized firms have not been transferred to new owners who could put their assets to the most efficient use. Instead, they ended up under the control of the "Russian Mafia," which derives its income not from increasing the market value of the firm, but from diverting revenues and engaging in asset-stripping.

The Americas

Venezuela

GDP: $335 billion; GDP per capita: $12,800

A founding member of the Organization of Petroleum Exporting Countries (OPEC) cartel in 1960, Venezuela's economy became firmly yoked to the volatile oil market in the 1970s and 1980s. Compounding the problems brought on by its oil dependency and lack of economic diversification, the country's political leaders mired it in corruption, inefficiency, and a bloated civil service. The country also suffered instability as an intermediate point for the illegal drug trade originating in Colombia. Austerity measures induced by decades of overspending and a sudden drop in oil prices in the late 1980s brought about civil unrest, and an attempted military coup in 1992. The leader of that coup, Hugo Chávez Frias, was democratically elected as a civilian leader in 1998 and again in 2000 on a pledge to stem corruption and spread economic development to rural areas.

Chile
GDP: $234.4 billion; GDP per capita: $14,400

In 1970 the socialist Salvador Allende was elected president of Chile, and immediately nationalized foreign corporations (which in the case of Anaconda and Kennicott copper had turned an $80 million investment into a $4 billion return for the North American owners). He also established redistributive policies and price controls, which scared off international investors. U.S. support helped bring about a military coup in 1973, which installed Augusto Pinochet; foreign investment was once again encouraged.

Despite attempts to gain immunity from prosecution, the Pinochet regime began to face criticism and growing unrest in the late 1980s. The military stayed in the background, and civilian-elected governments returned. While Pinochet, who had named himself senator for life, was on a medical visit to Britain in 1998, he was arrested and held by a Spanish judge for crimes against humanity. That act of international conscience brought the human rights community back to life in Chile, and although Pinochet was never jailed, he is no longer part of public conversation. There is substantial criticism of Chile's privatized social security, and little praise in Chile for the neoliberal economic model. However many Western economists think that Chile's economy makes it a logical target for expansion of the North American Free Trade Act.

Colombia
GDP: $320.4 billion; GDP per capita: $7,200

Although Colombia is the second biggest producer of coffee (after Brazil), its illegal drug trade is a major economic contributor. Trade balances can be made positive with illegal sales, even though they are negative for legitimate goods. Drug dealers spend money to grow their businesses, which sometimes benefits Colombians more than

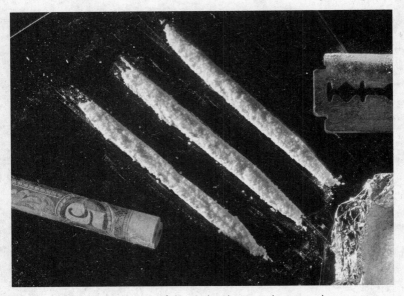

Cocaine is an integral part of the Colombian underground economy.

the legitimate economy does. By the end of the 20th century, opium poppy cultivation and heroin trafficking had increased considerably.

At present Colombia faces economic challenges including pension reform and reducing unemployment. The exportation of coffee and oil also face difficulties—the coffee harvest and prices are depressed, and to offset declining oil production, new exploration is needed. The threat of guerilla groups remains a concern for business leaders and investors.

Argentina

GDP: $523.7 billion; GDP per capita: $13,000

In 1989 Argentine president Carlos Menem implemented a staunchly neoliberal program of economic reforms that included rapid trade and capital account liberalization, and the widespread privatization of state enterprises. Privatization and the curtailment of the role of the state in the economy resulted in the rapid concentration of wealth, the erosion of the middle class, and the weakening of labor unions.

The cornerstone of Menem's policy was the Convertibility Plan, a monetary policy based on a fixed exchange rate between the Argentine and U.S. currency. It relied on heavy inflows of foreign capital, but the Mexican peso crisis of 1995 and the southeast Asian crisis of 1997 dried up those flows. The possibility of a balance of payments crisis emerged, and the IMF demanded the implementation of austerity measures. In 1998 the economy entered a recession that lasted until 2002.

In 2002 President Eduardo Duhalde declared an end to the fixed exchange rate, and the largest default of sovereign debt in history.

Mexico
GDP: $1.353 trillion; GDP per capita: $12,500

In August 1982 Mexico was the first domino to fall in the Latin American debt crisis. A recession engineered by the Reagan administration to reduce inflation in the United States resulted in a sharp increase in international interest rates, and a significant drop in the price of oil, Mexico's main export. Unable to make payments on its foreign debt, Mexico declared a moratorium. The International Monetary Fund stepped in with financial resources to make payments on condition that the country implement austerity measures and the liberalization of the economy. The administration of Miguel de la Madrid (1982–88) struggled to revive the domestic economy while implementing IMF policies. In 1986 Mexico joined the General Agreement on Trade and Tariffs and 743 state enterprises were privatized or shut down between 1982 and 1988. Nevertheless, de la Madrid was unable to control inflation until the implementation of the Pacto de Solidaridad in 1987, which froze wages and prices in an attempt to stave off inflation without further economic contraction.

The North American Free Trade Agreement (NAFTA) went into effect in 1994. The next year political instability and investor anxiety led to a sharp devaluation of the peso that required a $40 billion bailout by the IMF and the U.S. Treasury Department, launching a series of financial crises in emerging market economies.

Although the economy recovered rapidly from the 1995 crisis, growth has remained sluggish and highly dependent on the U.S. economy, which currently absorbs 90 percent of Mexico's exports. Under NAFTA Mexican manufactures have gained unrestricted access to U.S. markets, boosting the economies of Mexico's northern region where the infrastructure and semi-skilled labor necessary for industrial production is concentrated. However NAFTA has increased concerns about the fate of hundreds of thousands of peasants, primarily in the central and southern regions, whose survival is endangered by rising imports of subsidized U.S. corn. The intended beneficiaries of proposed infrastructure development in these regions (such as Plan Puebla-Panama), many of them indigenous people, are deeply rooted in their lands. Attempts to integrate them as wage laborers into a modern, export-oriented economy are likely to meet resistance as this represents a threat to their cultures.

Canada
GDP: $1.274 trillion; GDP per capita: $38,200

The Canada-USA Free Trade Agreement created a free trade zone in 1989. With suspicion toward the United States, many Canadian provinces opposed the project, but Québec was strongly in favor from the beginning. The North American Free Trade Agreement (NAFTA) was launched in January 1994 with the goal of fostering greater economic growth in Canada, the United States, and Mexico by removing barriers to trade and investment among the three nations. Even though commercial conflicts have appeared (such as the U.S. surtax on Canadian wood, and a series of American branches and factories closing in Canada to reopen in Mexico), free trade is still presented as a way of constructing closer commercial relations between neighbors. Although government measuring practices and methods about labor have changed during the 1990s, unemployment remains Canada's main challenge for the new century.

United States of America
GDP: $13.86 trillion; GDP per capita: $46,000

The world's largest economy is in the United States. A quick summary begins after World War II: One unfortunate result of the extended boom in the economy experienced after World War II was a rise in price inflation throughout the 1950s, 1960s, and 1970s, peaking in the early 1980s. Perhaps the most difficult period occurred in the 1970s when the nation experienced stagflation, an economic slowdown and rise in prices caused, in part, by a sudden spike in oil prices. The Vietnam War is also considered to be responsible for some of the economic problems of this period.

Inflation was a serious concern throughout the Eisenhower, Kennedy, and Johnson administrations, but not a major political issue until Nixon's presidency. Nixon tried to curb inflation by implementing a series of price controls on goods, wages, and rents. The subsequent inflation surge when controls were lifted discredited price controls as a tool for the federal government. During the Ford administration and every administration since, inflation has become the province of the American central bank, the Federal Reserve. The Fed used monetary policies to battle inflation, a less aggressive and often more successful tool than price controls.

Nevertheless, the Fed had only limited success. Inflation fell somewhat but the most dramatic effect was on unemployment. The problems of trying to moderate inflation without throwing the economy into recession became a major problem for the Fed, and a key political issue. This became even more problematic with the growing power of OPEC and the Arab oil boycott of the United States. The Carter administration faced stagflation, and later a crisis in Iran after the fall of the American supported regime of the Shah.

The Iran Hostage Crisis had a transformative effect on American politics, helping to elect Ronald Reagan to the presidency in 1980. The Reagan presidency was marked by aggressive foreign policy actions and rhetoric. In many ways, the Reagan presidency represented a return to the "big stick" policies that have epitomized

American foreign policy since the earliest days. The unprovoked invasion of the tiny island of Grenada, although not significant in military terms, demonstrated that the United States had emerged from the malaise that had followed the lost war in Vietnam. The Grenada invasion, interventions in Central America, and a general perception that the Reagan administration was willing to use force in order to achieve its objectives, played a key symbolic role in the resurrection of American superpower clout.

Subsequent administrations continued this approach, employing U.S. troops in Panama, the Persian Gulf, Kosovo, and other venues. In 2003 George W. Bush used U.S. troops to oust Saddam Hussein, dictator of Iraq, a strategically important Persian Gulf nation. The Iraq invasion was strongly opposed by many nations and, most significantly, by other permanent members of the U.N. Security Council. Thus, it marked a clear move away from multilateralism in a conflict beyond the Western Hemisphere.

A series of investment bubbles—the dot-com stock mania that burst in 2000, followed by the housing boom and bust—hurt the reputation of the Federal Reserve under Alan Greenspan, because its low interest-rate policy beginning in 2003 was central to creating the credit boom and subprime mortgage mania. Losses generated by the economic crisis of 2007–09 are estimated to exceed $2 trillion, more than the entire GDP of many countries.

Chapter 7

Must-Reading for Capitalists

Because capitalism encompasses so much, where you go from here is up to you. Maybe you are interested in the theory behind everything, either a historical text like Adam Smith's, or something a little more recent by John Kenneth Galbraith or John Maynard Keynes. Maybe you want to read about socialism's critiques of capitalism as presented by Marx or Schumpeter. Maybe something like Ayn Rand's *The Fountainhead* is more up your alley—a novel illustrating and lionizing her pro-capitalist views. To help you move on from here, we have some excerpts of major capitalist works—a taste of must-reading for capitalists.

1776
An Inquiry into the Nature and Causes of the Wealth of Nations
by Adam Smith

The Wealth of Nations, published in 1776, ranks as one of the most influential books ever written, and is still a useful source for economists today. One of his most important contributions to modern economic thought was the concept of the "division of labor," which he discusses in the excerpt below.

To take an example. . . the trade of the pin-maker. . . One man draws out the wire, another straights it, a third cuts it, a fourth points it, a fifth grinds it at the top for receiving the head; to make the head requires two or three distinct operations; to put it on, is a peculiar business, to whiten the pins is another; it is even a trade by itself to put them into the paper; and the important business of making a pin is, in this manner, divided into about eighteen distinct operations, which, in some manufactories, are all performed by distinct hands, though in others the same man will sometimes perform two or three of them. . . . Each person might be considered as making four thousand eight hundred pins in a day. But if they had all wrought separately and independently, and without any of them having been educated to this peculiar business, they certainly could not each of them have made twenty, perhaps not one pin in a day. . . . In every other art and manufacture, the effects of the division of labour are similar to what they are in this very trifling one; though, in many of them, the labour can neither be so much subdivided, nor reduced to so great a simplicity of operation. The division of labour, however, so far as it can be introduced, occasions, in every art, a proportionable increase of the productive powers of labour. The separation of different trades and employments from one another, seems to have taken place, in consequence of this advantage. This separation too is generally carried furthest in those countries which enjoy the highest degree of industry and improvement. . . .

1826

Elements of Political Economy
by James Mill

James Mill (1773–1836) was a Scottish economist, philosopher, and historian. He was one of the first modern thinkers to try to deal with the economic changes arising from the early phases of the Industrial

Revolution. In this excerpt from his 1826 masterwork *Elements of Political Economy*, Mill talks about the role of the laborer and how his wages should be apportioned.

Begin by supposing a certain number of capitalists, with a certain quantity of food, raw material, and instruments, or machinery; that there is also a certain number of labourers; and that the proportion, in which the commodities produced are divided between them, has fixed itself. . . .

Let us next suppose, that the labourers have increased in number one half, without any increase in the quantity of capital. There is the same quantity of the requisites for the employment of labour; that is, of food, tools, and material, as there was before; but for every 100 labourers there are now 150.

There will be 50 men, therefore, in danger of being left out of employment. To prevent their being left out of employment they have but one resource; they must endeavour to supplant those who have forestalled the employment; that is, they must offer to work for a smaller reward. Wages, therefore, decline.

If we suppose, on the other hand, that the quantity of capital has increased, while the number of labourers remains the same, the effect will be reversed. . . .

If it were the natural tendency of capital to increase faster than population, there would be no difficulty in preserving a prosperous condition of the people. If, on the other hand, it were the natural tendency of population to increase faster than capital, the difficulty would be very great.

There would be a perpetual tendency in wages to fall. The progressive fall of wages would produce a greater and a greater degree of poverty among the people.... By whatever proportion the population tended to increase faster than capital, such a proportion of those who were born would die: the ratio of increase in capital and population would then remain the same, and the fall of wages would proceed no farther. . . .

1857

Eyewitness to Wall Street

by David Colbert

The boom-and-bust cycles of American finance are a frustratingly well-established aspect of economic history. After a period of rapid growth in the 1850s, in the summer of 1857, stock prices began to fall from their inflated values, and banks began to fail. In this excerpt from David Colbert's *Eyewitness to Wall Street*, he discusses the Panic of 1857 as seen through the eyes of New York City lawyer and diarist George Templeton Strong.

People's faces in Wall Street look fearfully gaunt and desperate. There are two or three millionaire friends of mine whose expression is enough to knock off three per cent a month extra from the market value of their paper. I know of at least two "great houses" that are trembling to their foundations. No merchant or banker, no man who has an obligation outstanding, can feel sage unless he has the needful gold in his own custody. He may be worth any amount in stocks and bonds and land, yet be unable to raise five thousand dollars a week hence.

The Bowery Bank stopped yesterday. So did the little "East River Bank," I believe. . . .

Morning was cloudy. From Hanover Street to Nassau, both sidewalks were densely packed with business men, capitalists, and operators. It was a most "respectable" mob, good-natured and cheerful in its outward aspect but quivering and tingling with excitement. They laughed nervously, and I saw more than one crying.

October 14. We have burst. All the banks declined paying specie this morning, with the ridiculous exception of the Chemical, which is a little private shaving-shop of the Joneses with no depositors but its own stockholders.

October 22. Walking down Broadway you pass great $200,000 buildings begun last spring or summer that have gone up two stories, and stopped, and may stand unfinished and desolate for years, or on

The United States had bank runs in 1819, 1837, 1857, 1873, and 1893.

which six Celts are working instead of sixty. Almost every shop has its placards (written, not printed) announcing a great sacrifice, vast reduction of prices, sales at less than cost. In Wall Street every man carried Pressure, Anxiety, Loss, written on his forehead. This is by far the worst period of public calamity and distress I've ever seen, and I fear it is but the beginning.

1899

The Theory of the Leisure Class: An Economic Study of Institutions
by Thorstein Veblen

Thorstein Veblen (1857–1929) was a Norwegian-born American economist who used such diverse fields as psychology, sociology, and anthropology to develop the concept of evolutionary economics, the core ideas of which he illustrated in his 1899 work, *The Theory of the Leisure Class.*

Veblen argued that economics was driven by powerful forces rooted in a shared social past. In this excerpt, Veblen compares the laboring class's approach to work with that of the "superior" or ruling class.

These lower classes can not avoid labour, and the imputation of labour is therefore not greatly derogatory to them, at least not within their class. Rather, since labour is their recognized and accepted mode of life, they take some emulative pride in a reputation for efficiency in their work, this being often the only line of emulation open to them. . . .

But it is otherwise with the superior pecuniary class, with which we are here immediately concerned. For this class also the incentive to diligence and thrift is not absent; but its action is so greatly qualified by the secondary demands of pecuniary emulation, that any inclination in this direction is practically overborne and any incentive to diligence tends to be of no effect. The most imperative of these secondary demands of emulation, as well as the one of widest scope, is the requirement of abstention from productive work.

In order to gain and hold the esteem of men it is not sufficient merely to possess wealth or power. The wealth or power must be put in evidence, for esteem is awarded only on evidence. And not only does the [display] of wealth serve to impress one's importance on others and keep their sense of his importance alive and alert, but it is of scarcely less use in building up and preserving one's self-complacency. In all but the lowest stages of culture the normally constitute man is comforted and upheld in his self-respect by "decent surroundings" and by exemption from "menial offices." Enforced departure from his habitual standard of decency, either in the paraphernalia of life or in the kind and amount of his everyday activity, is felt to be a slight upon his human dignity, even apart from all conscious consideration of the approval or disapproval of his fellows.

1936

The General Theory of Employment, Interest and Money
by John Maynard Keynes

British economist John Maynard Keynes (1883–1946) was arguably the most influential force in 20th century political-economic thought. By the 1960s, "Keynesian economics" had largely overtaken the older theories of laissez-faire capitalism, mostly due to the principle laid out in his 1936 work *The General Theory of Employment, Interest and Money*, excerpted below. His General Theory introduced a generation of political leaders to the idea of macroeconomics and the role Keynes felt the government should play in the stabilization and development of their national economies.

In a given state of technique, resources and costs, the employment of a given volume of labour by an entrepreneur involves him in two kinds of expense: first of all, the amounts which he pays out to the factors of production (exclusive of other entrepreneurs) for their current services, which we shall call the factor cost of the employment in question; and secondly, the amounts which he pays out to other entrepreneurs for what he as to purchase from them together with the sacrifice which he incurs by employing the equipment instead of leaving it idle, which we shall call the user cost of the employment in question.

The excess of the value of the resulting output over the sum of its factor cost and its user cost is the profit, or as we shall call it, the income of the entrepreneur. The factor cost is, of course, the same thing, looked at from the point of view of the entrepreneur, as what the factors of production regard as their income.

Thus the factor cost and the entrepreneur's profit make up what we shall define as the total income resulting from the employment given by the entrepreneur. The entrepreneur's profit thus defined is, as it should be, the quantity which he endeavours to maximise when he is decided what amount of employment to offer. . . .

It follows that in a given situation of technique, resources and facto cost per unit of employment, the amount of employment, both in each individual firm and industry and in the aggregate, depends on the amount of the proceeds which the entrepreneurs expect to receive from the corresponding output. For entrepreneurs will endeavour to fix the amount of employment at the level which they expect to maximise the excess of the proceeds over the factor cost.

1942

Capitalism, Socialism & Democracy
by Joseph A. Schumpeter

Joseph A. Schumpeter (1883–1950) was a European economist and political philosopher who spent much of his career at Harvard. Because Schumpeter's economic ideas ran counter to the Keynesian principles coming into vogue at the height of his career, his contributions to economic philosophy have often been overlooked, but today he has many adherents. In this excerpt from his 1942 book *Capitalism, Socialism and Democracy*, Schumpeter discusses the ways in which economic necessity tends to produce rationality.

Capitalism develops rationality and adds a new edge to it in two interconnected ways.

First it exults the monetary unit—not itself a creation of capitalism—into a unit of account, a tool of rational cost-profit calculations, of which the towering monument is double-entry bookkeeping. We will notice that, primarily a product of the evolution of economic rational, the cost-profit calculus in turn reacts upon that rationality; by crystallizing and defining numerically, it powerfully propels the logic of enterprise. And thus defined and quantified for the economic sector, this type of logic or attitude or method then starts upon its conqueror's career subjugating—rationalizing—man's tools and philosophies, his medical practice, his picture of the cosmos, his outlook on life, everything in fact in including his concepts of beauty and justice and his spiritual ambition.

In the 15th century mathematics was mainly concerned with questions of commercial arithmetic and the problems of the architect. The utilitarian mechanical device, invented by men of the craftsman type, stood at the source of modern physics.

The rugged individualism of Galileo was the individualism of the rising capitalist class. The surgeon began to rise above the midwife and the barber. The artist who at the same time was an engineer and an entrepreneur—the type immortalized by such men as Vinci,

Alberti, Cellini; even Durer busied himself with plans for fortifications—illustrates best what I mean. By curing it all, scholastic professors in the Italian universities showed more sense than we give them credit for. The trouble was not with individual unorthodox propositions. Any decent schoolman could be trusted to twist his texts as to fit the Copernican system. But those professors quite rightly sensed the spirit behind such exploits—the spirit of rationalist individualism, the spirit generated by rising capitalism. . . .

1943

The Fountainhead
by Ayn Rand

Ayn Rand was a Russian-born American novelist and philosopher. An opponent of socialism, religion, and other forms of collectivism, Rand's works focused on individualism and the role of the individual in a capitalist society. Her 1943 novel *The Fountainhead* was her first major literary success. Her main protagonist, Harold Roark, is a promising young architect who would rather labor in obscurity than compromise his artistic vision. Toward the end of the novel, Roark is on trial for sabotage. The following excerpt is taken from part of Roark's argument to his jury.

No creator was prompted by a desire to serve his brothers, for his brothers rejected the gift he offered and that the gift destroyed the slothful routine of their lives. His truth was his only motive. . . .

"But the mind is an attribute of the individual. There is no such thing as a collective brain. There is no such thing as a collective thought. An agreement reached by a group of men is only a compromise or an average drawn upon many individual thoughts. It is a secondary consequence. The primary act—the process of reason—must be performed by each man alone. We can divide a meal among many men. We cannot digest it in a collective stomach. No man can use his lungs to breathe for another man. No man can use his brain to think for another. All the functions of body and spirit are private. They cannot be shared or transferred.

"We inherit the products of the thought of other men. We inherit the wheel. We make a cart. The cart becomes an automobile. The automobile becomes an airplane. But all through the process of what we received from others is only the end product of their thinking. The moving force is the creative faculty which take this product as material, uses it and originates the next step. This creative faculty cannot be given or received, shared or borrowed. It becomes to single, individual men. That which it creates is the property of the creator. Men learn from one another. But all learning is only the exchange of material. No man can give other the capacity to think. Yet that capacity is our only means of survival. . . ."

1944

The Road to Serfdom
by Friedrich A. Hayek

Friedrich Hayek (1899–1992) was a Nobel Prize–winning economist and political philosopher. His 1944 work *The Road to Serfdom,* excerpted below, became a bestseller despite wartime rationing, and even today is considered among the most influential books of the 20th century. Among it's fans were British Prime Minster Margaret Thatcher and President Ronald Reagan, both of whom folded Hayek's principles into their economic plans in the 1980s.

Our generation likes to flatter itself that it attaches less weight to economic considerations than did its parents or grandparents. The "End of the Economic Man" bids fair to become one of the governing myths of our age. . . .

Nor can their be much doubt that in their beliefs and aspirations men are today more than ever before governed by economic doctrines, by the carefully foisted belief in the irrationality of our economic system, by the false assertions about "potential plenty" pseudo-theories about the inevitable trend toward monopoly, and the impression created by certain much-advertised occurrences such as the destruction of stocks of raw materials or the suppression of invention, for which competition is blamed, though they are precisely the sort of thing which could not happen under completion and which are made possible only by monopoly and usually by government-aided monopoly.

. . . Though it is natural that, as the world around us becomes more complex, our resistance grows against the forces which, without our understanding them, constantly interfere with individual hopes and plans, it is just in these circumstances that it becomes less and less possible for anyone to fully understand these forces. A complex civilization like ours is necessarily based on the individual's adjusting himself to changes whose cause and nature he cannot understand; why he should have more or less, why he should have to move to another occupation, why some things he wants should become more difficult to get than others, will always be connected with such a multitude of circumstances that no single mind will be able to grasp them; or, even worse, those affected will put the blame on an obvious immediate and avoidable cause, which the more complex interrelationships which determine the change remains inevitably hidden to them. . . .

1958

The Affluent Society
by John Kenneth Galbraith

Harvard economist John Kenneth Galbraith (1908–2006) was a Keynesian adherent with a deep and abiding belief in American progressivism and liberalism, making him the perfect public face for the post–World War II generation. Written in 1958, *The Affluent Society* was the most popular of Galbraith's four major books and more than 1,000 articles, as he sought to define wealth in the new American economy. In the following excerpt, Galbraith explains that the widespread poverty of earlier eras was still defining American economic policy, even as society was growing in wealth and stability.

The ideas by which the people of this favored part of the world [the United States] interpret their existence. . . were the product of a world in which poverty had always been a man's normal lot and an other state was in degree unimaginable. This poverty was not the elegant torture of the spirit which comes from contemplating another man's more spacious possessions. It was the unedifying mortification of the flesh—from hunger, sickness and cold. . . .

. . . One would not expect that the preoccupations of a poverty-ridden world would be relevant in one where the ordinary individual has access to amenities—foods, entertainment, personal transportation, and plumbing—in which not even the rich rejoiced a century ago.

So great has been the change that many of the desires of the individual are not longer even evident to him. They become so only as they are synthesized, elaborated and nurtured by advertising and salesmanship, and these, in turn, have become among our most important and talented professions. Few people at the beginning of the 19th century needed an adman to tell them what they wanted.

It would be wrong to suggest that the economic ideas which once interpreted the world of mass poverty have made no adjustment to

John Kenneth Gailbraith at his desk in the 1940s.

the world of affluence. There have been many adjustments, including some that have gone unrecognized or have been poorly understood. But there has also been a remarkable resistance. And the total alteration in underlaying circumstances has not been squarely faced. As a result, we are guided, in part, by ideas that are relevant to another world; and as a further result, we do many things that are unnecessary, some that are unwise, and a few that are insane. Some are a threat to affluence itself.

1982

The Organization of Industry
by George Stigler

George Stigler (1911–91) was the recipient of the 1982 Nobel Prize and a key figure in the influential Chicago School of Economics. First published in 1982, *The Organization of Industry* is a collection of 23 essays written by Stigler over a period of more than 20 years. In this excerpt, Stigler discusses the role of competition in economics.

A main requirement of perfect competition is that the largest firm in an industry makes a trifling fraction of the industry's sales (or purchases), from which it follows that there are many firms in the industry. . . .

These many firms, no one of few of which account for an appreciable share of the industry's output, are assumed to act independently. . . . For it is a fact that there are insuperable difficulties in organizing an effective combination of many persons, when it is profitable for each person secretly to depart from the agreement. . . .

Such large numbers suggest that (perfect) economic competition is impersonal. In the economic race, there are 1,000 or 100,000 runners, and each gets a price proportional to his efforts. The fortunes of any one firm are independent of what happens to any other firm: one farmer is not benefited if his neighbor's crop is destroyed. The essence of perfect competition, therefore, is not strong rivalry but rather the utter dispersion of power to influence market behavior.

The power, for example, to restrict quantities sold and raise prices is effectively annihilated if it is spread over a thousand acres.

A third condition of perfect competition is complete knowledge of offers to buy and sell by the participants in the market. . . . The assumption that each seller knows what various buyers will pay, and vice versa, is necessary to keep the parties together—in the same market. . . .

These conditions of perfect competition are enough to insure that a single price will rule the market . . . and that this price is affected only negligibly by the actions of any one or few buyers or sellers. . . .The definition of perfect competition is therefore sometimes expressed in the equivalent form: the demand curve facing any one seller is infinitely elastic; and the supply curve facing any buyer is infinitely elastic.

1990

Barbarians at the Gate
by Bryan Burrough and John Helyar

The leveraged buyout of American conglomerate RJR Nabisco by Kohlberg Kravis Roberts & Company was one of the biggest business stories of the late 1980s and a prime example of corporate greed run amuck. In 1990, *Wall Street Journal* investigative reporters Brian Burrough and John Helyar published *Barbarians at the Gate: The Fall of RJR Nabisco*, their inside account of the buyout. In this excerpt, they talk about the public and private faces of the takeover.

Time magazine hit the newsstands Monday. . . . "A Game of Greed" the cover blared over a picture of a thoughtful Ross Johnson, hand on chin. "This man could pocket $100 million from the largest corporate takeover in history," it read. "Has the buyout craze gone too far?"

As bad as the cover was, the worst damage to Johnson was, as usual, self-inflicted. What about the outsize management agreement? "My job is to negotiate the best deal I can for my people." Does a chief executive deserve that kind of reward? "It's kind of Monopoly money." Wouldn't lots of people lose their jobs? Sure, Johnson said. "But the people that I have, particularly the Atlanta people, have very portable types of professions: accountants, lawyers, secretaries. It isn't that I would be putting them on the breadline. We have excellent severance arrangements."

That wasn't quite true. The special committee wanted each bidder to include employee-protection guarantees in their draft merger agreements, a notion the management group was stoutly resisting. The point would take on significance because a longtime employee was lobbying hard for the employee protection.

... Miller insisted on several points guaranteeing pay and benefits of RJR Nabisco employees for three years, giving remaining employees the right to quit with sweet severance packages if they were forced by RJR's new owners to move more than thirty-five miles, assuring that retirees' medical benefits would continue.

The Kohlberg Kravis lawyers didn't like Miller's ideas, but they negotiated them. The management group's lawyers wouldn't budge. Miller went back to the board members and peevishly let them know it. . . .

Johnson talked to Hugel Monday afternoon. "I won't even ask you if this will be a fair bid," he said. "If you ask me, 'Do I trust the people on the special committee' the answer is no."

2003 (covers 1880s on)
The Change-Makers: From Carnegie to Gates,
How the Great Entrepreneurs Transformed Ideas Into Industries
by Maury Klein

After the Civil War the American economy underwent tremendous development and change, which seemed to benefit owners and managers at the expense of the workers, who often toiled for long hours in dangerous conditions for low wages in the name of maximizing corporate profits. In this excerpt from Maury Klein's 2003 book *The Change-Makers: From Carnegie to Gates, How the Great Entrepreneurs*

Transformed Ideas Into Industries, the author explains why this concept of the greedy "robber baron" of the late 19th century is flawed.

Perhaps the worst fault of the "robber baron" concept is that it simply gets in the way of understanding who these men were and what they accomplished. As Michael Novak observed, "They left behind great institutions that have been socially productive for generations after their deaths. These men did more than make money. They were hugely ambitious, creative, sometimes vain, tough, and even ruthless ... and certainly not saints. . . The attempt to understand them under the heading 'greed' reveals both historical amnesia and ideological distortion."

Historian Joseph Frazier Wall, in his definitive biography of Andrew Carnegie, stressed that "whatever else Carnegie and Rockefeller may have been—ruthless, selfish, and wasteful of men and resources—they were ... empire builders, not extortionists, and it is that drive for imperium that distinguishes them from their partners."

There is a striking parallel between the rise of the great corporations and the process of political consolidation into nation-states. Both took place at roughly the same time in history; one sought to bring order out of economic chaos, the other out of political chaos. Both fused small, fiercely competing entities into large, more stable ones that did not eliminate competition so much as move it to a higher level. In both cases, successful leadership required a degree of vision and purpose lacking in petty chieftains. Put another way, the great entrepreneur is to a robber baron or businessman what a statesman is to a politician. Their greatness lies not only in what they do but in what they conceive.

2005
The World Is Flat: A Brief History of the Twenty-First Century
by Thomas Friedman

Award-winning author and *New York Times* columnist Thomas Friedman has been called the "high priest of free trade fundamentalism," and is among the most vocal modern advocates of globalism and environmentalism. In this excerpt from his 2005 bestseller *The World is Flat: A Brief History of the Twenty-First Century*, Friedman reports from Bangalore, India.

On the day we went to the Infosys campus around five p.m.—just when the Infosys call center workers were flooding into the grounds for the overnight shift on foot, minibus, and motor scooter, while many of the more advanced engineers were leaving at the end of the day shift. The crew and I were standing at the gate observing this river of educated young people flowing in and out, many in animated conversation. They all looked as if they had scored 1,600 on their SAT's , and I felt a real mind-eye split overtaking me.

. . . If all these Indian techies were doing what was their comparative advantages and then turning around and using their income to buy all the products from America that are our competitive advantage—from Corning Glass to Microsoft Windows—both our countries would benefit, even if some individual Indians and Americans might have to shift jobs in the transition. And one can see evidence of this mutual benefit in the sharp increase in exports and imports between the United States and India in recent years.

But my eye kept looking at all these Indian zippies and telling me something else: "Oh, my God, there are so many of them, and they all look so serious, so eager for work. And they just keep coming, wave after wave. How in the world can it possibly be good for my daughters and millions of other young Americans that these Indians can do the same jobs as they can for a fraction of the wages?"

. . . Just as I was getting worked up with worry, the Infosys spokeswoman accompanying me casually mentioned that last year Infosys India received "one million applications" from young Indians for nine thousand tech jobs.

Have a nice day.

Capitalist Glossary

An in-depth discussion of capitalism and its tools naturally requires a lot of specialized language. Much of that language is familiar, like "stocks," "bonds," and "IPO," but even if you can understand it in context, you may not be aware of a fuller definition. Other terms may be completely alien. We will not cover everything here—the world of finance has many nooks and crannies, and every subfield has its own jargon and alphabet soup of acronyms—but this glossary will provide you with the highlights of capitalist language.

absolute advantage: a situation that occurs when better natural endowments or production-related experience equip one nation with the ability to produce more of a good than another nation, even though both nations have equal quantities of resources. The existence of absolute advantage naturally leads to situations of specialization, a macro-scale version of the baker trading bread to the shepherd for sweaters. When two entities need two different things, and each can produce more of one of them than the other, trade benefits both of the parties.

ad valorem tax: a tax levied on a good, where the tax on each unit sold is determined by the value or price of that unit. Sales tax is the ad valorem tax encountered most often, but import tariffs, inheritance taxes, meal taxes, and property taxes are all found in the United States. In Europe, value-added tax (VAT) is more common; in the United States, only Michigan used this system, which applies a tax at every stage of production. In comparison a sales tax charges only the consumer at the time of purchase. Michigan's VAT—called the Single Business Tax—was repealed in 2008. Presidential candidate Mike Huckabee recently proposed the adoption of a 30 percent sales tax to replace the federal income tax, shifting the tax burden to outgo instead of income.

antitrust legislation: government laws aimed at preventing anticompetitive practices that firms may use to drive equally efficient rivals from an industry, or to perpetuate monopoly status against otherwise equally efficient competitors. While antitrust laws are technically in conflict with pure laissez-faire capitalism, they have been an accepted feature of capitalism since the early 20th century. They originated in the late 19th century in response to the anticompetitive nature of many of the robber barons, and in theory protect all businesses by restricting some businesses. In practice, there is always much debate about what exactly antitrust legislation should prohibit, what constitutes an anticompetitive practice, and what is merely good business.

appreciation: an increase in value. The appreciation and depreciation of assets can be important for tax purposes even when the assets aren't being transferred, as when a company car is claimed as a deduction over the period of years in which it loses value. Knowing how much something appreciates requires knowing its value, a difficult thing to state confidently without selling the asset—there's a reason people will tell you that a certain thing is worth whatever you can get for it. Currencies appreciate and depreciate in relation to one another in a floating exchange rate.

asset: money or any other good with value. Generally speaking, assets are a form of savings and help to determine the wealth of an individual or firm. Current assets are those that exist in liquid form (cash in bank accounts) or are expected to be cashed in, sold, or used over the course of the year—a business's inventory is a current asset. Intangible assets include things like franchises, patents, and other forms of intellectual property. Fixed assets or PPE (property/plant/equipment) include the land, buildings, and equipment owned by a company for the purposes of its operations, such as the cash registers in a retail store, or the kitchen in a restaurant.

automatic stabilizers: fiscal policy instruments enacted by government to "automatically" affect economic activity throughout the business cycle by supporting demand during recession, and restraining demand during periods of inflationary pressure. Because automatic stabilizers are already in place when Gross Domestic Profit or GDP changes, these instruments do not require any change in government policy.

budget deficit: when an economic system's government expenditure exceeds its income and tax revenues. A budget deficit of zero is referred to as a balanced budget. When the budget deficit of a country accumulates over multiple years, it's referred to as the national debt. Monetizing that debt—printing new currency to pay it off—tends to lead to rapid inflation, and so is rarely the recourse of healthy nations. Issuing bonds is a more stable way to deal with the debt. A budget surplus occurs when revenues are greater than government spending.

burden of a tax: the ability of a tax (for example, per unit tax) to both increase the price paid by demanders and decrease the price received by suppliers. The change in the price paid is considered the demander's tax burden, whereas the change in the price received is considered the supplier's tax burden.

capital flight: when the physical and financial assets of citizens from one country are invested in foreign nations. The term is particularly used when this happens rapidly and in response to some event, such as an economic crisis, a series of bank failures, political change, or a change in the interest rates offered to investors. An analogous term, human capital flight, is sometimes better known as "brain drain," describing the loss of individuals with particular skills or education as they leave their home areas for other places. Developing nations suffer from brain drain when their technically skilled students leave for jobs in industrial nations.

Coase theorem: a theory stating that individuals within the private sector can resolve an externality if property rights are well defined, and the bargaining costs associated with resolving the externality are low. British economist Ronald Coase was awarded the 1991 Nobel Prize in Economics for the theorem, which grew out of his study of the regulation of radio frequencies. The two claims of the theorem are: (1) that the prevailing outcome will be the most efficient one (because individuals will resolve it otherwise) and (2) that the prevailing outcome will be the same no matter to whom the property rights are initially granted.

collective bargaining: the negotiation process by which employers and labor unions reach agreements regarding wages, fringe benefits, hiring practices, and work and safety conditions. The right to collective bargaining, broadly recognized in the Western world, is protected in the United States by the 1935 National Labor Relations Act, which prevents employers from discriminating against workers on the basis of union membership. Organized labor blossomed in the days of the Industrial Revolution. When an employer holds sway over many workers, collective bargaining becomes necessary.

collusion: noncompetitive behavior designed to maximize the profits of an entire industry or set of firms, rather than the profits of one single firm. Collusion is behavior that allows separate firms to approximate the behavior of a monopoly, thereby raising the profits of all firms within the industry. Certain forms of tacit collusion—when there is no law-breaking or overt cooperation—are acceptable. For instance, all major fast food chains tend to charge about the same for soft drinks and hamburgers, even though this would be a very easy area in which to compete. By maintaining similar prices, no chain risks the losses of a price war. Cartels, on the other hand, are groups that collude according to explicit agreements to fix prices and create an effective oligopoly; they are prohibited by law.

complementary goods: goods related in consumption such that the two goods are purchased and consumed together. The demands for these goods are positively related, implying that increases in the demand for one good corresponds with increased demand for that good's complements. The strongest degree of complementarity is called a perfect complement, like right-handed and left-handed gloves, which are only sold together. Very similar to that would be hot dogs and hot dog buns, which are sold separately, but rarely consumed independently. There is also complementarity that is not mutual, though. While buying a Playstation game requires buying or already owning a Playstation, buying a Playstation does not require the customer to buy that specific game.

Consumer Price Index (CPI): a measure of the (weighted) average price of a particular set of consumer goods. The CPI tells consumers how the cost of these goods changes over time. The percent change in the CPI is a measure of inflation, and the CPI is one of the most closely monitored statistics in economics. In most countries, including the United States, the CPI is computed monthly. The accuracy of the CPI varies—in some nations, negative data are often excluded in order to keep from skewing the results of the average, and in some countries black market activity and the purchasing habits of rural populations may be excluded because the data simply isn't available.

In the United States, government benefit payments, such as Social Security, rise based on changes in the CPI.

cost object: an input involved in the production of a good or service, which incurs a cost. Labor and raw materials are cost objects, as are all the services that must be paid for in the course of production, such as the employ of a trucking company to transfer goods to selling points, the advertising used to sell the goods, and so forth.

corporation: a type of organization where the owners have purchased equity (stock) in the firm, with liability limited to the extent of the owner's investment in the firm. A corporation is ultimately a legal entity. While a company of any size can be a corporation, a single person can also do business as a corporation. The rules governing corporate behavior are designed to protect the interests of shareholders, who are themselves not liable. When the corporation is sued, it is the entity itself that is sued, not its officers. If Burger Land serves you a tainted hamburger, you don't sue its president and you don't sue the little old ladies who own a few shares of Burger Land stock: you sue Burger Land Inc. However if you win your suit, the shareholders may suffer the consequences insofar as the corporation will have to pay damages, and may see their stock drop because of negative publicity.

economic system: the means, in any given economy, of organizing demanders, suppliers, and the government in order to answer questions about what goods and services to produce, how to produce those goods and services, and then how to distribute the goods and services. Modern economic systems are some mix of capitalist and socialist systems. Planned economies are predominantly socialist, in which the government seeks to answer those questions and enforce their solutions; market or hands-off economies are predominantly capitalist, in which competitive market forces are left to determine solutions; mixed economies incorporate aspects of both.

economies of scale: cost advantages enjoyed when long-run increases in a firm's production or scale of operation leads to decreases in average costs. The opportunity for economies of scale is why some industries tend to encourage large businesses, even on an international scale. Coca-Cola has greater control over its costs, because it buys its ingredients in such quantity that it is less subject to market fluctuations than a local soft drink maker producing a few hundred bottles a month for his local region.

elasticity: a ratio of change or measure of how changes in one variable respond to changes in another related variable, where those changes are calculated in terms of percentage change. When the response is small (i.e., less than one), the relationship is said to be inelastic, whereas when the response is larger, it is elastic.

enlightened self interest: an assumption within economic analysis stating that individuals will behave in such a way as to maximize the net benefit of their actions. In ethics, enlightened self interest is discussed in terms of the potential of people to prosper while "doing good," sometimes by deferring gratification, which is where the "enlightened" part comes in—unlike animals or children, adult humans can recognize the ways in which good can come our way down the line, and so don't need to be immediately rewarded.

exchange rate: the price of one nation's currency in terms of another nation's currency. Exchange rates may be set by the foreign exchange market (for example, flexible exchange rates) or at specific levels by government (fixed exchange rates). The foreign exchange market is one of the largest markets in the world, where investors trade trillions of dollars worth of currency every day. An exchange rate can be spot (the current rate of exchange) or forward (with delivery and payment made at a future date). Many currencies with fixed exchange rates—such as many Asian currencies—are "pegged" to a specific foreign currency, often the American dollar.

Euroland: informal, but common term for the group of European Union (EU) member states that have adopted the euro as their currency: Austria, Belgium, Cyprus, Finland, France, Germany, Greece, Ireland, Italy, Luxembourg, Malta, Netherlands, Portugal, Slovenia, and Spain. Most EU nations are obliged to adopt the euro in a timely manner; the exceptions are the UK and Denmark, which were granted exemptions in the treaty that formed the EU. Sweden has no such exemption, but opted out of the euro anyway; the EU has made it clear that future members will be expected to adopt the euro. Mayotte, Monaco, San Marino, Saint Pierre and Miquelon, and the Vatican City all use the euro under an agreement with the EU; other nations are in talks to do the same.

fiscal policy: government policy designed to affect economic activity with changes in government expenditure and/or taxation. Spending and taxation are the two tools of fiscal policy that, according to Keynesian economics, are the best ways to kickstart overall economic activity. This was the idea behind the New Deal. The problem with such policy, and with evaluating the success of the New Deal, is that there is such a lag between the implementation of policy and its visible effects. The influence of other factors in the interim can't be dismissed.

free trade: when countries engage in international trade, exchanging goods and services, but without the existence of trade barriers like quotas and tariffs. The United States was traditionally opposed to free trade. "Under free trade," President William McKinley said in the early 20th century, "the trader is the master and the producer the slave." Protectionism—setting tariffs in order to make domestic goods more attractive and discourage people from buying imports—was a common practice, and "Buy American" bumper stickers are still a common sight. After World War II, as the United States achieved industrial dominance, it began to advocate free trade and an abolition of tariffs—the goal was to get other countries to buy American.

Gross Domestic Product (GDP): a measure of economic activity. GDP is calculated as the total value of all final goods and services produced in a given period within a nation's borders. When assigning value to these goods and services, an economist may use current prices (nominal GDP) or constant prices (real GDP), which eliminate the effects of inflation. The "gross" in the term refers to the fact that the depreciation of capital isn't taken into accounted. It's important to differentiate between GDP and Gross National Product, (GNP) which used to be referenced more frequently. The GNP includes the income generated by Americans working abroad, while ignoring the income of foreigners working in the United States; GDP focuses not on who, but on where the activity takes place.

impossible trinity: a fixed exchange rate, free capital movement, and an independent monetary policy. As hypothesized in the 1960s by Robert Mundell and Marcus Fleming, the trinity consists of those three things that cannot be simultaneously attained. In a capitalist society, the government must therefore choose between a fixed exchange rate to control currency volatility, and a monetary policy that keeps inflation under control. A central bank may go back and forth between the two like a cook multitasking in the kitchen. European states tend to favor stable currency; English-speaking countries tend to favor low inflation.

inflation: an increase in the average price of a group of goods and services. The inflation rate is the percentage change in the average price of a group of goods and services. Price indexes provide an approximation of the average price of a set of goods at a moment in time, whereas percentage changes in a price index approximate the inflation rate between periods. A term rarely seen is disinflation, which is a reduction in the rate of inflation—as opposed to deflation, which is the opposite of inflation, a decrease in average prices. Hyperinflation, which is usually limited to unstable economies at times of upheaval (such as the collapse of the Soviet Union, when

Russian inflation rose to more than 2,500 percent), is a very rapid and chaotic level of inflation. Stagflation, suffered by the United States in the 1970s, is the combination of inflation and economic stagnation.

instrument: a particular type of document. Though in all other fields, an instrument is an object, in law and finance it's a document. Legal instruments are those that confer a particular status, such as marriage licenses, wills, and court orders. Financial instruments document a transaction, such as bonds, stock certificates, and mortgages. Financial instruments include cash instruments, the value of which is determined directly by the market, and derivative instruments that derive their value from underlying assets. Futures and options are both derivative instruments, for instance. Negotiable instruments document an obligation to pay money, such as a promissory note or a check.

intellectual capital: a form of capital asset that produces intellectual property—such as copyrighted works, patents, and trademarks. Thinkers and artists, creative types, problem-solvers, scientists and engineers who produce "outside the box" solutions—these are the typical creators of intellectual capital.

interest rate: the percentage of borrowed funds that must be repaid to a lender in exchange for the privilege of borrowing those funds. Essentially, when you borrow money, buy something on credit, or defer payment on something in accordance with a store's credit plan, you are renting someone else's money. The debt you are taking on requires you not only to replace that money with your own, but to pay the "rent" on it for the time you took it. There are two types of interest, simple and compound. Simple interest is calculated based only on the unpaid portion of the principal; compound interest adds the interest charges to the unpaid balance, so that every time it compounds, you are now paying interest on the interest.

Laffer curve: a graphical bell-shaped relationship between (income) tax rates and tax revenues. When the tax rate is zero, government receives no tax revenues. However, as tax rates are adjusted, government revenues rise to a maximum point and then decline again. It was named for economist Arthur Laffer, though the principle has been known for centuries and both Keynes and von Mises wrote about it. Laffer introduced the curve—drawn on a napkin over lunch—to Dick Cheney and Donald Rumsfeld in 1974, when Rumsfeld was President Ford's chief of staff and Cheney was a deputy assistant in the White House. It became integral to supply-side economics, which was developing at the time.

liability: items or money that one person, firm, or group potentially owe another person, firm, or group. For example, when borrowing money from a lender, the amount loaned is considered a liability for the borrower because the money must be repaid. Current liabilities are those expected to be repaid over the course of the year, like the wages a company pays its employees and the rent on its buildings. Long-term liabilities include bonds that have been issued, the obligations incurred by employee pensions, and warranties issued to customers.

Lorenz curve: a graphical means of illustrating how income or wealth is distributed within an economic system. The curve is often used to measure the proportion of income earned by a cumulative percentage of the population within that economic system. The Lorenz curve is the source of statements about distributive inequality, like "the top 10 percent of the population controls 90 percent of the wealth" (hypothetically speaking). Developed by American economist Max Lorenz in 1905, while he was still a graduate student, it remains his most famous work.

macroeconomics: the study of how the whole economy allocates goods and services. Macroeconomics focuses on the behavior of variables like GDP, inflation, unemployment, and long-run economic growth. As a discipline, macroeconomics developed principally in the 20th century, though it built on work that had come before. Especially characteristic of macroeconomics is the attempt to understand business cycles; macroeconomics was essentially born in the wake of the Great Depression, and was greatly influenced by Keynes' study of such.

microeconomics: the study of how specific parts of the whole economy (for example, individual industries) allocate goods and services. Microeconomics focuses on variables like output and price. Price theory and supply and demand are concepts from microeconomics. Labor economists study employment and wages, health economists study the role of health insurance and the medical profession, and public finance economists study the economic effects of government spending and taxation.

monetary policy: when government chooses to affect economic activity with changes in the money supply and/or interest rates to accomplish specific macroeconomic goals. While fiscal policy guides the economy through taxation and expenditure, monetary policy is usually either expansionary or contractionary—that is, it either increases or decreases the money supply. Unemployment is generally fought with expansionary tactics, like lowered interest rates and a decline in bank reserve requirements. Inflation is countered with a contraction in money supply and higher interest rates.

money: any good that fulfills the functions associated with facilitating the exchange of products and services. Money is described as simultaneously functioning as a unit of account, a medium of exchange, and a store of value. While all currency is money, not all money exists in the form of currency. In fact, much of it exists "only on paper"— most of your money is probably in one account or another, not as a stack of bills or a sack of coins.

monopolistic competition: an industry that consists of many small firms which produce goods that are slightly different from firm to firm, but where the barriers to entry and exit are few. The prevalence of monopolistic competition leads to the building of brand identities, and the industries in which it is most common are also the ones we are the most used to seeing ads for: restaurants, especially national chains; convenience foods, from pudding cups to cereal; soft drinks and beer; sneakers; and toiletries. Though there is often little difference between products, advertising will often be engaged to create distinctions between nearly-identical products— paper towels may be praised for their absorbent abilities, and so on—or to associate the product with a particular brand identity like "trustworthy" or "cool."

monopoly: an industry that consists of one firm serving the entire market, where the barriers to entry are high enough to keep all other firms out for some period of time. A natural economy is one with significant economies of scale through some relevant range of market demand. Monopolies are discouraged by American law because of their anticompetitive nature, and a company may be targeted for government intervention even when it has not broken the law. AT&T's monopoly on the long distance phone market was eliminated in 1982 when the government broke it up into seven new companies covering the various regions of the country, known as the Baby Bells.

national debt: the sum of all of a nation's previous budget deficits. This sum represents the total amount owed by the nation's government, both internally (to citizens of its country) and externally (to foreign entities). National debt is the result of budget deficits, when more money has been spent than taken in through revenue. Keynesian economics (named after John Maynard Keynes) defended national debt as a salve during lean times, though it also called for paying it off in times of plenty; but like individual credit card debt, national debt has become something we tend to treat as something we simply live with, tolerating its perpetual existence even in the best economic times.

natural rate of unemployment: the level of unemployment associated with a stable or constant inflation rate, reflecting the choice by workers not to work at the existing wage. It is believed that all unemployment is voluntary at the natural rate of unemployment.

non-price competition: when firms compete using methods other than prices (like product quality) to attract consumers. Coca-Cola and Pepsi, for instance, first competed by price (Pepsi, the newcomer, offered its product at half the price) but for almost 100 years have sold at essentially identical prices, competing mostly via advertising and brand image. The creation of those brand images is an example of sustainable competitive advantage: what Coca-Cola and Pepsi both have over other colas is the familiarity and iconic appeal of their brands. Their use of exclusive contracts with restaurant and movie theater chains is another form of such competition.

normative economics: economic analysis that explains or predicts outcomes on the basis of moral judgments, opinions, or beliefs. Normative is a term from philosophy, meaning "to say what should be." The difference between normative and positive economics is the same as that between prescriptive and descriptive grammar: prescriptive grammar, the kind you learn in junior high, tells you "the right thing to do." Descriptive grammar tells us what people actually say when teachers aren't there. The recommendations of normative economics have to be considered in light of the values being held; a capitalist and a Communist will have different goals and different recommendations.

Okun's Law: as stated by economist Arthur Okun in 1962, an inverse relationship between the change in the rate of unemployment and the GDP gap, or the difference between actual and potential real

GDP. For every one percent that the actual unemployment rate goes over the natural rate of unemployment, real GDP is reduced by two to three percent.

oligopoly: an industry consisting of a few large firms and fairly high barriers to entry. Oligopolistic firms are often characterized as being mutually interdependent, which implies that strategic interaction may exist within oligopolistic industries. Collusion among oligopolistic firms leads to a circumstance indistinguishable from a monopoly, from the consumer's perspective, but within legal bounds such cooperation can also stabilize the industry's market and benefit both investors and customers. In the 21st century the entertainment industry is the most obvious example of an oligopoly, with half a dozen movie studios and music labels taking in the overwhelming majority of the revenue. Related to oligopolies is the oligopsony, in which there are many sellers but only a small number of buyers, such as in the defense or nuclear energy industries.

partnership: a type of organization where two or more individuals create a firm. Unlike corporations, where liability is limited to the extent of an individual's investment in the firm, partnerships are characterized as having unlimited liability. In the United States, there are three types of partnerships. General and limited partnerships are very similar except that a limited partnership includes limited partners, who do not have management responsibilities and carry less liability than the general partners. Limited liability partnerships consist only of limited partners, like a corporation managed directly by its shareholders. There are no federal laws governing partnerships, and so ordinances vary from state to state.

patent: a legal means of appropriating a return on innovative activity, whereby an inventor is allowed to operate as the only seller of an innovation for a specific period of time. A patent is generally owned by the inventor of the property it covers, but can be sold to another individual or corporation; if it isn't sold, the rights to produce the product can be sold. Patents also prevent the invention of technologies that depend on the product of the patent. Patents generally expire after 20 years, though extensions can be granted. Some people don't file for patents because it would mean disclosing the specifics of the process or product being patented, which then become public property when the patent expires. "Secret blends of herbs and spices," the original formula for Coca-Cola—these are trade secrets that can theoretically be preserved forever without patent, simply by concealing them.

perfect competition: an industry that consists of many small firms that, as individual firms, are unable to influence the market price. Perfectly competitive firms produce identical products (standardized goods) and operate in industries where the barriers to entry or exit are nonexistent. Perfect competition exists only in theoretical models, sort of like pointing out that gridlock can be avoided if everyone travels at the same speed with a consistent distance between cars—it may be true, but it will never happen. Perfect competition is most closely approximated by the online auction website eBay, where the barrier to market entry is negligible, and competitive advertising is not feasible.

per unit tax: a tax levied on the sale of a good, wherein each unit sold is taxed at the same rate (for example, an excise tax). This is the opposite of an ad valorem tax, which is determined by unit price. Examples of per unit taxes encountered in consumers' daily lives are gasoline and cigarettes. Per unit taxes can have interesting effects. Because in some states cigarettes are taxed on a per pack basis but tobacco is not, it can be significantly cheaper to buy your own tobacco and rolling papers, subject only to ad valorem sales tax. Because the demand for cigarettes is steady, there is a thriving black market in cigarettes without tax stamps, which can be sold cheaper to the customer while still making a profit for the seller.

Phillips Curve: the inverse relationship between unemployment rates and the rate of inflation, named for Aban Phillips. Economists often debate the nature of this relationship, in terms of whether the relationship is negative, positive, or even possibly nonexistent. Phillips's original paper was used in support of Keynesian economic policies, and the notion that high inflation was acceptable since it would lead to low unemployment. The curve came under attack in the 1970s, because the prevailing stagflation seemed impossible under a Phillips model.

positive economics: economic analysis that explains or predicts outcomes in an objective manner. That is, analysis that is more descriptive than prescriptive. Positive economics examines behavior and is interested in the causes and effects of economics, and certainly in being able to say that doing X will lead to Y, but its principle concerns are not moralist—it remains neutral on the determination of the right course of action.

predatory pricing: the act of pricing below cost with the intent of reducing or eliminating competition within an industry. "Intent" is the key here, since the term describes a motivated action. A video game console may sell below cost because the company creates customers that way, and recoups on licensing and the sale of game CDs. That's not automatically anticompetitive. But when Microsoft offered Internet Explorer for free, it came under scrutiny because predatory pricing can be a violation of antitrust laws, and its motive—since there was no Microsoft-profiting product associated with IE—seemed to be to put Netscape and its $30 browser out of business.

price control: when a government imposes a specific price on a good or service, often different from the price that would have otherwise arisen in the market. Price ceilings represent a maximum price that can be charged per unit. Rent control, common in New York City but rare elsewhere, is a price ceiling imposed on property rental, to keep landlords from taking advantage of high demand. A price floor is a minimum that can be charged; the minimum wage law is a price floor on wages.

price discrimination: the act of charging different prices to different consumers, but not on the basis of differences in cost. Despite the connotations of the word "discrimination," this is not always a bad or immoral thing, nor is it always inconvenient for the customer. Certain business travelers pay extra for air travel, without a difference in the product purchased. Certain discounts are offered at many businesses for students, minors, or senior citizens, and entertainment venues like aquariums and movie theaters almost universally charge different prices according to age, even though there is no difference in cost to the provider. In some parts of the country, discounts are offered to the military, veterans, firefighters, or off-duty police officers.

price elasticity of demand: a measure of the percentage change in the quantity of a good sold relative to the percentage change in the price of the same good. In the case of most types of goods, a drop in price will mean an increase in demand. The inelastic or sticky goods are usually those that have no substitute, such as a particular antibiotic or disease treatment. Currency is the classic example of a perfectly elastic good: you would never pay $5 for a quarter, but you'd always pay a quarter for $5, and do so until the supply was exhausted.

privatization: the process of converting government-owned enterprises into private sector firms. Proponents believe that subjecting the enterprise to market forces will result in a better and cheaper product, often conjuring up the notion that government is made inefficient by bureaucracy and red tape, or overpriced. The private sector also doesn't have to worry about pleasing all the people all the time, which in many democracies can hamstring the public sector. On the other hand, opponents point out, the profit motive can lead to cutting corners and unethical behavior—as was the case among aggressive mortgage lenders during the recent credit boom.

property rights: the legal right to determine how a good or service is used. Private individuals, firms, and government (acting on behalf of society as a whole) may each possess the property rights for various goods and services within an economy. The three types of property are real property (land), personal property (other physical goods), and intellectual property. The term *real estate* generally refers to the land, plus any buildings located on it.

public good: any good that may be consumed by more than one individual at a specific moment in time, where one person's consumption does not exclude others from consuming the same good. Not to be confused with "public interest" or "the common good"; "good" here is used in its economic sense, not the opposite of "bad." Nonexcludability is another common feature of public goods. Broadcasts, for instance, are available to anyone with a receiver—television and radio content providers who want control over access to their content seek out subscription models (such as cable television and satellite radio) instead of broadcast models. Lighthouses and street lights are often used as examples of public goods since they function in such a way that there is no way to exclude anyone from receiving their benefits; law enforcement and the national defense are likewise public goods.

pure capitalism: an economic system where ownership and decision-making is predominantly the responsibility of private individuals, rather than the government. Even the most strident capitalists rarely advocate pure capitalism, because the 19th century taught that a completely unregulated market will actually lead to anticompetitive situations. When industrial tycoons and robber barons dominated their industries with monopolies and cartels, taking advantage of both consumers and workers. But there are many who think that government involvement should be limited to protecting free enterprise, rather than restricting it.

pure Communism: an economic system where ownership of human and nonhuman resources, as well as all decision-making, is bestowed on society as a whole. As with pure capitalism, this doesn't exist in practice, though Marxism does consider it an end goal synonymous with "stateless Communism": the predicted postsocialist stage of history when nations, states, and class have disappeared.

rationing: the process of allocating goods and services among demanders, typically on the basis of a person's willingness to pay a specific price to obtain the good. In economics, most rationing is price-rationing—setting a particular price ensures that the good goes to those who want it most, or can most easily afford it. A great many goods were rationed by the government during World War II, when wartime needs and production created shortages of staple foods and raw materials with military applications. But nonprice rationing also occurs in the private sector. The Boston Red Sox, for instance, play in one of the smallest ballparks in the country and have sold out every game for several seasons, with most tickets selling out the day they go on sale. A number of schemes have been attempted to try to distribute tickets as widely and fairly as possible, including setting tickets aside for residents of certain states, offering free raffles for the chance to buy tickets to particular games, and limiting each transaction to a small number of tickets.

real: adjusted for inflation, as in real GDP, real dollars, and real cost.

recession: a fall in economic activity that can be observed through decreases in real GDP over two consecutive quarters, and increases in unemployment. Though a depression is a severe or prolonged recession, there's no clear divider between the two, and often what one generation would have called a depression (or will call a depression in hindsight) is kept in the recession camp by the powers that be, for the sake of appearances. The United States succumbs to a recession only when the National Bureau of Economic Research—a private company that has been performing official research for the federal government since 1930—says so. Its criteria are based on a significant drop in GDP, income, employment, production, and sales, over "more than a few months."

Say's Law: Say's Law of Markets, named for Jean-Baptiste Say, proposes that supply creates its own demand in that any given amount of output produced will influence demand to the degree that demanders will purchase all of any existing output. There is no demand without supply. Specifically, Say was arguing against the suggestion (in the early 19th century) that the economy was suffering because people didn't have money, and that more money should thus be printed; by Say's Law, printing more money would only result in inflation. "Products are paid for with products," Say said. Print more money, and the product one man buys with the profit from the other product he sold will simply cost more.

services: intangible, nonmaterial goods that have value to demanders. Medical care consists of both services (a doctor's time and expertise) and goods (medicine), as for instance does a meal at a restaurant. Teachers, lawyers, performing musicians, stage actors, plumbers, maids, and therapists are all predominantly providers of services, though they may produce or require the purchase of goods in the course of their work. Financial advice is a service, though brokering a trade involves the transfer of goods. Most goods fall somewhere between pure good and pure service. A service is said to be perishable, because the time set aside for it cannot be reallocated: a teacher does not get paid less just because half the students are absent, and your minimum-wage job at the convenience store does not dock your pay just because business is slow and you haven't had to do anything for the last hour. You agreed in advance to be available during that time, and could have made other arrangements with it: you are entitled to the money.

social costs: the sum of private and external costs. Private costs are those paid by the individual; external costs are the burden of others or society as a whole. The water you use to keep your lawn green during a drought imposes a private cost on you, but an external cost on the rest of us when you exacerbate the shortage. The total of those costs is the social cost of your well-trimmed greenery. Likewise, manufacturing a widget costs the J. Widget Corporation a certain private cost, but imposes an external cost by polluting public air and water. Social cost is integral to many arguments for government regulations; there is little reason to think that competition alone will lead J. Widget and its competitors to eliminate their pollution, even if enlightened self-interest implies that they would benefit from doing so.

socialism: an economic system where the government has ownership over productive (nonhuman) resources, and is responsible for the predominant amount of decision-making. Though Karl Marx was a socialist and in turn influenced socialism, it's important to remember that socialism is not mutually exclusive with capitalism. Though socialism has been under attack since the late 1970s and the generation of Reagan and Thatcher, the United Kingdom has been ruled by the socialist Labour Party since the 1990s, which explicitly seeks to promote a capitalist economy and entrepreneurship, while still pursuing the traditional aims of social welfare through government involvement.

sole proprietorship: a business or operation in which the owner has no partners, and in which the business has no separate existence from the individual. A sole proprietor is a self-employed person operating his or her own business account. Registering a trade name (such as

John Doe Enterprises) lets you operate under a business name rather than just your legal name, and open bank accounts in that name, which also simplifies interactions with customers if the sole proprietorship later expands. A sole proprietorship involves unlimited liability, and therefore greater risks than a single-member corporation or a limited liability company.

sticky: resistant to change, and especially resistant to change in one direction or another. Something that is "sticky upward" is unlikely to rise despite changes in conditions; something that is "sticky downward" is unlikely to fall. In many cases, prices are sticky downward: even when production costs are reduced, companies are unlikely to offer their products cheaper unless competition forces them to do so. This is less true in consumer technology—prices of DVD players and computers fall, even as they add more features.

supply-side economics: a school of macroeconomic thought that developed among conservatives in the mid to late 1970s, and thus became associated with the Reagan-Bush era. Supply-side economics calls for the creation of incentives for suppliers—such as tax reduction—in order to create economic growth by freeing up money in the marketplace. The argument made at the time, amidst the problem of stagflation, was that a more active economy would lead to more government revenue through volume. President Richard Nixon's refusal to reduce taxes was blamed for exacerbating stagflation. Supply-side policies were first implemented by the Reagan administration.

tariff: a tax levied on imported goods. An ad valorem tariff exaggerates the effect of foreign economies on the price of imports, but a specific tariff (a flat amount per unit) needs to be updated manually, so to speak, in order to be reasonable. Tariffs can also be defined by motive: revenue tariffs exist purely to raise money for the government, and are generally levied on goods that can't be produced domestically. Protective tariffs are usually levied only on those goods which can be and are produced domestically, and are deliberately high in order to make the imports noncompetitive with the domestic product. Up until the adoption of the federal income tax, tariffs were the main source of revenue for the federal government.

tax: a fee imposed on an individual or entity by a government. Taxes account for much of a government's revenue, although not all fees charged by governments are considered taxes (for instance, the fee to renew your driver's license is not thought of as a driving tax). Common taxes include income taxes, sales taxes, tariffs on imports, tolls on roads and bridges, per unit taxes on items like fuel and cigarettes, property tax, and the various taxes that apply to nonwage income (such as the capital gains tax, inheritance tax, and gift tax). The federal government takes most of its tax revenue in the form of income tax, while state and local governments rely (generally) on sales and property taxes.

transaction costs: sometimes called "the cost of doing business," transaction costs are the loss of time, effort, and other resources directly related to the initiation and completion of trade and exchange. Sometimes this is literally a cash cost, as in the fee assessed by a broker when completing a stock trade, or a real estate sale. There are many transaction costs that we don't account for in our individual lives, though, like the cost of driving to the supermarket, not only in fuel but in the wear and tear on the car, the eventual medical expense of our rising blood pressure in the midst of traffic, the tax burden of road repair because of the distance we've chosen to drive. We don't account for these things, but that doesn't make them free.

unemployment: to be unemployed is to be without work, but capable of working or looking for work. The unemployment rate is the percentage of such unemployed people in the labor force—the part of the population over working age and under retirement age (16 and 65, in the United States). There is persistent debate about the causes and importance of unemployment and its relationship to economic cycles. Keynesian economics tie unemployment to business cycles, and to the recession stage when wages do not meet an equilibrium rate because of a lack of sufficient demand for labor. Unemployment is also affected by the fact that the desirability of a job is affected by factors other than the success of a company.

value: one of the most fundamental economic concepts, that of "what is it worth," is actually the most difficult to determine. 'The value of a thing can only be determined by its sale or trade. While value may seem synonymous with price, we speak sometimes of an "actual value" that is derived only from utility, without consideration for supply and demand: no matter how rare it is, a record album is worth nothing to a person with only a DVD player.

variable costs: the economic cost associated with hiring variable inputs to produce goods and services. Variable costs change with changes in output, whereas fixed costs do not change with changes in output. Variable costs include but are not limited to direct costs, which are associated with a particular cost object like the labor and raw materials required to produce the good; most indirect costs (such as taxes and equipment rental) are fixed, but there are exceptions.

wealth: the value of the physical and financial assets owned by an individual, less the accumulated liabilities (for example, debt) carried by that individual. Despite this neutral definition, use of the word usually connotes abundance; we wouldn't speak of the poor as having "low wealth." While income is a flow, wealth is a snapshot, and we sometimes speak of wealth in terms of how long they could maintain their current expenses and lifestyle without further income. Although capitalism strives for a circumstance in which all wealth is earned, the moral and societal imperative to assist the poor is one counter-example, while the inheritance of wealth by the earner's descendants is rarely complained about.

welfare economics: a branch of microeconomics that analyzes and addresses the well-being (welfare) of a society in terms of the economic activity of individuals within that society. Welfare economics is both positive and normative. Its positive side studies economic efficiency and the measure of social welfare by which these things are true: no individual's situation can be improved at the expense of others; increasing the production of a good can only occur by decreasing the production of another; and production matches consumer demand. Welfare economics considers income distribution and the problems created by vast inequalities of wealth.

Appendix B

Capitalist Resources

There are hundreds of worthwhile books on capitalism, finance, economics, and business history—though of course those hundreds are sometimes hard to find among the thousands of less worthwhile ones. This list of resources presents some of the cream of the crop—many of the better business histories (think of them as biographies of a company), economics texts, biographies, and history books. There are web pages, too—it goes without saying that the Internet is a dynamic and ever-changing resource, and so in particular our list of Websites can not be considered complete, since new things go up every day.

Centers and Societies

The Center on Capitalism and Society
(Columbia University)
http://www.earthinstitute.columbia.edu/ccs/
The aim of the CCS is to develop a theory of capitalism in which the discovery of viable ideas is the crucial activity, and in which novice and veteran entrepreneurs, venture capitalists, and other financiers are key actors.

The Center for the Advancement of Capitalism
http://www.moraldefense.com/
An objectivist organization.

BB&T Center for the Study of Capitalism
(Wake Forest University)
http://calloway.wfu.edu/
An academic initiative from Wake Forest's Calloway School of Business and Accountancy.

Ayn Rand Institute
http://www.aynrand.org
Ayn Rand, a novelist and philosopher, founded Objectivism (which among other things, advocates pure laissez-faire capitalism).

Elfenworks Center for the Study of Fiduciary Capitalism
(St. Mary's College of California)
http://stmarys-ca.edu/fidcap/
An academic organization dedicated to producing both academic and action-oriented research that explores the implications of the rise of institutional investors as the owners of equity and debt capital.

Clemson Institute for the Study of Capitalism
(Clemson University)
http://business.clemson.edu/bbtcenter/cci/

The Clemson Institute is specifically concerned with the moral foundations of capitalism, and by extension the moral concerns of government and its relationship with the individual.

Magazines and Newspapers

Fortune Magazine
The magazine is known for its compilation of various lists, such as the Best Companies to Work For, the Most Admired Companies, and the Fortune 500 (ranking U.S. public corporations by revenue).

Inc.
Creator of the Inc. 500, measuring the fastest-growing private companies in the United States.

Entrepreneur
Focuses on small business management.

Money
A personal finance magazine, also known for its annual list of the "Best Places to Live."

Smart Money
The *Wall Street Journal*'s personal finance magazine.

The Economist
A weekly, international news magazine with a focus on economic issues; the premier publication of its kind.

The Financial Times
Great Britain's leading business newspaper, and co-owner of *The Economist*.

The Wall Street Journal
The United States's leading business newspaper, published daily.

The New York Times
The newspaper of record, including extensive business coverage.

Barron's
A weekly business and investment newspaper published by the Dow Jones company.

BusinessWeek
Business news, stock market analysis, and financial advice.

Books: Biographies of Capitalist Leaders

Chandler, Alfred Dupont and Stephen Salsbury. *Pierre S. Du Pont and the Making of the Modern Corporation* (2000).
This biography of Pierre S. du Pont, head of the Du Pont Company and later General Motors, describes how the Delaware scion took a loosely run, family gunpowder factory and turned it into a giant corporation.

Chernow, Ron. *Titan: The Life of John D. Rockefeller* (2004).
"Unflaggingly interesting . . . brings John D. Rockefeller Sr. to life through sustained narrative portraiture of the large-scale, 19th-century kind." (*New York Times*)

Deutschman, Alan. *The Second Coming of Steve Jobs* (2000).
"Steve Jobs did not succeed so much because he made better widgets but because, at some deep level, he understands us. If he is a jerk, he is our jerk. To understand Jobs, then, is to understand not just his personality—vain, petulant, cruel, yet irresistibly seductive even to those he abuses most—but his aesthetic." (*New York Times*)

Hagstrom, Robert J. *The Warren Buffett Way* (2004).
"Financial consultant Hagstrom, who did not interview his subject but obtained permission to quote from his Berkshire Hathaway annual reports, here outlines Buffet's iconoclastic tenets for invest-

ing. Unlike many entrepreneurs who take over companies to sell them off in bits, Buffet buys and holds. He rejects the 'efficient market theory'; he doesn't worry about the stock market; and he buys a business, not a stock. He manages with a small staff, no computers and a 'hands off' strategy." (*Publishers Weekly*)

Kaufman, Michael J. *Soros: The Life and Times of a Messianic Billionaire* (2002).
"A flinty-eyed exposition of a brilliant capitalist, devoted provocateur and accidental humanitarian. You come away believing it is possible to be a really rich man and a really good man after all." (*New York Times*)

Morris, Charles. *The Tycoons: How Andrew Carnegie, John D. Rockefeller, Jay Gould, and JP Morgan Invented the American Supereconomy* (2005).
"Morris skillfully assembles a great deal of academic and anecdotal research to demonstrate that Andrew Carnegie, John D. Rockefeller, Jay Gould and J. P. Morgan did not amass their fortunes by trampling on the downtrodden or ripping off consumers—though he does concede that Carnegie and Gould could be scoundrels in their personal lives." (*New York Times*)

Ross, Ian Simpson. *The Life of Adam Smith* (1995).
"Scottish economist Adam Smith, who laid the foundation of classical economics with his model of a competitive, self-regulating market, was described by contemporaries as having a harsh voice, huge teeth and a conversational style tantamount to lecturing. In London, Smith, a policy adviser, urged the British government to jettison its colonial system of restraints, and the publication of his classic *Wealth of Nations* in 1776 was timed, suggests Ross, to convince Parliament to support a peaceful resolution of the conflict with the rebellious American colonies. Ross's rounded intellectual biography gives us all sides of the man." (*Publishers Weekly*)

Stross, Randall E. *The Wizard of Menlo Park: How Thomas Alva Edison Invented the Modern World* (2007).
"In this entertaining biography, biographer Stross approaches the life of Thomas Edison from an atypical angle: where scores of other biographers have focused on the genius's technical career, Stross presents Edison as the first self-conscious celebrity, a man deeply aware of the media's power and who wasn't afraid to use 'the press's hunger for more sensational discoveries for his own ends.'" (*Publishers Weekly*)

Strouse, Jean. *Morgan: American Financier* (2000).
"Seamlessly weaves Morgan's exploits as America's leading banker with his frenetic social life . . . The Morgan who emerges from these pages is, for all his hard ambition and ruthlessness, not merely ruthless and greedy." (*Publishers Weekly*)

Wallace, James and Jim Erickson. *Hard Drive: Bill Gates and the Making of the Microsoft Empire* (1992).
An unauthorized biography of Gates, written and published at the start of Microsoft's antitrust troubles. Investigative reporters Wallace and Erickson follow Gates from his days as a 13-year-old computer hacker, to his current status as a billionaire CEO. "The book recalls, in interesting fashion, how Microsoft bought 86-DOS, the disk-operating system that was the germ of the cash cow, from Seattle Computer Products for a mere $50,000 in 1981. The biography also records, justly, that Paul Allen, who left Microsoft in 1983, has received less than his share of attention, perhaps because he has a life beyond Microsoft." (*New York Times*)

Wheen, Francis. *Karl Marx: A Life* (2000).
"While he hasn't dug up many new facts, Wheen has engagingly reinterpreted Marx's exhaustively annotated life. . . . Wheen's portrait of Marx's life is artfully shaped and makes delectable reading." (*New York Times Book Review*)

Books: Company Histories

Auletta, Ken. *World War 3.0: Microsoft and Its Enemies* (2001).
"Painstakingly recreates the broader context of the conflict, not only Microsoft's allegedly predatory behavior toward Netscape Navigator, but also its supposedly bullying treatment of companies like Apple, Intel, Sony, Sun Microsystems, Oracle and even, arguably, IBM." (*New York Times*)

Birla, Madan. *FedEx Delivers: How the World's Leading Shipping Company Keeps Innovating* (2005).
An inside look at leadership practices that enabled the world's leading shipping company to outthink and outperform its competition. Using firsthand accounts, the book explains how the company became an international powerhouse and one of the most trusted global brands by using leadership practices that tapped into the creativity and commitment of its employees.

Burrough, Bryan and John Helyar. *Barbarians at the Gate: The Fall of RJR Nabisco* (2008).
"One of the finest, most compelling accounts of what happened to corporate America and Wall Street in the 1980s." (*New York Times Book Review*)

Carlson, W. Bernard. *Innovation as a Social Process: Elihu Thompson and the Rise of General Electric, 1870–1900* (1991).
"Carlson has examined the broader issues of technical innovation as a social process by taking the life of Thomson as a case study. . . . The approach gives useful insights into the relationship between innovation and the extraordinary rise of technologically based business in late 19th-century America." (*Nature*)

Cohen, Adam. *The Perfect Store: Inside eBay* (2005).
"What is most notable about Cohen's book is his willingness to stray from the classic business narrative and into the gnarlier issues of

community and idealism. He portrays Omidyar as an earnest dreamer, who began AuctionWeb (as eBay was first called) in the hope that he might create, in Cohen's words, 'a perfect, global marketplace that everyone comes to on an equal basis.'" (*New York Times*)

Marquard, William H. and Bill Birchard. *Wal-Smart: What It Really Takes to Profit in a Wal-Mart World* (2007).
"Whether or not one likes it, Marquard says, it's a Wal-Mart world we live in, and astutely choosing how to respond to Wal-Mart, and other industry big dogs like it, can mean the difference between a business's success and failure. Marquard, who helped Wal-Mart devise its very first business strategy and has since worked for other businesses competing against that strategy, knows his subject intimately and describes the controversial retail goliath with admirable neutrality." (*Publishers Weekly*)

Pendergrast, Mark. *For God, Country and Coca-Cola: The Definitive History of the Great American Soft Drink and the Company that Makes It* (2000).
"Freelance business journalist Pendergrast, granted access to Coca-Cola company files, has produced an entertaining, fair-minded history without much scandal. He traces the roots of 'the world's most widely distributed product' as a patent medicine, describes the development of the unique 'Hobbleskirt' bottle and depicts the canny use of advertising, which enabled Coke to 'permeate every aspect of American life.'" (*Publishers Weekly*)

Quinn, Bill. *How Wal-Mart is Destroying America (and the World)— and What You Can Do About It* (2005).
Texas newspaperman Bill Quinn provides detailed accounts of retail giant Wal-Mart's sometimes questionable business practices and lawsuits, vendor issues, and efforts to stop expansion, arguing that Wal-Mart is the most feared and despised American corporation in the world.

Rose, Frank. *West of Eden: The End of Innocence at Apple* (1990).
"As Mr. Rose tells it, Apple was built on an ideology, or more accurately a lifestyle: young, individualistic, countercultural. 'One person—one computer' was Apple's motto. The phrase, Mr. Rose writes, was 'born of Jobs's conviction that the democratization of computer power would alter the balance between the individual and the institution.'" (*New York Times*)

Schultz, Howard & Dori Jones Yang. *Pour Your Heart Into It: How Starbucks Built a Company One Cup At a Time* (1999).
"A chatty history of Starbucks by its CEO, who announces that he considers the company to be only in its third chapter (which is nowhere near the eleventh). Schultz first heard of Starbucks in 1981 when he sold to the fledgling business a number of expensive coffeemakers, and he fell in love with the company immediately." (*Kirkus Reviews*)

Vise, David A. and Mark Malseed. *The Google Story* (2005)
"Washington Post reporter Vise and researcher Malseed give a serviceable rundown of the company's rise from grad-student project to web juggernaut, its innovative technology and targeted advertising system, its savvy deal-making and its inevitable battles with Microsoft." (*Publishers Weekly*)

Yergin, Daniel. *The Prize: The Epic Quest for Oil, Money and Power* (1993).
"Energy consultant Yergin limns oil's central role in most of the wars and many international crises of the 20th century." (*Publishers Weekly*) A Pulitzer winner and PBS miniseries.

Books: History and Philosophy

Aaronovitch, Sam and Jan Toporowski. *Political Economy and the New Capitalism: Essays in Honour of Sam Aaronovitch* (2000).
Examines key developments in capitalist economies at the end of the 20th century, and brings together essays by leading economists in

honor of the late Sam Aaronovitch, the veteran left-wing economist. In his work, Aaronovitch emphasized the need to take into account the most recent developments in capitalist economies.

Barnes, Peter. *Who Owns The Sky?: Our Common Assets and the Future of Capitalism* (2001).
"Barnes, cofounder and former president of the 'socially responsible' financial services company Working Assets, argues that natural resource management urgently needs rethinking, since the atmosphere's capacity for absorbing carbon gas emissions is severely tested every day. While not an alarmist, he cites recent statistics and insists that we need new solutions." (*Publishers Weekly*)

Baumol, William J., Robert E. Litan, and Carl J. Schramm. *Good Capitalism, Bad Capitalism, and the Economics of Growth and Prosperity* (2007).
Documents four different varieties of capitalism, some "good" and some "bad" for growth. The authors identify the conditions that characterize good capitalism—the right blend of entrepreneurial and established firms, which can vary among countries—as well as the features of bad capitalism.

Bell, Daniel. *The Cultural Contradictions of Capitalism* (1996).
This analysis of Western liberal capitalist society contends that capitalism—and the culture it creates—harbors the seeds of its own downfall by creating a need among successful people for gratification.

Bernanke, Ben S. *Essays on the Great Depression* (2000).
By the chairman of the Federal Reserve's central bank.

Bernstein, Michael A. *The Great Depression: Delayed Recovery and Economic Change in America, 1929–1939* (1987).
"This book makes an excellent case for the argument that sectoral transformation was an important contributing factor to the length of

the Great Depression. It also points out the importance of including sectoral change in all economic histories of the 20th century." (*Journal of Economic History*)

Bogle, John C. *The Battle for the Soul of Capitalism* (2005).
"In this book, Bogle abhors what he sees as rampant cheating among his peers—not only mutual fund managers but brokers, bankers, lawyers and accountants. It's not just a few bad apples, he says: 'I believe that the barrel itself—the very structure that holds all those apples—is bad.'" (*New York Times*)

Bordo, Michael D., Claudia Dale Goldin, Claudia Goldin, and Eugene Nelson White. *The Defining Moment: The Great Depression and the American Economy* (1998).
To what extent was the Depression a watershed period in the history of the American economy? This volume organizes 12 scholars' responses into four categories: fiscal and monetary policies, the economic expansion of government, the innovation and extension of social programs, and the changing international economy.

Brinkley, Alan. *The End of Reform* (1996).
"Mr. Brinkley suggests that when the liberals of the late 1930s abandoned hope for a far-reaching overhaul of the American economy and instead embraced the Keynesian notion that government's principal duty was to protect national economic health by underwriting aggregate consumer demand, they in fact beat a craven retreat from 'genuine' reform. They deferred to a later day the moment when state power would have to be applied to the economy in more vigorous and intensive ways." (*New York Times*)

Bruner, Robert F. and Sean D. Carr. *The Panic of 1907: Lessons Learned from the Market's Perfect Storm* (2007).
"Though business professors Bruner and Carr approach their subject, the spectacular financial crisis that gave America the FDIC and

the Federal Reserve, with grave pedantry, they devote the majority of the book to the more colorful events and personalities of the crisis, which even academic prose cannot dull." (*Publishers Weekly*)

Chafe, William Henry. *The Achievement of American Liberalism: The New Deal and Its Legacies* (2002).
"With this volume, editor Chafe (history, Duke), a prominent historian of postwar America, honors William Leuchtenburg, perhaps the leading New Deal historian, with a collection of eleven new essays assessing the course of American liberalism from the 1930s to date." (*Library Journal*)

Chow, Rey. *The Protestant Ethnic and the Spirit of Capitalism* (2002).
Chow proposes that ethnicity be examined in conjunction with Max Weber's famous theory about the Protestant work ethic and capitalism (see below), which holds that secular belief in salvation often collaborates effectively with the interpellation, disciplining, and rewarding of subjects constituted by specific forms of labor.

Cohen, Jere. *Protestantism and Capitalism: The Mechanisms of Influence* (2002).
Drawing on both new and underutilized older evidence on Puritan preachers and merchants, Cohen evaluates the impact of English Puritanism on the development of modern capitalism.

Davies, Glyn. *A History of Money: From Ancient Times to the Present Day* (1994).
"If you want a chronological history of money, here it is. If the development of banking is required, that is available. And if you want to worry about the exploding world population, the book provides some interesting theories." (*Banking World*)

Deffeyes, Kenneth S. *Hubbert's Peak: The Impending World Oil Shortage* (2001).

"This is an oilman and geologist's assessment of the future, grounded in cold mathematics. And it's frightening." (*Scientific American*)

Dine, Janet and Andrew Fagan. *Human Rights and Capitalism: A Multidisciplinary Perspective on Globalisation* (2006).
Brings together two important facets of the globalization debate and examines the complex relationship between human rights, property rights, and capitalist economies.

Eichengreen, Barry J. *Golden Fetters: The Gold Standard and the Great Depression, 1919–1939* (1992).
"Important and convincingly argued. ... Even those who are not sympathetic to the arguments and conclusions of this book will agree that it is destined to be an important work for all future students of the gold standard." (*Journal of Economic Issues*)

Friedman, Milton and Rose D. Friedman. *Capitalism and Freedom* (2002).
How can we benefit from the promise of government while avoiding the threat it poses to individual freedom? In this classic book, Milton Friedman provides the definitive statement of his immensely influential economic philosophy—one in which competitive capitalism serves as both a device for achieving economic freedom and a necessary condition for political freedom.

Friedman, Thomas L. *The World is Flat: A Brief History of the Globalized World* (2005).
"The metaphor of a flat world, used by Friedman to describe the next phase of globalization, is ingenious. It came to him after hearing an Indian software executive explain how the world's economic playing field was being leveled. For a variety of reasons, what economists call 'barriers to entry' are being destroyed; today an individual or company can collaborate or compete globally. What created the flat world? Friedman stresses technological forces." (*New York Times*)

Frydman, Roman, Kenneth Murphy, and Andrzej Rapaczynski. *Capitalism with a Comrade's Face: Studies in the Postcommunist Transition* (1998).
"Those looking for a sharper insight into what makes post-Communist countries tick are well-served by this snappily-written examination of the central questions . . . the authors range well beyond narrow economic analysis . . . nicely spiced with real-life examples." (*The Economist*)

Fulcher, James. *Capitalism: A Very Short Introduction* (2004).
The crisis tendencies of capitalism—including the southeast Asian banking crisis, the collapse of the Russian economy, and the 1997–98 global financial crisis—asking whether capitalism is doomed to fail.

Galbraith, John Kenneth. *The Essential Galbraith* (2001).
Selections from the great economist's key texts, including *The Affluent Society*, the book in which he coined the term *conventional wisdom*.

Gaudiani, Claire. *The Greater Good: How Philanthropy Drives the American Economy and Can Save Capitalism* (2003).
"Declaring 'no people on earth are as generous with their money as Americans are,' Gaudiani posits 'citizen generosity' as not just an alternative to government spending or corporate investment, but an integral fulfillment of the nation's "democratic imperative" of upward mobility." (*Publishers Weekly*)

Gersemann, Olaf. *Cowboy Capitalism: European Myths, American Reality* (2005).
Europeans and many American pundits believe that while the U.S. economy may create more growth, Europeans have it better when it comes to social opportunities like to job security and other factors. Olaf Gersemann, a German reporter who came to America, found the reality quite different.

Heilbroner, Robert L. *21st Century Capitalism* (1994).
"Economics, often vilified as the 'dismal science' offers, in Heilbroner's deft book, an exhilarating exploration of ideas. In this study, based on lectures from the fall of '92, he ponders the possibilities for 21st-century capitalism in a sweeping examination of the 'idea of progress,' capitalism as a social and political system, class struggle, capital accumulation, the challenge of growth, the marketplace, the collapse of the Soviet Union and the unpredictability of human behavior." (*Publishers Weekly*)

Hertz, Noreena. *The Silent Takeover: Global Capitalism and the Death of Democracy* (2003).
"Cambridge University economist Hertz asserts that Reagan's and Thatcher's brand of free market capitalism has had dire social and political repercussions, although it has triumphed as the dominant world ideology and brought prosperity to many." (*Publishers Weekly*)

Klein, Naomi. *The Shock Doctrine: The Rise of Disaster Capitalism* (2008).
"Privatization, free trade, slashed social spending are catastrophic in two senses, argues this polemic. Because their results are disastrous… their means must be cataclysmic, dependent on political upheavals and natural disasters as coercive pretexts." (*Publishers Weekly*)

Kovel, Joel. *The Enemy of Nature: The End of Capitalism Or the End of the World* (2007).
"Anyone certain of capitalism's complete triumph has not as yet encountered Kovel . . . who believes it possible as well as desirable to overthrow capitalism for a world ecosocialist regime with values." (*Library Journal*)

Kunstler, James Howard. *The Long Emergency: Surviving the End of Oil, Climate Change, and Other Converging Catastrophes of the Twenty-First Century* (2006).

"Kunstler notes signs that global oil production has peaked and will soon dwindle, and argues in an eye-opening, although not entirely convincing, analysis that alternative energy sources cannot fill the gap, especially in transportation. The result will be a Dark Age in which 'the center does not hold' and 'all bets are off about civilization's future.'" (*Publishers Weekly*)

LaFeber, Walter. *Michael Jordan and the New Global Capitalism* (1999).
"LaFeber understands the nearly universal celebrity of Michael Jordan and the global profitability of the sportswear manufacturer Nike as something ... insidious." (*New York Times Book Review*)

Lakwete, Angela. *Inventing the Cotton Gin: Machine and Myth in Antebellum America* (2003).
"With careful use of vivid illustrations and keen analytic skills, Lakwete captures the relationship between technology and human initiative." (*Times Literary Supplement*)

Marable, Manning. *How Capitalism Underdeveloped Black America* (2000).
A work of political history, on racial and economic inequality.

Mason, Matt. *The Pirate's Dilemma: How Youth Culture Is Reinventing Capitalism* (2008).
"Music journalist Mason, a former pirate radio and club DJ in London, explores how open source culture is changing the distribution and control of information and harnessing the old system of punk capitalism to new market conditions governing society." (*Publishers Weekly*)

Nicholson, Philip Yale. *Labor's Story in the United States: An Introduction to the History of Labor* (2004).
Nicholson considers American labor history from the perspective of institutions and people: the rise of unions, the struggles over slavery,

wages, and child labor, and public and private responses to union organizing.

Owen, Thomas C. *Dilemmas of Russian Capitalism* (2005).
"Provides a fascinating insight into the economy, politics and culture on Russia in the period following the Crimean War. Owen integrates the genre of biography with a thorough analysis of economic ideas, political and legal institutions. The volume is a valuable contribution to the debate on how economic and cultural institutes form economic performance and business culture, and to the studies on economic nationalism as well." (*Business History*)

Perelman, Michael. *The Invention of Capitalism: Classical Political Economy and the Secret History of Primitive Accumulation* (2000).
"Perelman's study of the ideological support for primitive accumulation raises a set of significant issues at the conjunction of liberal political thought and classical political economy that deserve further investigation." (*Theory and Event*)

Pretzer, William S. *Working at Inventing: Thomas A. Edison and the Menlo Park Experience* (2002).
A study of research and development at Thomas Edison's Menlo Park (New Jersey) laboratory during the six years between 1876 and 1882 that transformed American life.

Pryor, Frederic L. *The Future of U.S. Capitalism* (2002).
"An in-depth look at the long-term economic, social, cultural, and political forces shaping the United States." (*Futurist*)

Rawley, James A., and Stephen D. Behrendt. *The Transatlantic Slave Trade: A History* (2005).
"This first-rate new study discusses the size and profitability of the slave business, the people who engaged in it, and its consequences in European and American history." (*The New Yorker*)

Schlesinger, Arthur Meier. *The Politics of Upheaval* (1988).
The Politics of Upheaval, 1935–1936, volume three of Pulitzer Prize-winning historian and biographer Arthur M. Schlesinger, Jr.'s Age of Roosevelt series, concentrates on the turbulent concluding years of Franklin D. Roosevelt's first term.

Sklair, Leslie. *Globalization: Capitalism and Its Alternatives* (2002).
Sklair focuses on alternatives to global capitalism, arguing strongly that there are other alternative futures that retain and encourage the positive aspects of globalization, while identifying what is wrong with capitalism.

Soros, George. *The Crisis of Global Capitalism: Open Society Endangered* (1998).
"This book is sometimes hard sledding, particularly in the first section, where Soros explains his theory of reflexivity, which essentially argues that reality affects perceptions and in turn is affected by those perceptions. It is an idea that seems obvious, and readers may be tempted to skip over much of that. But when Soros gets down to financial market business, and explains how we got to where we are now, he does an excellent job." (*New York Times)*

Stiglitz, Joseph E. *Globalization and Its Discontents* (2003).
"Stiglitz's critique of the market-driven '90s still resonates, especially when the business pages are full of stories about white-collar crime and the stock market seems stuck in a perpetual rut. Even the United States cannot blithely assume that financial markets will work on autopilot. It is testament to the salience of Stiglitz's arguments that many economists—even some Bush administration officials—now embrace his view that economic change in the developing world must evolve more with local conditions." (*New York Times)*

Index

A

absolute advantage of goods, 235
acquisitions, 23–24, 88, 138, 148
ad valorem tax, 236, 250, 257
Adams, John, 150
advertising, 100, 111, 147–48, 248
Affluent Society, The (Galbraith), 99, 227–29
Afghanistan, 67, 204
Africa, 158–59
AIG bailout, x, 25
airline industry, 115–18, 146
Aldrich-Vreeland Act, 160–61
Alger, Horatio, Jr., 77, 80–*81*
Allen, Paul, 104
American Capitalism (Galbraith), 100
AMEX (American Stock Exchange), 25
Amoco, 120
Amsterdam Stock Exchange, 49, 50
Anglo-Iranian Oil Company, 118–19
antitrust issues
    of Boeing, 117
    legislation of, 236
    of Microsoft, 105–6
    of Northern Securities, 84
    of Standard Oil, 88

of United Aircraft and Transport, 116

See also monopolies

AOL (America Online), 138

appreciation, 236

arbitrage, 30–31

Argentina, 212–13

Arkwright, Richard, 53–54, 57

Asian developmental countries, 194–95

Asian financial crisis, x, 175–82

    Association of Southeast Asian Nations and, 179

    causes of, 178

    countries involved in, 176–77, 181, 198, 201–2, 213

    financial contagion in, 179–82

    IMF assisting in, 180–81

    pegged exchange rates and, 178

Asia's Four Tigers, 176–79, 200

assets

    appreciation of, 236

    arbitrage and, 30

    of British Petroleum, 120

    capital flight and, 238

    current, 237

    defined, 237

    depreciation of, 236

    distressed, 186

    financial liberalization and, 178

    fixed, 22, 237

    intellectual property as, 237, 244

    liquid, 28, 237

    protecting, 37, 106

    short-term, 22

    for subprime mortgages, 182–83

    Trouble Assets Relief Program for, 186

Association of Southeast Asian Nations, 179

AT&T, 122, 247

audits, 34–36

Australia, 98, 114, 202–3

automatic stabilizers, 237

automobile industry, 62–63, 94–97, 112–15

B

balance-of-payments crises, 175

Baldwin, Jerry, 139

Banco Ambrosiano, 194

bankruptcy, 36–37
bank(s)
    bailouts of, 22–23, 171
    central, 18–20, 243
    collapsing during Great Depression, 165
    commercial, 21–23
    credit, 33
    deposits, 21–22, 159–60, 173
    deregulation of, vii
    Emergency Banking Relief Act for, 166
    of England, 19
    European Central Bank and, 19, 206
    FDIC for. *See* FDIC (Federal Deposit Insurance Corporation)
    Federal Reserve, 9, 19, 22, 160–61, 172
    financial liberalization and, 178
    investment, 23–25, 184–86
    Islamic, 192
    loans, 22
    national, 161
    nationalizing, 185
    offshore, 197
    Panic of 1857, 220
    Panic of 1907, 159–61
    panics, 19, 84, 157, 159–61, 221
    run on, 19, 23
    S&L crisis and, 171–74
    stock market crash and, 161–63
Barbarians at the Gate: The Fall of RJR Nabisco (Burrough/Helyar), 230–31
bartering, 38–40, 44
Bentham, Jeremy, 4
Berkshire Hathaway, 103, 104
Bernanke, Benjamin, 182
Bill and Melinda Gates Foundation, 104, 106
bill of exchange, 48
biofuel, 183, 184
Black Friday panic, 84
black markets, ix, 40–41, 204–5, 239, 250
Boeing, x, 115–18
Bolshevik Revolution, 11, 67
bonds, 27–29, 32
brain drain, 238
Bretton Woods System, 20, 98
British Petroleum, 118–21
Brown, Gordon, Prime Minister, 206

Bryan, William Jennings, 156, 158
budget deficit, 237
Buffett, Warren, 69, 102–4, 103, 106, 153
Burke, Edmund, 75–77
Burrough, Bryan, 230–31
business cycles, 10–12. *See also specific topics*

C
Canada, 142, 214
Candler, Asa, 109–11
Capital (Marx), 5–6, 76, 79
capital flight, 238
Capitalism, Socialism & Democracy (Schumpeter), 5, 224–25
Capitalism and Freedom (Friedman), xiii–xiv
Carnegie, Andrew, 82–83, 232
cartels, 87, 210, 239, 254
cash flow, 37–38
certificates of deposit, 32, 173–74
Chamberlain, Chancellor Neville, 169
Change-Makers: From Carnegie to Gates, How the Great Entrepreneurs Transformed Ideas Into Industries (Klein), 231–32
Chevron, 118, 121
Chile, 170, 211
China
    cheap labor in, 178, 182
    economy of, xvi, 195–96
    free market in, xviii, 69, 107
    Hong Kong and, 199–200
    poverty in, xv
    Silk Road to, 13, 46–47
    Wal-Mart in, 142
    See also Communism
Citigroup, x
classes, social, 59, 80. *See also* leisure class; middle class
classical economics, 2–4, 73, 93, 102
Coase theorem, 238
Coca-Cola, 103–4, 108–12, 241
Coinage Act of 1873, 156
coincident indicators, 17–18
Colbert, David, 220–21
Cold War
    affecting markets, 27
    airline industry during, 116
    end of, xiv

internet and, 68
    military spending for, 65
collateral, 22, 25, 32
collective bargaining, 96, 168, 238
collusion, 3, 238–39, 249
colonialism, 52, 75, 159
Communism
    Communist Manifesto, The (Marx/Engels) and, 59, 79–80
    fall of, xv–xvi, 67
    Karl Marx and, 5–6
    labor and, 59
    pure, 254
Communist Manifesto, The (Marx/Engels), 59, 79–80
company towns, 57–58, 60
competition, 229–30
    in free market, 6, 99
    monopolies and, 247
    perfect, 250
computer industry
    AOL in, 138
    eBay and, 143–45
    FedEx and, 145–46
    Google and, 147–49
    IBM and, 128, 130–31
    Macintosh and, 137
    Microsoft and, 104–6, 135–38
conglomerates, 127, 194–95, 200, 230–31
ConocoPhillips, 118
conservatism, 7
Conservative Coalition, 169
Continental Illinois Bank, 22–23
Control Data Corporation, 131
Convertibility Plan, 213
corporations, 38, 240, 249–50, 256–57
cost object, 240, 259
cotton gin, 56–57
Cournot, Augustin, 16
CPI (Consumer Price Index), 28, 239–40
credit
    bank, 33
    cards, 22, 65–67, 173, 247
    consumer, 33
    defined, 32–34
    for goods and services, 33

history, 45, 182
instruments of, 33
interest rates for, 244
as liability, 31
line of, vii–viii, 134
in Long Depression, 155
markets, viii, 156
rating, 34, 179
risk, 183
stock value and, 163
CTR (Computing-Tabulating-Recording), 128
Cultural Revolution, 195–96
currency
bill of exchange as, 48
bimetallism of, 156, 158
Coinage Act of 1873 and, 156
crises, 175
debasing coins and, 49
defined, 246
euro, 205–7, 242
exchange rates, 17, 31, 85–86, 175, 213, 236, 241
first-generation, 175, 178
inflation affecting, 102
pegged, 175, 177–78, 241
permanent income theory of, 102

D
D'Arcy, William Knox, 118
Darwin, Charles, 63–65
de la Madred, Miguel, 213
debt
defined, 31–32
and French Revolution, 76
for goods and services, 31
and inflation, 237
instruments of, 24, 27, 32
as liability, 31
in Long Depression, 155
national, 237, 247–48
short-term, 178
deflation, 243
democracy, 5, 34, 67, 71, 83, 99, 224
deposits
bank, 21–22, 159–60, 173

brokering, 173–74
    certificates of, 32, 173–74
deregulation(s)
    after Great Depression, xv
    of airline industry, 146
    of banks, vii
    international, 198, 208
    Washington Consensus advocating, 180
    See also regulation(s)
discount rate, 20
dividends, 25, 85
division of labor, 39, 53, 74, 217–18
dot-com industry, 69, 163, 174, 216
double coincidence of wants, 39
Drew, Daniel, 84
Dust Bowl, 165–66
Dutch East India Company, 47

E
eBay, 143–45
economic crisis of 2007–2009
    affecting oil prices, 183
    affecting regulations, 25
    Emergency Economic Stabilization Act of 2008 for, 186
    Fannie Mae/Freddie Mac bailout during, 185
    food prices affecting, 183–84
    Goldman Sachs during, 185–86
    IndyMac Bank failing during, 185
    investment banks in, 184–85
    Lehman Brothers failing during, 184–86
    MBS (mortgage-based securities) affecting, 183–85
    Morgan Stanley during, 185, 186
    subprime mortgage affecting, 182–83
    Trouble Assets Relief Program for, 186
    Washington Mutual failing during, 186
Economic Union, 203
economic(s)
    auctions in, 143–44
    boom-bust cycle of, 178, 220
    classical, 2–4, 73, 93, 102
    crisis of 2007–2009. *See* economic crisis of 2007–2009
    cycles of, 11–12, 98, 178, 246
    for developing countries, 13–14
    evolutionary, 221

financial contagion and, 175–76
financial liberalization and, 178
game theory in, 15–17
indicators of, 17–18, 168
Keynesian, 101, 222–23, 242, 247, 251, 259. *See also* Keynes, John Maynard
laissez-faire, 2–3, 7–9, 64, 101, 166, 172, 222–23
macro, 9, 20, 44, 206, 223, 245–46, 257
Marxian theory of, 5–6
micro, 9, 44, 246, 260
neoclassical, 4–5
neo-liberal, 211–12
normative, 248, 260
positive, 248, 251
pure capitalism and, 253
social market, 209
supply and demand. *See* supply and demand
supply-side, 245, 257
theories of, 2–9
unemployment and, 98, 157, 168, 170, 207, 248, 258–59
See also economy; free market
Economics of The Peace, The (Keynes), 97
economy
goods and services in, 240, 245, 246
mixed, xiii, xviii, 240
natural, 247
planned, 240
See also economic(s)
Edison, Thomas, 61–62, 90–92, *91*, 132–33
elasticity, 241, 252
electrical power, 61–62, 90
Elements of Political Economy (Mill), 218–19
Emergency Banking Relief Act, 166
Emergency Economic Stabilization Act of 2008, 186
EMU (Economic and Monetary Union), 205–6
Engels, Friedrich, 59, 79
enlightened self interest, 179, 241, 256
entrepreneur, 38, 102–3, 139, 223–25, 232
EU (European Union), 205, 242
euro, 205–7, 242
Euroland, 242
European Central Bank, 19, 206
ExxonMobil, 118, 121–24
Eyewitness to Wall Street (Colbert), 220–21

F

factories

American, 57, 59–60, 78

assembly line in, 62, 74, 95–96

building cars, 95–96

labor in, 58

mass production in, 60

TPS (Toyota Production System) for, 112–14

Fannie Mae/Freddie Mac bailout, 25, 185

fascism, 99, 171

FDIC (Federal Deposit Insurance Corporation), 167, 174, 185

Federal Reserve, 19

controlling inflation, 215

creation of, 9, 160–61

role with banks, 22

S&Ls borrowing from, 173

stagflation and, 172

Federalist Papers, 77

FedEx, 145–47, 146

FHLBB (Federal Home Loan Bank Board), 174

financial contagion, 175–76, 179–82

FIRREA (Financial Institutions Reform and Recovery Enforcement Act), 174

fiscal policy, 102, 237, 242, 246

Fisk, James, 84, 85

Fleming, Marcus, 243

Ford, Henry, 62, 94–97, 95

Fountainhead, The (Rand), 225–26

France

economy of, 207

laissez-faire economics in, 7

Physiocrats of, 7

rise of middle class in, 149, 150

using euro, 242

Franklin, Benjamin, 150

free market

Carnegie supporting, 83

competition in, 6, 99

Edmund Burke supporting, 76

failure of, 6

global spread of, xviii

international, xviii, 69, 107, 198, 200

Organization for Economic Cooperation and Development supporting, 191

profits in, xvi–xvii

Say's Law and, 255

self-correcting, 73

French Revolution, 75–76, 150

Frias, Hugo Chávez, 210

Friedman, Milton, xiii–xiv, 98, 101–*2*

Friedman, Thomas L., x, xviii, 232–33

From Canal Boy to President (Alger, Jr.), 81

FSLIC (Federal Savings and Loan Insurance Corporation), 173, 174

G

GAAP (Generally Accepted Accounting Principles), 35

GAAS (Generally Accepted Auditing Standards), 35

Galbraith, John Kenneth, 99–101, *100*, *228*

game theory, 15–17

Gates, Bill, x, 104–6, *105*

GATT (General Agreements on Trade Tariffs), 13–14, 117, 213

GDP (Gross Domestic Product)

    black markets and, 40–41

    defined, xiv, 243

    economic indicators and, 17

    of goods and services, 243

    growth of, 11, 12

    and inflation, 243

    macroeconomics and, 245–46

    Okun's Law and, 248–49

    real, 243, 254

    recession and, 254–55

    venture capital and, 29

GEAR (Growth, Employment and Redistribution plan), 203

General Electric, 91, 132–35

General Motors, 95, 96

General Theory of Employment, Interest and Money (Keynes), 222–23

Germany, xviii, 40, 56, 75, 97, 99, 209

Gerstner, Louis, 132

GNP (Gross National Product), 243

gold standard, 8, 19–20, 85–86, 156, 158, 167, 170

Goldman Sachs, 185–86

goods and services

    absolute advantage in, 235

    ancient, 44

    complementary goods, 239

    debt and, 31

    defined, 255

    in economy, 240, 245, 246

    in free trade, 242

GDP of, 243
 inflation of, 243
 of OPEC countries, 192
 price control of, 251–52
 price discrimination of, 252
 price elasticity, 252
 sticky, 252, 257
 supply and demand of, 4, 9
 value of, 259
Google, 147–49
Gorbachev, Mikhail, 67
Gospel of Wealth, The (Carnegie), 83
Gould, Jay, 83–85, *84*
Graham, Benjamin, 103
Great Depression
 banks collapsing during, 165
 as business cycle, 11
 causes of, 161–63, 165, 169
 Dust Bowl years of, 165–66
 Hayek predicting, 98–99
 laissez-faire economics and, 9
 New Deal policies of. *See* New Deal
 President Hoover during, 162, 165–66
 result of, 3–4
 Smoot-Hawley Tariff Bill affecting, 162, 169, 171
 stock market crash and, 65, 161–63, *162*, 169, 175
 trade during, 162, 170
 unemployment during, 165, 168
 World War II and, 170–71
Great Gatsby, The (Fitzgerald), 93
Greenspan, Alan, 41, 183
Gross Domestic Product. *See* GDP (Gross Domestic Product)

H
Hamilton, Alexander, 77–79
Hammurabi, code of, 45–46
Hayek, Friedrich August von, 98–99, 226–27
healthcare, national, 169
Heinze, F. Augustus, 159
Helyar, John, 230–31
History of the Standard Oil Company, The (Tarbell), 88
Hobbes, Thomas, 2
Hong Kong, 176, 198–200
Hoover, President Herbert, 162, 164–66, 169, 171

Hume, David, x, *72*, 76
hyperinflation, 243
Hyundai Group, 195

I
IBM, 127–32, *128*
IMF (International Monetary Fund), 13, 65, 98, 180–81, 191, 213–14
impossible trinity, 243
India
    cheap labor in, 182
    economy of, 202
    free market in, xviii
    outsourcing to, 67–68
    United States trade with, 233
    Wal-Mart in, 143
Indonesia, 176–77, 191, 197–98
Industrial Revolution
    affecting classical economics, 4–5
    American, 57, 78
    assembly line and, 74
    James Mill on, 218–19
    middle class during, 149–51
industrialized countries, 170, 191, 198, 208
IndyMac Bank, 185
inflation
    defined, 243
    Federal Reserve controlling, 215
    Galbraith warning against, 101
    monetizing debt causing, 237
    and Phillips Curve, 251
    S&L crisis and, 172
    Say's Law and, 255
    unemployment and, 248
initial public offerings (IPOs), 23–24
Inquiry into the Nature and Causes of the Wealth of Nations, An (Smith), x, 73, 217–18
Institutionalism, 92, 94
instruments
    defined, 244
    financial, 48, 244
    fiscal policy, 237
intellectual capital, 244
intellectual property
    as assets, 237, 244

rights for, 253
  WTO rules for, 190
interest
  altering rates of, 20, 246
  arbitrage affecting, 31
  bonds and, 27–28
  coupon rate of, 28
  defined, 244
  Islamic banking and, 192
International Monetary Fund (IMF), 13, 65, 98, 180–81, 191, 213–14
Internet, 68–69
invisible hand, 53, 73, 92
IPOs (initial public offerings), 23–24
Iran, 118–20, 172, 191, 204–5, 215
Iraq, 216
Islam, 13, 120, 192, 204, 205
Italy, 159, 206, 208–9, 242

J
Japan
  Bank of, 19
  economic development of, 194–95, 200–201
  free market in, xviii
  Microsoft in, 135–36
  as model economy, 176
  trade, 199, 204
Jefferson, Thomas, 8, 78
Johnson, Ross, 230
Johnson & Johnson, 126–27
Julius, the Street Boy (Alger, Jr.), 81

K
Keating Five, 174
Kessler, Jean-Baptiste, 121
Keynes, John Maynard, 97–98, 222–23. *See also* economic(s), Keynesian
Klein, Maury, 231–32
Knickerbocker Bank, 159
Kohlberg Kravis Roberts & Company, 230–31

L
labor
  cheap, 178, 182
  collective bargaining with, 238
  division of, 39, 53, 74, 217–18

employment fluctuations of, 12
Homestead Strike of, 60–61
international, 196–98, 205, 207–8, 214
James Mill on, 218–19
Karl Marx and, 59
during Long Depression, 154
minimum wages for, 167
National Labor Relations Act for, 238
New Deal policies for, 168
unemployment and, 98, 157, 168, 170, 207, 248, 258–59
unions, 58–61, 96, 168, 200, 238
Laffer curve, 245
lagging indicators, 17–18
laissez-faire economics, 2–3, 7–9, 64, 101, 166, 172, 222–23
law of one price, 30
laws of motion, 6
leading indicators, 17–18
Lehman Brothers, 25, 184–86
leisure class, 92–94, 221–22
lender of last resort, 18–19
leveraged buyout, 24, 29
liability
    in cash flow, 37
    of corporations, 240, 249
    defined, 245
liberalism, 2–3, 7, 8, 100
Locke, John, 2, 7
Lockheed Martin, 116, 118
Long Depression, x, 60–61, 154–58
Lorenz curve, 245

M
Macao, 196
Macintosh, 137
macroeconomics, 9, 20, 44, 206, 223, 245–46, 257
Malaysia, 176–77, 197
Mao Zedong, Chairman, 195–96
marginal revolution, 4–5
marginal utility, 4
markets. *See* free market
Marx, Karl, 5–6, 59, 76, 79–80, 256
MBS (mortgage-based securities), 183–85
McDonnell-Douglas, 116, 117
McKinley, William, President, 156, 158, 242

Medicaid, xiv
Medicare, xiv
mercantilism
    Adam Smith and, 7, 48, 73
    colonialism and, 52
    David Hume rejecting, 72
    history of, ix, 47–49
mergers, 24, 117, 121–25, 128–29, 133
Merrill Lynch, 25
Mexico
    economy of, 213–14
    illegal immigrants from, 41
    NAFTA and, 15, 213–14
    oil industry in, 120
microeconomics, 9, 44, 246, 260
Microsoft Corporation, 104–6,
    135–38, 233
middle class
    after World War II, 66
    erosion of, 212–13
    government role with, 150
    international, 203, 207, 208, 212–13
    origin of, 149–50
    rise of, 107–8, 149, 150
    work ethic of, 151–52
Mill, James, 218–19
MMF (money market funds) accounts, 22
Monetary Authority of Singapore, 197
Monetary History of the United States, A (Friedman), 102
monetary policy, 20, 243, 246
monopolies
    antitrust legislation for, 236
    AT&T, 122, 247
    collusion and, 238–39
    competition and, 247
    defined, 247
    oligopoly and, 249
    problems with, 3, 5, 253–54
    railroad, 8
    restrictions on, 9
    Rockefeller oil, 88
    See also antitrust issues
Morgan, J.P., 83–86, 132, 160
Morgan Stanley, 25, 185–86

Morgenstern, Oskar, 15
Mundell, Robert, 243

N
NAFTA (North American Free Trade Agreement), 14–15, 213–14
NASDAQ, 25–26
National Bureau of Economic Research, 255
National Labor Relations Act, 238
National Monetary Commission, 160
Navigation Acts, 51, 52
NCR (National Cash Register Company), 127–31
neoclassical economics, 4–5
Nestlé, 124–26
New Deal, 97–98, 101, 166–69
    fiscal policy of, 242
    instituting minimum wages, 167
    for labor, 168
    removing gold standard, 167
    Social Security Act and, 168
    WPA and, 168
New York Clearing House, 160
New York Stock Exchange (NYSE), 25–27
    crash of 1907, 159–61
    crash of 1929, 65, 161–63, 162, 169, 175
    crash of 1997, 181
    See also stock market
Nobel Prize winners, 99, 102, 133, 182, 226, 229, 238
Northern Securities Company, 84, 86
Novak, Michael, 232
NOW (Negotiable Order of Withdrawal) accounts, 22
Nye, Joseph, 12

O
Office of Thrift Supervision, 174
oil industry, 87–88, 118–24, 172, 191, 210, 215
Oil Pollution Act, 123
Okun's Law, 248–49
oligopoly, 239, 249
Omidyar, Pierre, 143
OPEC (Organization of Petroleum Exporting Countries), 121, 172, 191–92, 210, 215
Organization for Economic Cooperation and Development, 191
Organization of Industry, The (Stigler), 229–30
outsourcing, 67–68, 131

P
panic, Black Friday, 84
Panic of 1857, 220–21
Panic of 1873, 21, 156–57
Panic of 1893, 157
Panic of 1907, 159–61
patents, 54, 89, 108–9, 249–50
philanthropy, 83, 86–89, 106
Philippines, 146–47, 176–77, 198
Phillips Curve, 251
Physiocrats, 7
Pinochet, Augusto, 211
Political Discourses (Hume), 72
Populists, 8, 85
Portugal, 159, 196, 208, 242
price
    control, 251
    discrimination, 252
    elasticity of demand, 252
    predatory, 251
    rationing, 254
Principles of Biology (Spencer), 63–64
privatization
    defined, 252
    failure of, 210
    international, 13, 197–98, 202–3, 207–8, 210, 212
    Washington Consensus and, 180
profits
    falling, 6
    from interest, 21
    of investment banks, 23
    Keynes on, 223
    See also dividends
property, xvi, 7, 253

R
racism, 150, 158
railroad industry
    bankrupt, 157
    Corsair compact for, 85
    early, 56
    lines, 84, 157
    in Long Depression, 156–57
    monopolies, 8

    robber barons of, 84, 86
    Rockefeller supporting, 87
Rand, Ayn, 225–26
rationing, 254
Reagan, Ronald, President, 102, 172, 206, 213, 215–16, 226
recession(s)
    of 1937, 169
    of 1990s, 174
    of 2007-2009, 182
    automatic stabilizers in, 237
    defined, 11, 254
    international, 70, 169, 175, 208, 213
    unemployment in, 258–59
    in United States, 171, 177–78, 215
Reconstruction, 154–55, 158, 180, 204
Reflections on the Revolution in France (Burke), 75
regulation(s)
    Asian financial crisis and, 180
    black markets and, 41
    economic crisis of 2007–2009 affecting, 25
    Galbraith and, 100–101
    Great Depression affecting, xiv–xv
    of interest, 22
    market, 41
    of stock markets, 25
    See also deregulation(s)
Rhode Island System, 57–58
Risen from the Ranks (Alger, Jr.), 81
RJR Nabisco, 230–31
Road to Serfdom, The (Hayek), 99, 226–27
robber barons, 84, 86, 93, 231–32, 236, 253–54
Rockefeller, John D., 86–89, 87, 123, 232
Roosevelt, Franklin D., President, 65, 97–98. *See also* New Deal
Royal Dutch Shell, 118, 121–22
Russia
    black market in, 40
    economics of, 99, 210
    mafia of, 210
    See also Soviet Union

S
S&L (Savings and Loan) crisis, 171–74, 181
Samuelson, Robert J., xiii–xix
Saudi Arabia, 191, 205

Say's Law, 255

Schumpeter, Joseph, xvii, 5, 224–25

SEC (Securities and Exchange Commission), 23, 167

securities trade, 26–27

securitization, 24–25

sharecropping, 154–55

Silk Road, 13, 46–47

Singapore, 176, 194–97, 200

Single Business Tax, 236

Smith, Adam, 73–75
    as classical liberal, 8
    on David Hume, 72
    describing supply and demand, 74
    Inquiry into the Nature and Causes of the Wealth of Nations, An by, x, 53,
        217–18
    invisible hand and, 53, 73, 92
    mercantilism and, 7, 48, 73

Smoot-Hawley Tariff Bill, 162, 169, 171

social costs, 256

Social Darwinism, 63–65

Social Security Act, 168

socialism
    defined, 256
    Hayek warning against, 99
    Labour Party and, 256
    Marx founding, 79, 256
    rise of, 11
    See also Communism

Socony (Standard Oil of New York), 122–23

sole proprietorship, 256–57

South Africa, 203

South Korea, 176, 194–95, 200

Soviet Union
    fall of communism in, xv–xvi, 67
    hyperinflation in, 243–44
    poverty of, xv
    See also Russia

Spain, 52, 159, 207–8, 242

speculating
    affecting S&L crisis, 173
    affecting Thailand currency, 177
    of Jay Gould, 84

Spencer, Herbert, 63–64

spice trade, 47–48, 198

stagflation, 172, 215, 244, 251
Standard Oil Company, 87–88, 121–23
Starbucks, 139–41
steam engine, 54–56, *55*
sticky goods, 252, 257
Stigler, George, 229–30
Stiglitz, Joseph, 182
stock market
    crash, 65, 159
    crash of 1907, 159
    crash of 1929, 161–63, *162*, 169, 175
    crash of 1997, 181
    credit and, 163
    defined, 25–27
    reacting to news, 178–79
    regulations of, 25
    volatility, 20
    See also New York Stock Exchange (NYSE)
Strive and Succeed (Alger, Jr.), 81
subprime mortgages. *See* economic crisis of 2007–2009
supply and demand
    Adam Smith describing, 74
    defined, 9–10
    of goods and services, 4, 9
    Say's Law of, 255
Switzerland, 209

T
Taft, Senator Robert, 169
Taiwan, 176, 194–95
Tarbell, Ida, 88
tariffs
    after World War II, 242
    Alexander Hamilton creating, 77, 78
    defined, 257–58
    GATT and, 213
    Great Depression and, 170
    mercantilism and, 49
    protective, 257–58
    Smoot-Hawley Tariff Bill and, 162, 169, 171
tax(es)
    ad valorem, 236, 250, 257
    audits, 34
    defined, 258

income, 8–9, 258
   Laffer curve and, 245
   problems with, 7
   sales, 236, 250, 258
   sur, 214
   value-added, 236
   See also tariffs
Tesla, Nikola, 61–62, 90, 92, 132
textiles, 57–58
Thailand, 176–77, 201–2
Thatcher, Margaret, Prime Minister, 102, 206, 226, 256
Theory of Games and Economic Behavior, The (von Neumann/Morgenstern), 15
Theory of the Business Enterprise, The (Veblen), 94
Theory of the Leisure Class: An Economic Study of Institutions (Veblen) , 92–94,
   221–22
Thoughts and Details on Economic Scarcity (Burke), 76
Toyoda, Sakichi, 112
Toyota, x, 112–15
Toyota Production System (TPS), 112–14
trade
   free, 53, 75, 158, 242
   free market, 232–33
   GATT and, 213
   during Great Depression, 162, 170
   international, xviii–xix, 75, 190, 198–99, 204, 209, 242
   NAFTA and, 14–15, 213–14
transaction costs, 258
Trouble Assets Relief Program, 186
tulip mania, ix, 49–51

U
unemployment, 98, 157, 168, 170, 207, 248, 258–59
unions, 58–61, 96, 168, 200, 238
United Aircraft and Transport Corporation, 115–16
United Copper Company, 159
United Kingdom, 33, 102, 142–43, 204, 206–7, 256
United States, 215–16. *See also specific topics*
UNIVAC, 131
U.S. Treasury, 28, 86, 213–14
"Use of Knowledge in Society, The" (Hayek), 99

V
value, 163, 236, 259
Vanderbilt, Cornelius, 84

Vatican, 192–94, 242
Veblen, Thorstein, 92–94, 93, 221–22
Venezuela, 191, 210–11
venture capital, 23, 29–30, 69, 143, 146–47
vertical integration process, 82, 83, 118, 131
Vienna Stock Exchange, 158
Vietnam, 145, 172, 201, 215, 216
von Neumann, Jon, 15

W
Wal-Mart, 141–43
Walton, Sam, 141
Washington Consensus, 13–14, 180
Washington Mutual, 186
Watson, Thomas Jr., 130
Watson, Thomas Sr., 127–28
Watt, James, 54
Welch, Jack, 134
Westinghouse, George, 61–62, 89–91
Whitney, Eli, 56–57
World Bank, 13, 65, 98, 189–91
World is Flat: A Brief History of the Twenty-First Century (Friedman), x, 232–33
World Trade Organization. *See* WTO (World Trade Organization)
World War I, 19–20, 96, 97, 118
World War II
    business cycles and, 12
    Great Depression and, 170–71
    inflation after, 101
    middle class after, 66
WPA (Works Progress Administration), 168
WTO (World Trade Organization), 13, 14, 117, 184, 190–91, 196

X
XBox, 138
Xenix operating system, 136

Photo Credits: Library of Congress: 3, 21, 73, 75, 77, 79, 82, 84, 87, 89, 91, 95, 100, 109, 162, 221, 228; Photos.com: 55, 151, 177, 193, 199; Getty Images: 185; Harvard News Online (staff photo by Jane Reed): 100; Free to Choose Media: 102; Microsoft: 105; Stock.xchng: 139; Wikimedia: 63, 72, 81, 85, 93, 97, 103 (photo by Mark Hirshey), 115, 119, 128, 146; iStock: 50, 66, 212.

Acknowledgements
The Capitalist's Bible was produced using some rewritten text from the *Encyclopedia of Capitalism*, published by Facts On File for the library reference market.